HELL BROKE LOOSE,

Could Not More Appall the Good People of the Capital City

Than the Dark and Damnable Deeds Done in the Blackness of Night By Fiends.

The crimes still remain a mystery. They are abnormal and unnatural, as compared to ordinary crimes among men. No one, not even the expert skilled in the detection of crime, can find a plausible motive.
**Austin Mayor John W. Robertson
November 10, 1885**

DEAD MEN DO TELL TALES SERIES

"I Want to Come Home Tonight" (2017)
Blood, Guns & Valentines (2023)
Bloody Chicago (2006)
Bloody Hollywood (2008)
Bloody Illinois (2008)
Dead Men Do Tell Tales (2008)
Fallen Angel (2013)
Horribly Mutilated (2021)
Blood, Bullets & Booze (2023)
Murder by Gaslight (2013)
Murdered in Their Beds (2016)
One August Morning (2015)
One Midnight in Texas (2024)
One Night at the Biograph (2016)
Suffer the Children (2018)
Two Lost Girls (2016)
Until Death Do Us Part (2024)
Victims of the Ax Fiend (2020)
Without a Trace (2020)

DEAD MEN DO TELL TALES

ONE MIDNIGHT IN TEXAS

THE TRUE STORY OF THE SERVANT GIRL ANNIHILATOR

TROY TAYLOR

AN AMERICAN HAUNTINGS INK BOOK

ONE MIDNIGHT IN TEXAS
THE TRUE STORY OF THE SERVANT GIRL ANNIHILATOR

© Copyright 2024 by Troy Taylor

All Rights Reserved.
ISBN: 978-1-958589-18-2
First Edition

Published by American Hauntings Ink
P.O. Box 249 - Jacksonville IL - 62651
www.americanhauntingsink.com

Publisher's Note:
No part of this publication may be reproduced, distributed, or transmitted In any form or by any means, including photocopying, recording, or other electronic or mechanical methods, without the prior written consent of the publisher, except in case of brief quotations embodied in critical reviews or other noncommercial uses permitted by copyright law.

Cover Design by April Slaughter
Interior Design by Troy Taylor

Printed in the United States of America

AUSTIN, TEXAS
DECEMBER 31, 1884

IT WASN'T SUPPOSED TO BE THIS COLD IN TEXAS.

That was a thought on many peoples' minds in Austin during the early morning hours of New Year's Eve 1884. The telegraph lines had been buzzing for days before the cold front arrived, promising chilly weather, ice, and maybe even snow. It was heading southeast from Canada, freezing the Great Plains, slowing down trains, and keeping folks bundled up at home.

When the cold reached the Texas state capital, the bracing wind snuck under doors, slipped through cracks around windows, and slid down chimneys like St. Nicholas did just a few days earlier.

But it didn't knock on doors.

So, who was bothering Tom Chalmers in the middle of the night? Tom was lying in bed at the home of his brother-in-law on the west side of Austin when he was awakened by the sound of rapping at the front door.

Then he heard the voice of a man. "Help me," it croaked.

Tom and his wife lived on a ranch outside of town and had come into town earlier in the week to celebrate the holidays. They were the only ones at the house on West Pecan Street that evening. Tom's brother-in-law, William Hall, an insurance agent, was visiting friends with his wife down in Galveston, where they'd once lived.

The knocking at the door continued, and the man's voice called out again, louder this time. "Help me!"

Tom was more aggravated than he was concerned by the late-night knocking. He was a tough man and afraid of little. He had once been a Texas Ranger and had been featured in the local newspaper when he was thrown by a horse and landed on his face, breaking his front teeth. The newspaper praised his fortitude, noting that he spit out the broken teeth, got back on the horse, and rode away.

But he was not enthused about leaving his warm bed on this cold night. Then the front door creaked open.

William Hall's home was one of the finest in Austin. It was large, with two chimneys, 10-foot ceilings, and a grand entryway that led to a curving staircase. Tom and his wife were sleeping in the bedroom at the back of the house. Tom quietly climbed out of bed, crept to the doorway, and peered down the hall toward the foyer. He had no weapon – his gun was in the library – but he needed to find the intruder. He silently walked down the hall, and in the deep gloom of the foyer, he saw a man move past a window and stagger in his direction.

The man cried out, "Mister Tom, Mister Tom, for God's sake, help me! Somebody has nearly killed me!"

Tom lit a match and held it up to see who was speaking. The light flickered across the face of Walter Spencer, a 29-year-old African American man who worked as a laborer at Butler's Brick yard.

Walter was Mollie Smith's boyfriend. Molly worked as a maid and cook in the Hall home for the past few months. The pretty 23-year-old was well-liked by the family and referred to as a "yellow girl," a phrase that white people used in those days to describe a light-skinned black person. Mollie worked six days a week for the Halls and received a monthly salary of $12 and a free place to live, a small apartment in the backyard behind the kitchen.

The apartment was apparently where Walter had come from. He was barefoot and wearing only a nightshirt. There was blood on his face and running out of several cuts in his head. He stumbled as though he was having trouble keeping his balance. He told Tom that he must've been attacked while he was sleeping next to Mollie. He'd been hit in the head and knocked unconscious.

When he woke up, Mollie was gone. Whoever had hit him must've taken her, he said. He'd looked for her in the front and back yard, even up and down the street, but he couldn't see anything without a lantern.

Walter seemed terrified. He was gasping for air, and the blood from his head wounds was still running down his face and into his mouth, making it hard for him to talk. He was having trouble keeping his head up.

"Mister Tom, please..." he pleaded.

But Tom Chalmers had no intention of going outside in such weather to look for some black man's missing girlfriend. That was something that could certainly wait for daylight.

Tom told Walter, as he led him back to the front door, that he needed to wrap a bandage around his head before he bled to death. They'd see about Mollie in the morning. He gently pushed the man out of the house, closed the door, cleaned up the blood on the floor, and went back to bed.

BUT MOLLIE SMITH WOULD BE FOUND THE next morning, and her murder would be the start of a year-long reign of terror by a vicious and diabolical madman. The killer traveled the city, striking by moonlight, using axes, knives, and even steel rods to rip women apart.

The story of the Austin murderer became one of the great American murder mysteries of the nineteenth century – perhaps made most famous because he was never caught.

Also, no matter how you look at it, he was America's first real serial killer. There had been other multiple murderers that came before him – and perhaps claimed as many victims as he did – but he was truly the first that would fit the criteria established a little less than a century later about what makes a serial killer what they are.

For the first time on record, an American city was forced to confront a vicious monster who was, for some unknown reason, driven to murder women in a ritualistic fashion. The string of murders in Austin would set a standard for what was to come in the twentieth century when serial killers chose their hunting ground and hunted their prey.

The Austin killer eluded the police, who were almost helpless to stop him. He taunted them for their failures, ensuring they couldn't predict where he'd strike next.

Worried citizens came up with increasingly desperate plans to stop the murders, suggesting things like giving all the women of the city a guard dog or lighting the entire city with newly invented "arc lamps" so the killer would have no place to hide.

Private detectives descended on Austin in droves, all hoping to find the killer and claim the sizable reward that was offered by the city's businessmen and by the governor of Texas himself.

Even a group of "alienists" from New York – as experts in the study of mental illness were referred to in those days – gathered at the New York Academy of Medicine to discuss the killer's methods, hoping they might somehow uncover his identity.

Before it all came to an end, at least a dozen men were arrested for the murders. There would be three different murder trials for three different suspects, all of whom claimed to be innocent – and undoubtedly were.

This is a story of violence, madness, bloodshed, and terror, and the story of a town that was pushed to the brink in response to one man's terrible crimes.

And it's also a story of the failure of a police force hampered by the inherent racism of the day. In fact, it was a year after the first attack when the murders finally stopped – only after the Austin killer slaughtered two *white* women. After that, the investigation finally began to be taken more seriously. For an entire year, the killer had targeted only African American women, so white families never imagined that the brutality would ever touch them. Meanwhile, black families in Austin were living in fear, terrified that a mother, sister, female relative, or friend might be attacked and killed while they slept.

Ultimately, this is a story about America's first serial killer and how he managed to elude capture and vanish into history. He was never punished, and the murders he committed remain unsolved.

The name of the Austin killer – or as he would come to be dubbed by the press, "The Servant Girl Annihilator"–has always been a mystery. We don't know who he was or why he went on that rampage in 1884 – 1885 that ended with so many dead. Was the killer a crazed drifter who found the city to be a fertile hunting ground? Was he, as so many Austin locals believed, a deranged black man?

Or was he well-known in society and lived an everyday life but occasionally felt the urge to murder women? And if so, was it true, as one rumor stated, that he was quietly captured and locked away to avoid public scandal for his well-connected family?

Or could the killer have been someone peripherally involved in the case, often present around the murder scenes but never seriously considered a suspect? There was at least one man who not only had an in-depth knowledge of the murders but had a connection to the investigators, was in a position to cover up his role in the crimes, and also murdered his entire family just a decade after the "Servant Girl" murders came to an end. Could he have been the killer that haunted Austin during that year of terror?

And could the killer have disappeared after the Austin murders only to resurface again later to carry out another series of murders and attacks?

As you'll see, anything seems to be possible.

FOR NOW, PREPARE YOURSELF FOR another book in my ongoing series of titles about unsolved ax murders. This is my third and will undoubtedly not be my last, as my fascination with murders committed by what was a "weapon of convenience" in the nineteenth century seems to know no bounds.

This volume is a little different, however. This one isn't about small towns in Iowa, Kansas, Illinois, and Texas that a mysterious stranger who traveled by train visited. It wasn't the early twentieth century when police officers – even in small towns – were a little more knowledgeable about crime and had greater access to assistance from larger departments and cities.

This is about a police force that might have been as modern as just about any department in the United States at the time. But even so, when these murders occurred in 1884 and 1885, the authorities in Austin – as those in pretty much anywhere else in America at the time – were unprepared for a killer like this. He came in the night, and he vanished without being seen. His victims were poor, mostly servant girls, so robbery was never the motive. He was committing murders just for the sake of killing.

He tasted blood on the night of December 30, 1884, and he found that he wanted more.

LEAVE THE LIGHTS ON and the doors locked for this one.

Troy Taylor
Late Winter / Spring 2024

1. AMERICAN CITY

LESS THAN A HALF-CENTURY BEFORE THE "Servant Girl" Murders, the city of Austin was nothing more than a scattering of houses and a primitive settlement on the frontier. A handful of traders and a few farmers were there, along with their families.

They'd arrived in 1838, just two years after the end of the Texas Revolution, which turned the Republic of Texas into an independent state. A man named Edward Burleson had surveyed the site and called the place "Waterloo." It was a name that wouldn't last.

In 1839, Texas was looking for a place to put its capital. It had been moving around over the past two years – a lot. Not surprisingly, President Sam Houston had moved it to Houston, named in his honor. However, shortly after the election of the new president, Mirabeau B. Lamar, the Texas Congress started searching for a permanent site. Lamar recalled a place of natural beauty that he'd visited the previous year on a buffalo hunt and suggested Waterloo. With its central location, nearby Colorado River, and many natural resources, the community made the cut.

But it wasn't without opposition. The new state capital site was far away from most population centers, which made it vulnerable to attacks from both Mexican troops and Native Americans. This made a lot of Texans – Sam Houston among them – unhappy with the choice. It was nearly abandoned a few times before Lamar prevailed, insisting the city would be a prime location to intersect roads that led to San Antonio and Santa Fe.

Officially chartered in 1839, Waterloo was renamed in honor of Stephen F. Austin, the beloved "Father of Texas," who had helped bring many of the first white settlers to the region. The first government buildings were crude log cabins, but after a

An early depiction of Austin and (below, right) the official plans for the city, created in 1839.

newspaper was started and a church was built by a group of Presbyterians, it seemed the new capital was on its way.

Judge Edwin Waller directed the planning and construction of the new city. He chose a 640-acre site on a bluff above the Colorado River, surrounded by other hills and rolling prairie. Austin became a picturesque place.

Yet life in the new capital was far from easy. In addition to the Comanche periodically attacking the residents, masked bandits robbing stores and stagecoaches that traveled back and forth to San Antonio, and wild hogs that slept in the downtown streets, frequent rainstorms made everything so muddy that wagons were able to traverse the rough roads.

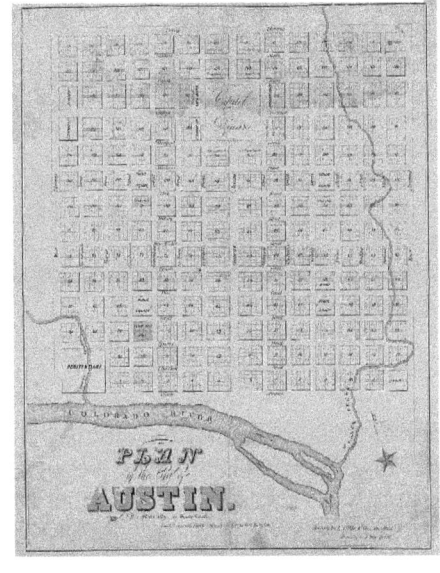

When Sam Houston regained the presidency in 1841, he announced that the national archives needed to be transferred back to Houston for safekeeping after Mexican troops captured

Texas President Sam Houston

San Antonio in March 1842. Convinced that removing the republic's diplomatic, financial, land, and military service records was the same as picking a new capital, Austin residents refused to give them up. Houston moved the government anyway, first to Houston and then to Washington-on-the-Brazos, which remained the seat of government until 1845.

When Houston sent a group of supporters to steal the archives one night in December 1842, they found themselves confronted by a group of armed residents, including a woman named Angelina Eberly, who fired a six-pound cannon at the men. The archives stayed in Austin.

Austin survived, but just barely. With no political function for over three years, the town languished, the population dropped, and the buildings deteriorated.

Even after Texas was annexed by the United States in 1845 – making it the twenty-eighth state in the union – Austin remained a dusty cow town with a ramshackle, wood-framed capitol building where the state legislature met every two years. The city would recover – or it would die.

Growth slowly began to happen. In five years, the population nearly quadrupled. By 1850, Austin's population had reached 854. Two hundred twenty-six of them were enslaved people, and one was a free black man. Nearly half the families in town owned enslaved people. The city was starting to recover, but not fast enough for some. In 1850, cities like Waco and Houston vying for the right to be the new capital made challenges. However, Austin decisively triumphed in that year's election, which determined the site of the capital for the next 20 years.

Finally, Austin began to grow. For the first time, the government constructed permanent buildings, including a new capitol building in 1853 and a governor's mansion in 1856. Asylums for the deaf, blind, and mentally ill were erected by the state on the outskirts of town. Congregations of Methodists, Baptists, Episcopalians, and

Austin in the 1850s

Catholics built new churches, and the city's politicians, businesspeople, and social elite built Greek Revival mansions to showcase their wealth. By 1860, the population had climbed to more than 3,500 people; one-third were slaves.

Then came the Civil War.

When Texas overwhelmingly voted to secede from the Union and join the Confederacy in 1861, Travis County – which includes Austin – was one of the few counties in the state to vote against secession. However, Union sympathies waned once the war began. By April 1862, about 600 local men had joined volunteer companies fighting for the Confederacy. During the war, Austin was never seriously threatened by Union troops. However, the city did experience a severe shortage of goods, spiraling inflation, and casualties and deaths among the men who left to fight.

After news that the Confederacy had surrendered reached Austin in late April 1865, civil order began to break down. Governor Pendleton Murrah vacated his office and fled to Mexico with other officials, leaving Lieutenant Governor Fletcher Stockdale to step up and serve in his place.

But Austin's biggest safety threat wasn't in the state house. In May, Captain George R. Freeman was forced to organize a company of 30 volunteers to protect the city from bandits and looters.

On June 11, a group of 50 men broke into the state treasury, and a gun battle ensued when Captain Freeman arrived with his men. One of the bandits was mortally wounded, and the others fled west with $17,000 in gold and silver. The escaping robbers – and their loot – were never found.

The aftermath of the war brought Union occupation troops as well as a large population of newly emancipated African Americans to the city. They established their own communities and soon numbered as much as one-third of the city's population again.

But Austin was in sad shape after the war. There was practically no industry left in 1865 except for a sawmill. About the only businesses that prospered were saloons, gambling parlors, and brothels. When the fence around the governor's mansion collapsed, there was no money to build a new one. Cattle wandered around town, grazing in yards, and the ever-present hogs were still a nuisance in the city's streets.

Elizabeth Custer, who accompanied her husband, General George Armstrong Custer, to Austin after the war, wrote: "Jayhawkers, bandits, and bushwhackers had everything their own way. The lawlessness was terrible."

The first railroad arrived in Austin in 1871 and changed the history of the city.

But all that changed in 1871 when the Houston and Texas Central Railway arrived and connected Austin to the rest of the state. By becoming the westernmost railroad terminus in Texas – and the only railroad town for miles around – Austin was transformed into the trading center of a vast area.

The city began to grow once more, and dramatic changes came to Austin. In the downtown area, wooden stables and saloons began to be replaced by solid masonry structures that still stand today. As construction boomed, the population more than doubled. Many new arrivals were immigrants from Mexico, Germany, Ireland, and Sweden.

Accompanying these changes were civic improvements, like gas streetlamps in 1874, the first mule-drawn streetcar line in 1875, and the first elevated bridge across the Colorado River in about 1876.

Although a second railroad – the International and Great Northern – arrived in Austin in 1876, the town's fortunes had already taken a downturn. The Texas economy had gone into free fall when the price of cotton, the state's largest commodity, collapsed from 30 cents to just 13 cents per pound. Land values fell, incomes dropped, and the state government nearly went bankrupt. Governor Richard B. Hubbard slashed state spending, but it didn't help. Within a year, the state's debt had risen from $3 million to $4 million. Half of the state remained unsettled, undeveloped, and lawless. As one news editor wrote, Texas seemed to be "headed straight for hell."

Cotton was the main crop of Texas and thousands of acres were grown across the state. Many fortunes in Austin rose and fell with the fortunes of the market.

By 1880, the price of cotton was rising again, and not only that, but Austin had also solidified its position as the capital after an election settled its location once and for all. In 1888, a new Texas State Capitol was completed in Austin, 31 feet taller than the National Capitol building in Washington, D.C.

In the early 1880s, cotton production in the state doubled, cattle brought in more money than ever, and a full-fledged economic boom began positively affecting every part of the state, especially Austin.

The Texas legislature had just agreed to fund the building of the long-planned state university in Austin. This four-story Gothic building would be called the University of Texas.

More and more passenger trains were arriving at the city's Union Depot, bringing lawyers, doctors, bookkeepers, clerks, and

Congress Avenue in downtown Austin, with the State Capitol in the background. This was the city's main business district and plays a major part in the story of the murders.

every kind of skilled laborer imaginable. New homes were built, along with boarding houses, hotels, offices, schools, factories, restaurants, and, of course, more saloons.

Some gunsmiths offered "Winchester Repeating Arms," and stores sold fine leather goods like "horse's saddles" and "cowman's boots." An art instructor named Doris Barker opened a studio to teach portrait and landscape painting to ladies of local society. Julien Prade opened an ice cream parlor that used a steam engine to blow air over blocks of ice to "air-cool" the parlor during the summer. Another clever businessman named Gus Barnett built a roller coaster, a "modern marvel of flight and speed" that he claimed was "exactly like the one at New York's Coney Island." His customers climbed stairs to the top of a tower, got into small open-air railroad cars, and raced down a 500-foot-long track in an exhilarating 16 seconds.

By January 1, 1885, Austin was four square miles in size, and it was predicted that the population would soar to at least 20,000 within another year. Compared to New York or Chicago, Austin still looked like a small western town, but no one could deny that the city was changing.

It was true that herds of cattle were sometimes still seen just east of the city as they were pushed from the southern Texas ranches to the Fort Worth and Kansas cattle markets, but Austin was no longer simply a dusty Cowtown.

Streetcars, shoppers, and traffic on Congress Avenue in Austin.

On every afternoon – except for Sunday – the city's main boulevard, Congress Avenue, teemed with shoppers, children on bicycles, and brightly painted, mule-driven streetcars. Members of Austin society – men in their best suits and Stetsons and women in feathered hats and grand dresses – walked up and down the Avenue's wooden sidewalks. Young women peered in windows at the fashionable mannequins that were on display. Young men stood outside the barber shop, where they'd just had their mustache waxed, to discuss the latest news. Shoeshine boys buffed gleaming pairs of boots, newspaper sellers called out the headlines, traveling salespeople hawked their wares, and fortune tellers offered passersby the chance to sit at their tables as they flipped their cards and unveiled the future.

On Saturday afternoons, downtown Austin was the scene for chess tournaments, rope-jumping contests, and even horse races. At the fairgrounds, the city's semi-professional baseball team – with the unimaginative name "The Austins" – faced off against teams from other Texas cities. Usually, as many as 50 runs were scored during an average game, primarily due to lively competition, tiny gloves, and terrible pitching.

One weekend, two "midget" sisters from Chicago came to Austin to perform musical duets. On another weekend, the famed boxer John L. Sullivan put on an exhibition at Millett's Opera House, inviting a group of hopeful Austin men into the ring to challenge him one by one.

The champ remained undefeated.

Mollie Bailey became known as the "Circus Queen of the Southwest" and she often brought parades through Austin in the 1880s to publicize her shows.

Local circus owner "Aunt Mollie" Bailey occasionally brought parades to the Avenue, showing off her clowns, painted ladies, sword swallowers, camels, trained canaries, and an elephant, who left behind droppings the size of cannonballs. Mollie also employed the "Boy Rope Walker," whose actual name was William Iry, who would string a rope between tall buildings on the Avenue and walk calmly back and forth, waving at the cheering crowds that were 30 feet below.

William Sidney Porter, who'd later gain fame as writer O. Henry.

One young man who had moved to Austin in 1884 – William Sydney Porter, a North Carolina native with dreams of being a writer – was so fascinated with the streets of downtown Austin that he sometimes slipped away from the cigar store where he worked to wander around. Two decades later, after he'd moved to New York, changed his name to O. Henry, and become one of the nineteenth century's most popular short story writers, he used his time in Austin as inspiration for some of his fiction.

And it's no surprise that he did. Austin was a town that seemed on the verge of a golden new era in the mid-1880s. Mayor John W. Robertson told anyone who would listen that the city was about to fulfill its destiny as a great American city with new-fangled telephones, electric lights, and even roller coasters.

IN THE MONTHS AND YEARS TO COME, newspaper reporters from all over the country would arrive in Austin. Many would ask the residents if they sensed anything terrible would happen in their city during those last hours of 1884.

In every case, the answer was "no."

They shook their heads, believing everything Mayor Robertson told them was true. Austin was a city that would become known all over America. And they were right; it would.

It just wouldn't be for any of the reasons that they imagined.

2. NEW YEAR'S EVE - 7:28 A.M.

THE SUN ROSE OVER AUSTIN AT 7:28 THAT morning. By then, the storm front had passed over the city, but a frigid chill remained. Few of the city's residents, who were not used to such temperatures, ventured out that morning if they didn't have to.

Just after 9:00, the telephone began ringing at the Austin Police Department, which was in a large room on the second floor of City Hall. It contained a few tables and chairs, a large stove, and a couple of tarnished brass spittoons for those who used chewing tobacco. It wasn't exactly a well-equipped police force, but it was about as modern as most city departments were in those days.

The day clerk, Bart DeLong, answered the telephone call by picking up the receiver, turning the crank, and shouting, "Police!"

There was static over the phone – usually caused by overhanging wires getting tangled when it was windy – but then the voice of an operator from the downtown exchange came through. She told DeLong she was patching through a call from the phone box at Ravy's Grocery on the west side of town.

After more static, DeLong heard the voice of Dr. Ralph

Steiner, a surgeon who'd worked in Austin for at least two decades. Dr. Steiner apparently didn't say much because the only thing DeLong wrote down in the daily police log was, "Doctor Steiner reports a woman lying near Ravy's store and wishes an officer sent out to take charge."

In the 1880s, the Austin Police Department was located on the second floor of City Hall.

There were 12 men on the Austin Police Department payroll. Only a few of them were in the office that morning. Grooms Lee, the city's young marshal, was home in bed, suffering from the flu. The number two man in the department, Sergeant John Chenneville, had taken the morning off because he was scheduled to work the streets that evening, keeping watch on the New Year's Eve celebrations. That left William Howe, a young officer in his mid-twenties, and DeLong directed him to the grocery store to find out what happened.

Howe was not a detective. He did patrol work, working the downtown streets and handing out tickets to citizens who left their horses hitched too long in front of a business or drove their carriages faster than a "slow trot." He arrested vagrants, shoplifters, and pickpockets. He collared drunks who urinated in alleys behind saloons and prostitutes who left the confines of the city's vice district in the southwest part of downtown.

Howe didn't investigate murders. Austin might have four or five murders in a year, but those cases – along with every other major case -- were handled by Sergeant Chenneville.

Maybe this wasn't murder. Dr. Steiner didn't say anything about murder – only that it was a dead woman. Perhaps she fell on the ice during last night's storm and died from exposure. That would be a minor investigation, Howe thought. He could handle that.

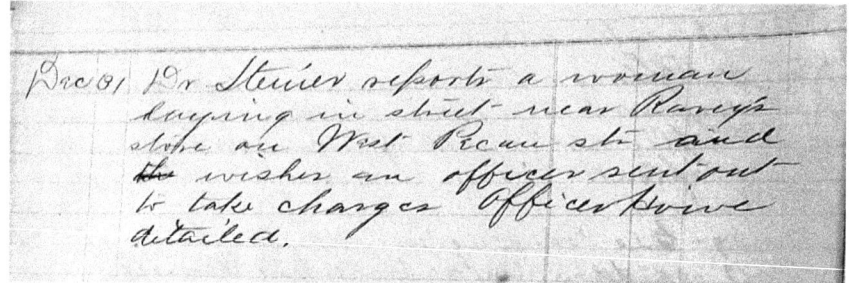

The original log book from the Austin Police Department, noting the report of Mollie Smith's murder by Dr. Steiner

    Howe hurried out the door in his department-issued Stetson hat and double-breasted overcoat with two vertical rows of buttons and a tin police badge pinned to the chest. He mounted his horse and rode to Ravy's, a half-mile from downtown. When he arrived, he was directed across the street to the home of insurance man William Hall.

    There, he found Tom Chalmers and Dr. Steiner, who lived a couple of houses away, waiting for him. There were other men from the neighborhood standing nearby. Tom told Howe about Walter Spencer coming to the house the night before, looking for his girlfriend, Mollie Smith, and begging for help. Dr. Steiner said that Walter had come to his house next, and he had bandaged his head and sent him on his way.

    Tom Chalmers picked up the story again and said that just after daylight, a man who worked for one of the Halls' neighbors was in the back alley picking up firewood when he saw a "strange-looking object" on the ground behind the Halls' outhouse. At first, he thought it was a dead animal, but then he realized it was the scrap of a nightdress. When he looked closer, he also saw the legs that were coming out of the nightdress – human legs covered with blood. That was when he started screaming.

    According to Chalmers, he, Dr. Steiner, and some other neighbors had come outside when they heard the screams, hurried to the outhouse, and saw what the man had found. Steiner walked over to Ravy's to call the police.

    Howe walked into the servant's apartment behind the Halls' kitchen. He saw that two or three pieces of furniture in the cramped space had been turned over, and a mirror had been knocked to the floor and broken. The sheets and pillows on the bed were soaked with blood – so much blood that it had dripped off one side of the bed and puddled on the floor. On the wall by the door leading into the backyard was a bloody handprint.

At the foot of the bed was a bloodstained ax.

Howe opened the door, followed the trail of blood more than 50 feet, got to the outhouse, and stopped.

Mollie Smith was lying on her back. Her head had been nearly split in two with the ax, and then she had been repeatedly stabbed in the chest and abdomen. Some of the gashes were so deep that her organs spilled out. Blood was everywhere. There was so much blood around her, flowing out into the alley, that she was resting in a pool of it.

It appeared that Mollie had been struck with the ax while lying in bed – just as Walter Spencer apparently had been – and then was dragged 50 feet from the house. Outside, she was not only stabbed repeatedly but was also struck by the ax several more times, leaving her body in such a state that it would not hold together in her coffin. After the killer slaughtered the young woman, he returned to the apartment and left the ax where it would be easily found. He must have assumed that Walter was dead or had no interest in mutilation of his body.

A reporter from the *Austin Daily Statesman* called the attack on Mollie Smith "one of the most horrible murders that ever a reporter was called on to chronicle – a deed almost unparalleled in the atrocity of its execution."

There is no police record of what happened next, but Officer Howe likely used the telephone at Ravy's to ask for help at the scene. Other officers soon arrived, including Sergeant Chenneville, who brought along his two bloodhounds, often used to track criminals on the run.

If there was a murderer on the loose, Chenneville – or his two slobbering dogs – was sure to find him.

JOHN CHENNEVILLE WAS IN HIS LATE THIRTIES at the time of the murders. He was a massive man with huge shoulders, big arms, a walrus-like mustache, and, according to local gossip, a handshake firm enough to crack corn. Whenever he walked into City Hall, staff members never had to look up to know he'd arrived because of the heavy thud of his boots. He could be fearsome when angry, but he was widely respected throughout the city.

Most people in town fondly called him "Ronnie O Johnnie." He'd been raised in New Orleans and spent his teenage years on a Confederate ship on the Mississippi River during the war. He arrived in Austin in the mid-1870s, joined the police department, and quickly became the city's most industrious officer. He was often seen roaring down streets, chasing after troublemakers with his holstered revolver slapping against his thigh. He never hesitated when he needed to push his way into saloons to break up fights. Chenneville also maintained a network of informants throughout the city who, for a few coins, would keep him notified about the activities of the more disreputable characters in town.

He was so dedicated to police work in Austin that he even traveled out of town to do it. Back in November, he'd gone down to San Antonio to get a look at all the thieves working the horse races there. He said he wanted to memorize their faces in case they decided to come to Austin's annual fair in December. When the fair ended without a single crime, the newspaper praised Chenneville for his vigilance.

The burly sergeant was also a member of Austin's fire department for about 20 years, serving in the Hook and Ladder Company and then as foreman of the Washington Fire Company No. 1.

Even now, a decade after he'd arrived in Austin, little about "Ronnie O Johnnie" had changed. He was just as big and just as tough as he'd always been, and he continued to work the streets at night so the city's riffraff would know he was still in charge. Each day, he rode his horse through downtown – once in the morning and once in the afternoon – so that he'd be spotted by those who never dared cross him.

He walked into the Halls' backyard and went to the outhouse to look at Mollie's body. Unlike Officer Howe, he'd seen more than his share of dead bodies – in every kind of state a person could dream up in their worst nightmare – but he'd never seen anything like this.

Mollie Smith had been slaughtered like an animal.

Despite all his years chasing criminals, Chenneville was not a homicide detective. Almost all the murders he'd investigated had occurred in Austin's saloons and poor neighborhoods, where liquor and a handy weapon could often lead to a killing. None were planned, and almost all happened in front of witnesses. Usually, the killer never even tried to run, and when he sobered up, he regretted what he'd done. All Chenneville typically had to do was show up, take away the gun or knife, and escort the perpetrator to jail.

But on this day, Chenneville had no killer waiting to be arrested. None of his informants could help him, and there was no forensics to help him study the scene. That kind of science hadn't even been invented in 1884. There was some inkling that every person's fingerprints were different and could be used to identify someone, but no procedure had been devised that allowed the police to put that knowledge to use.

As part of a standard murder investigation, police officers looked for footprints around a body. Sometimes, the prints were measured and sketched on a piece of paper or dug from the ground and preserved with plaster, hoping they might later be matched with a suspect's prints. But if there had been any prints around Mollie's body, they'd already been destroyed by the boots of Tom Chalmers, Dr. Steiner, and the other men from the neighborhood who'd come over to get a look at the body.

The only investigative tool that Chenneville had that New Year's Eve morning was his two bloodhounds. Howling loudly, the dogs were led to Mollie's body, then Mollie's apartment, where they dropped their heads and sniffed the floor, the bed, the wall with the bloody handprint, and the ax.

But like their owner, the dogs had never encountered such a scene, and all they seemed able to smell was the slain woman's blood. They picked up no sign of the elusive killer.

Reporters would play an important role in the way the story of the murders spread across the county – and created a feeling of panic in Austin.

AROUND THE SAME TIME CHENNEVILLE was discovering his bloodhounds wouldn't be much help in the case, he heard hoofbeats and carriage wheels from the front of the house – the press had arrived. There was a reporter from the *Austin Statesman*, another from the soon-to-be-defunct *Austin Daily Sun*, and a few more from Dallas, Houston, Galveston, and Fort Worth, all of which had bureaus in Austin to report about politics in the state capital.

One of the telephone operators who connected the calls to the police station must have alerted a newsman about the dead woman, and, with little else to do on New Year's Eve morning, they decided to check out the story.

Chenneville recognized many of the reporters that were soon standing in the yard behind the Hall house. They were usually a cocky, talkative bunch, but today, they were silent. To keep from throwing up, one of the men walked to another part of the yard, unable to look at what had once been Mollie Smith. They whispered among themselves. A couple of the older reporters had seen things like this in the past – before the

Comanche had been sent away to a reservation in Oklahoma – but he knew this was no Indian attack.

Maybe, one of the men suggested, Mollie's boyfriend, Walter Spencer, had invented the story about waking up and finding her missing. Perhaps they'd gotten into an argument, and he'd killed her with an ax and a knife – then hit himself in the head and face with the ax to make it look like he'd been attacked, too.

But those who knew Walter couldn't imagine him doing anything like that. Except for an arrest for disturbing the peace back in 1881, he'd never been in trouble with the law. His employers at the brickyard considered him an excellent employee. Each black laborer was tasked with carrying 500 bricks daily to the delivery wagons outside the yard. If he didn't do so for any reason – even illness or injury – he didn't receive his daily pay of 75 cents. Walter always made his quota.

The case for his innocence was bolstered when Nancy Anderson, an African American woman who worked as a part-time nurse for the Halls, told the police and reporters that Walter and Mollie had a "peaceful relationship." Walter did anything Mollie asked him to do, and the couple was on "the best of terms."

Tom Chalmers had to admit that Walter certainly hadn't acted like a man who'd committed a murder when he came into the house early that morning. He had to have known the risk he was taking when he walked unannounced into a white family's home. If Tom had shot him in the foyer, there would have been no arrest and no questions asked. Yet, instead of running away like a normal killer would have, Walter had looked for help and seemed genuinely concerned about Mollie's fate.

When the reporters and policemen began comparing notes – a common practice at the time – someone brought up a former boyfriend of Mollie's named William "Lem" Brooks. He worked at one of the city's downtown saloons, washing and drying glasses, and on his nights off, he called out steps at the city's black dances. Brooks first got to know Mollie in Waco, where they'd both been born. As a teenager, Mollie had been involved with another man and had given birth to a son. At some point after having the baby, she'd broken up with that man and started seeing Brooks. But when Mollie's son died from an untreated illness when he was only six, she decided to start her life over and moved to Austin. Brooks had followed her, hoping to rekindle their romance, but by then, Mollie was already involved with Walter Spencer. Brooks was supposedly so upset that he tried to fight Walter when they recently ran into each other downtown.

When Chenneville and the other officers heard this story, they immediately left for downtown, looking for Brooks. They found him sleeping at the home of his new girlfriend, Rosa Brown.

After being hauled out of bed, Brooks stammered out an alibi – he had spent the evening at a dance on the city's east side, two miles away from the Hall home. He'd been there until 4:00 A.M. and had two dozen witnesses who could prove it.

But Chenneville arrested him anyway. Brooks – the jealous ex-lover – was the only suspect he had. The man was brought to the station under "suspicion of murder," which under the criminal code of the time was not the same as being arrested for murder. It only meant the police wanted to keep a suspect in custody while the investigation continued.

Brooks was the first person arrested for the murders, but he wouldn't be the last.

The City-County Hospital, where the bodies of all the victims were taken for autopsy.

BY THE TIME BROOKS WAS LOCKED UP, it was early afternoon. The temperature was still below freezing, so the wheels of the wagon traveling up the alley behind the Hall house made a cracking sound on the frozen earth. A black man who volunteered as the undertaker for the local African American community had arrived to pick up Mollie's body and take her to the "dead room" at the City-County Hospital for an autopsy.

The man found this to be a difficult task. According to one reporter's account, when the undertaker tried to pick up Mollie and place her in a crude, wooden casket, her body didn't "hold together."

After regaining his composure, the man tried again. It took several trips between the place where the body lay and the horse-drawn wagon to remove every part of Mollie's corpse. When he was finished, the undertaker called out to his horse, and the animal trudged forward, disappearing down the narrow alleyway until the clip-clop of its hooves faded into the distance.

Meanwhile, Tom Chalmers had started cleaning the blood off the walls and floors of Mollie's room. He threw out the sheets and blankets, tossed her clothing in the trash, and discarded the broken mirror that had fallen from the wall. Tom wanted everything to be clean and order restored by the time his brother-in-law returned to Austin.

He wanted to ensure this unfortunate incident was behind them, so they'd never have to think about it again.

3. NEW YEAR'S EVE - CELEBRATION

WHEN DUSK DESCENDED ON AUSTIN THAT day, the city's lamplighter, Henry Stamps, began making his rounds of the downtown district. Using a long wooden pole with a dangling wick, he walked up and down Congress Avenue and Pecan Street, lighting the gas lamps that lined the sidewalks.

The owners of saloons and restaurants – preparing for the busiest hours of New Year's Eve – began stoking the fires in their stoves and scraping the ice from the wooden sidewalks in front of their doors. A few of the more prosperous proprietors turned on their new, electrically powered, incandescent light bulbs. The filaments inside the bulbs – guaranteed to last for an astonishing six hours – hissed to life, and light poured from windows, almost reaching the other side of the street.

By 7:00 P.M., Austin residents were heading downtown on horseback, in carriages, or by horse-drawn taxi. The wealthiest among them had reservations at Simon and Bellenson's, the city's finest restaurant.

Others made their way to Millett's Opera House to see "The Banker's Daughter," a comedy performed by a traveling theatrical troupe about a young woman stuck marrying a man old enough to be her father.

Millett's Opera House

Others paid the 25-cent admission fee to attend a "Dancing and Roller-Skating Carnival" at Turner Hall, which offered music performed by the 14-piece Manning Rifle Band. Couples whirled in a giant circle around the wooden floor in their metal skates, the women giggling and shrieking as they tried to maintain their balance in the thick skirts they wore. At intermission, there was a half-mile race for men. The winner received a basket of apples.

Turner Hall in the early 1800s

All evening, the saloons were packed with customers. The Gold Room held a raffle for a gold-plated shotgun worth $125, and the Crystal Room offered billiards on its three tables, which had been shipped to Texas from New York City. Over at the Iron Front, Austin's oldest saloon, which had an oak bar the length of a railroad car and a massive buffalo head on the wall, bartenders were offering a new brew from St. Louis called Budweiser. Each glass was only a nickel. Upstairs, the Iron Front's gambling parlor offered games of Monte, faro, chuck-a-luck, poker, and keno.

That night, the biggest party in Austin was the New Year's Eve Phantom Ball at the Brunswick Hotel. It was a masquerade party with women in evening gowns and black masks sweeping through the ballroom, followed by their husbands in masks, black capes, and carrying wooden swords. Wait staff stood by each door, offering flutes of champagne and glasses of lemonade for those who abstained from liquor. In the center of the ballroom, water poured from the top of the hotel's famous "rustic fountain" and ran downward through a jungle of fake foliage before landing in a tub filled with glistening rocks. A small band was on hand to entertain throughout the night, mostly playing a selection of German polkas. At the stroke of midnight, everyone raised their glasses and toasted to the future of their thriving city.

Outside on the street, as midnight arrived, children shot off Roman candles and sent "sky lanterns" – paper containers with small candles suspended at the bottom – into the night. Several men who were filled up with liquor staggered out of the saloons and fired their pistols into the air. The crowd cheered. Men and women kissed. Music filtered out into the street from the open doors of restaurants and taverns.

The entire city was celebrating the arrival of the New Year.

Autopsies in the 1880s were very different than those conducted today. Without the scientific advances that would come in the next century, doctors like William Burt could only examine a victim's wounds and write notes on what he observed.

PERHAPS NOT THE ENTIRE CITY.

While residents of Austin – both rich and poor – were welcoming in the New Year, Mollie Smith's body was being taken down into the basement dead room at the city's hospital. The smell of her blood, combined with the acrid chemicals in the bottles on the shelves, was a much harsher aroma than could be found in even the meanest saloons in the city.

Dr. William Burt, the hospital's staff physician, wasn't celebrating the New Year – not yet anyway. He had been asked to perform an autopsy on the murdered woman who had been found that morning. Even though she was African American, and most doctors would have waited until after the holiday to perform the grim task, Dr. Burt wanted to get the examination over with. His wife was waiting for him. Like everyone else in town, Dr. Burt had engagements that night to mark the end of the year.

He recorded Mollie's height and weight on a sheet of paper and then looked over her hands, fingernails, wrists, and the inside of her upper arms. Then, he carefully examined Mollie's wounds. Not sure what else he could do, Dr. Burt took a few more notes, pulled a sheet over the body, and left the dead room. A short time later, he was on his way home.

Mollie Smith wasn't going anywhere, and Dr. Burt likely felt the same way the police did – there were few murders in the city of Austin, and Mollie's, like all the rest, would undoubtedly be solved soon.

4. RINGING IN THE NEW YEAR

ON JANUARY 1, 1885, PEOPLE ALL OVER AUSTIN were celebrating their good fortune. They lived in a thriving American city and were convinced the new year would bring Austin prosperity and happiness.

That morning, there were at least a dozen "calling parties" at homes throughout the city. Wealthy and middle-class men alike dropped in at the homes of single young women in hopes of beginning a new relationship in the new year. They were usually accompanied by friends and family, giving the occasion a festive air. Wealthier folks were shuttled from one house to the next by what were known as "black and bays" – black boys who drove carriages pulled by chestnut-colored horses. Standing at the front doors to greet the guests were the young, unmarried women wearing gowns ordered months in advance from Austin dressmakers. The men handed out calling cards, which were six inches long and two and one-half inches wide, to the young ladies, who led everyone inside for hot drinks and refreshments.

Governor John Ireland

Later in the day, Texas Governor John Ireland hosted his annual New Year's Day open house at the governor's mansion, which was at that time the largest in the country and built on a small hill overlooking the city.

Texas Governor's Mansion

Ireland was handsome with a high forehead, broad-ridged nose, and a well-groomed beard. He was once described as "a great favorite with the ladies." Just two months earlier, he had been reelected to another two-year term as governor, and there was already talk that he might be considering a run for the U.S. Senate in 1886.

On this day, he was in a fine mood. Earlier that morning, he had signed pardons for a handful of convicts at the state prison who he believed had served enough time. He had met with Reverend Abraham Grant, the pastor of Austin's all-black African Methodist Episcopal Church, to hear his complaints about the railroads in Texas ordering black customers to buy first-class tickets but forcing them to ride in second-class cars. Ireland had also met with a delegation of children from the state's Institute for the Blind, who presented him with brooms they'd made in the institute's factory.

William Swain

That afternoon, with Anna, his wife, wearing a black silk gown and standing beside him, he greeted his many guests, which included members of the Texas legislature, judges from the state's supreme court, members of his administration, and a legion of admirers, well-wishers, and even the man who wanted to replace him.

William Swain was the state's comptroller, in charge of revenue and taxes. In November, he'd been reelected to office by the largest majority of votes ever cast for any candidate for public office in Texas history. Almost every newspaper in the state predicted a gubernatorial victory for Swain in the 1886 election. He was well-liked by nearly everyone who knew him, and the *Fort Worth Gazette* noted that Swain had "that dignity of intellect and personal bearing which would make him a leader of men anywhere."

Throughout the afternoon, Ireland, Swain, and other important men of Texas downed their cordials, spoke grandly about the state's future, and likely glanced many times at the young women in their gowns on the other side of the room. The smell of their cigar smoke mixed with the aroma of roasted pigs and turkey wafting up from the kitchen.

After dinner and after the open house ended, the governor's guests made their final toasts, gathered their coats, and walked out the front door to the mansion's vast front porch to await the arrival of their carriages.

From the porch, the guests could look off into the distance and see the grounds where the new capitol building was being constructed. They could see the freight trains arriving at the depot and hear the clang of their bells, their whistles, and the lurching and rumbling of their wheels as they steamed into position to unload the goods that would soon be sold in the shiny stores downtown.

None of the guests standing on the porch that evening would have dreamed that Austin was about to descend into chaos.

AT GOVERNOR IRELAND'S OPEN HOUSE, AT THE various calling parties, and all the other gatherings that took place in the city that day, it's likely that the murder of Mollie Smith was a topic of conversation.

The murder had, after all, been featured prominently on page three – the page devoted to local news – of the *Daily Statesman*. The headline was both eye-catching and lurid:

BLOODY WORK. A FEARFUL MIDNIGHT MURDER ON WEST PECAN – MYSTERY AND CRIME. A COLORED WOMAN KILLED OUTRIGHT, AND HER LOVER ALMOST DONE FOR.

An unnamed reporter for the newspapers detailed the killing and described Mollie's body as "a ghastly body to behold" and added that "a horrible hole on the side of her head" was the cause of death.

The reporter then mentioned he had interviewed Walter Spencer, whom he'd found at his brother's apartment. His brother was a cook at Newton's Restaurant downtown, and he lived above it. Walter was in great pain, with five deep gashes in his head and a wound under his eye that had fractured his orbital bone. In a weak and halting voice, he told the newsman that after Tom Chalmers and Dr. Steiner had thrown him out of their homes, he'd staggered around the neighborhood, still looking for Mollie, before he went to his brother's place.

When asked about Lem Brooks, Walter did say that he and his romantic rival had confronted one another in October, but it hadn't turned physical. Walter added that he didn't think Brooks would have killed Mollie. "I don't know who did it," he said. "But anybody could have got into Mollie's room easily through the door connecting it with the kitchen."

The reporter had also gone to the jail to interview William Brooks. The young man said he liked Mollie and Walter and had gotten over his ill feelings about Mollie leaving him. He told the reporter, "I'm innocent of the murder, and can prove by any number of witnesses that I was at the ball at Sand Hill until four o'clock in the morning. They've got a hold of the wrong man, for sure."

Brooks may not have felt as friendly toward Walter and Mollie as he claimed, but the reporter found several witnesses who swore that Brooks was definitely at the dance until 4:00 A.M. when Tom Chalmers said Walter had awakened him. If those men were telling the truth, the reporter stated, then Brooks would have had to have run two miles from Sand Hill to the Halls' house at "almost lightning speed" to have knocked Walter unconscious and cut Mollie to pieces. It just didn't seem possible.

And why, the reporter asked, would Brooks take the time to slash apart his former girlfriend and leave her new lover alive but unconscious?

The article did point out that there had been some speculation about Walter himself being the killer but added that it seemed unlikely. Even so, "the reader is left to draw his own conclusions," he concluded. "Whether slain by her love, or some party outside, is as yet a mystery that envelops as four a deed as was ever done in Austin."

LATER THAT DAY, THE CORONER'S INQUEST was held with a jury of six men who assembled to listen to statements from witnesses, police officers, and doctors. The inquest would decide if the death was unusual, unexplained, or suspicious. After the testimony was concluded, the jurors would declare what they believed was the cause of death.

Mollie Smith's inquest was privately held, but newspaper reporters who lingered outside the courtroom doors strained to pick up whatever new information they could. They learned that no one who testified could name anyone but William Brooks who might have had reason to harm Mollie. It was also suggested – probably by Sergeant Chenneville -- that Brooks could have killed Mollie before he went to the dance that night.

After some deliberation, the inquest jurors returned to the courtroom, and the foreman announced they believed William "Lem" Brooks had inflicted the injuries that killed Mollie Smith.

Why hadn't he killed Walter Spencer, too? The jurors speculated that perhaps Brooks left him alive because he wanted the police to believe Walter was the killer. Or maybe he planned to return to the apartment and use the ax on him when he finished cutting up Mollie and was scared away by something, perhaps a noise.

Obviously, the inquest jury had no more ideas about who killed Mollie than the police did. They decided, just like Chenneville did, that Brooks was the only suspect, so he must have done it.

THAT SAME AFTERNOON, WHILE THE INQUEST WAS taking place at the courthouse, the undertaker returned to the hospital's dead room, placed Mollie's broken body into his wagon, and drove to the Colored Ground, the African American section of the city cemetery.

Located at the bottom of a hill, the Colored Ground was the most scenic part of the cemetery – until heavy rain came and flooded all the graves.

A few of Mollie's friends came to witness her burial, shivering in the cold air. After singing some spirituals, they returned home to their little houses and shanties, unable to come to grips with the brutality that had occurred.

After the funeral, the cemetery's elderly caretaker, Charles Nitschke, was in his office near the front gates and opened the ledger that recorded the names of everyone buried at the cemetery. He wrote Mollie's name in one column and marked her birthplace as Waco in another.

But the kindly older man felt no purpose would be served by detailing the young woman's murder. Under the column that listed the cause of death for the deceased, he wrote only that Mollie had died from "a broken skull."

University of Texas

AND THAT WAS THE END OF MOLLIE'S STORY, or so most people in Austin believed. Days passed. Students began arriving at the University of Texas. Performances continued at Millett's Opera

House. People dined in restaurants, drank in saloons, and went on with everyday life.

When the state's cattlemen arrived for their annual convention in Austin, city officials welcomed them with banners stretched across Congress Avenue that spelled out messages of congratulations. At the Cattlemen's Ball, the highlight of the convention, decanters of whiskey were placed on every table, and they dined on steaks as thick as a man's arm. They danced with what one newspaper called "Austin's most beautiful belles" – single women who had been invited to the ball – and at the end of the night, some of them slipped away to the Variety Theatre to watch Ida St. Clair, a scantily-dressed blond who "commanded the admiration of every cowboy from Austin to the Rio Grande." Other cattlemen visited the brothel of the vice district's most prominent madam, Miss Blanche Dumont, who promised all sorts of wonders with her girls upstairs in a fake British accent.

Life in Austin moved on.

In late January 1885, there was a brief mention in the *Daily Statesman* about William Brooks being released from jail. The police hadn't found anything that could link him to Mollie's murder, and a county grand jury had decided there wasn't enough evidence against him to indict him.

But no one in the city – at least no one who was white – was concerned about the news of Brooks' release. The few white residents who still had an interest in the case were convinced that Mollie's death was nothing more than a "Negro killing" committed by a "jealous or deceived Negro lover." That kind of unseemly behavior was of no interest to them.

However, an Austin reporter for the *Galveston Daily News* had a helpful suggestion for Pastor Abraham Grant. He wrote that instead of the reverend meeting with the governor to ask for improved seating arrangements on trains, maybe he "would serve his race better by addressing his efforts to the suppression of their murderous instincts."

AS THE WEEKS PASSED, THERE WERE, OF COURSE, more parties, including an "onion sociable" at the home of one young woman. During this somewhat scandalous event, the young woman and five of her female friends went into a bedroom, where one of them took a bite of an onion, after which they were each kissed by a young man who tried to guess who had onion breath.

There were performances at Turner Hall and a stunt show at the fairgrounds that was put on by Miss Louise Armaindo of New York City, who was billed as the finest female bicyclist in the world. She sped down the track before an enthusiastic crowd, traveling a quarter mile in just 46 seconds and beating a horse racing against her by a full length. Later that evening, she put on a weight-lifting exhibition.

At the temporary state capitol building, legislators gathered for their session, offering grand proposals to improve the state. Money was demanded for public education, railroad tracks, a deepened harbor at Galveston, and a radical plan proposed by Temple Houston – son of Sam Houston – suggesting that half the clerks employed in the state's main offices be women. Newspapers reported that "scores of handsomely dressed and intelligent ladies" came to the capitol to show their support for the bill and applauded loudly when Houston rose to speak. Although the bill had no chance of passing, the women were thrilled, believing that women's rights would soon be coming to Texas.

Maybe, they dared to dream, they might someday even gain the right to vote.

On February 12, a wedding was held in Austin at what seemed on the surface to be an unlikely location – the State Lunatic Asylum. However, the bride was Ella Denton, the 19-year-old daughter of the asylum's superintendent, Dr. Ashley Denton.

The Texas State Lunatic Asylum was a three-story, classical-style building with Corinthian columns, long windows, and a massive porch. On either side of the main building were dormitories for men and women. A third dormitory for the "male colored lunatics" was a short distance away, while "female colored lunatics" were housed in the basement of the main hall. Farther away was the Cross Pits, a small building with barred cells where the most violent patients were held. The asylum was just over two miles away from downtown, away from the business and residential districts. Only a lone dirt track – called Asylum Road – connected the asylum with the rest of the city.

In the past, very few people in Austin would go anywhere near the asylum. Even as recently as 1880, conditions were reported as terrible – dirty, overcrowded, and odors so stifling that it was hard

The Texas State Lunatic Asylum was located two miles from downtown Austin and was the first hospital of its kind in the state.

to breathe. But after Dr. Denton was appointed as superintendent in 1883, he began a massive renovation program to transform the asylum from a place where the mentally ill were warehoused and kept away from society to what he called "a refuge for those unfortunates whose voices cannot be heard."

Dr. Denton used a generous grant from the state to buy new beds for patients' rooms, paint all the walls a gleaming white, and landscape the grounds, adding lily ponds, gazebos, benches, flower beds, statuary, and curving paths – which were considered more therapeutic than straight ones.

He removed the 10-foot-high fence surrounding the building and replaced it with a lower one. He moved the asylum's cemetery, where the unclaimed dead were buried, away from the main building and to the

Patients were encouraged to spend time on the manicured grounds with the belief that being outdoors could cure various kinds of mental illness.

other side of a hill so that his patients wouldn't have to see it and be "overcome by morbid thoughts."

He set up a daily schedule that had the inmates awake before dawn when they were given a hearty breakfast – a leading theory of the time was that insanity was caused by malnutrition – and then sent off to work. The asylum had a 120-acre farm and a 15-acre orchard to keep them busy. He encouraged them to read books and newspapers at the end of the day, sing songs around the piano, play cards, chess, billiards, or go bowling on the single lane in the basement.

While staff members wore gray uniforms with long sleeves and high necks, the patients were allowed to wear ordinary clothing to promote high esteem. He also ordered fresh flowers to be placed in the hallways and allowed cats and dogs to roam the asylum grounds.

Dr. Ashley Denton, the groundbreaking superintendent of the State Hospital for the Insane.

Unlike past officials, Dr. Denton took in anyone brought to him, regardless of their ailment, which filled the hospital with more than 500 patients suffering from every kind of nervous disorder of the day. Denton believed that within the quiet sanctuary of the asylum, all his "unfortunates" had a better chance at regaining at least some of their sanity and might someday return to the outside world.

Dr. Denton envisioned the wedding of his daughter, Ella, to his young assistant superintendent, Dr. James P. Given, as the ideal opportunity to introduce his new, modern asylum to members of Austin society. Dressed in their most fashionable clothes, his wealthy guests traveled along Asylum Road, passed through the iron gates, and climbed the front steps to the wedding venue.

More than a few guests likely felt apprehensive as they got their first look at the nearly fenceless asylum. A few of them likely even peeked into the Cross Pits building, which housed 52 violent patients on that day, including a madman named Lombard

Stephens, who'd sent a letter to the governor vowing that he'd eat his brains if he weren't given $500,000.

But when assembled in the high-ceiling foyer, Dr. Denton assured them they had nothing to fear. He pointed out the bell in front of the main building, which was rung whenever a patient escaped but told them it hadn't been used in months.

The Asylum dining hall

The wedding ceremony was held in the asylum's chapel, where Ella, dressed all in white, was given away to her new husband. Dr. Given was a striking man – tall, athletic, with dark brown hair and a handlebar mustache. An Episcopalian minister conducted the service, and then the entire entourage left the chapel and went to the dining hall, where servers, some of whom were patients at the hospital, served breakfast.

Friends lifted glasses in honor of the bride and groom, and then Dr. Denton made a toast, asking that good fortune follow them for the rest of their lives. At the end of the breakfast, Denton led the guests to the front porch to watch the newlyweds ride off in a carriage to the train station, where they'd depart to spend their honeymoon in New Orleans and St. Louis.

Everyone cheered and waved, and the asylum patients, their faces pressed against the windows of their dormitories, cheered and waved along with them. The wedding had been a remarkable success for Dr. Denton, much better than he could have dreamed. For a few hours, he had welcomed the sane into the world of the insane, and no one had been afraid. He truly believed at that moment that he was on the verge of removing the prejudices that the people of Auston held against his asylum, his refuge for the unfortunate.

But events were conspiring against his grand dreams. Soon, the asylum would become the center of controversy in the city as Austin residents began to fear that one of Denton's patients was on the loose, murdering his way through the young women of the town.

Or worse, that Denton was shielding a patient from prosecution for the murders. And not just any patient – but one uncomfortably close to home.

5. THE MARCH 1885 ATTACKS

ON MARCH 2, 1885, THE ANNIVERSARY OF TEXAS' independence from Mexico, Mayor Robertson and other city leaders put on the biggest event in the city's history – a lavish parade up Congress Avenue for the laying of the 16,000-pound granite cornerstone for the new state capitol building.

For weeks, advertisements had appeared in newspapers all over the state, encouraging everyone to come to Austin to see the cornerstone lowered into the ground. Letters had been sent to Texas public schools, inviting students and teachers, and more than 3,000 invitations had gone out to prominent people outside of Texas – even one to the president of Mexico.

Before the parade began, it was estimated that at least 25,000 people lined the downtown streets. The upper floors of buildings along Congress Avenue were filled with women and children in holiday attire, leaning out the windows for a better view. The buildings themselves were draped with bunting and Texas flags.

Somewhere in the distance, the Manning Rifle Band began to play, and at the stroke of noon, a whistle blew to mark the official start of the parade, which lasted for nearly an hour. The crowd roared as Governor Ireland, Mayor Robertson, and dozens of other government officials passed in open-topped buggies. They were followed on foot by men from Austin's trade unions, professors and students from the University of Texas, athletes who train at the Austin Athletic Association, Jewish and German immigrants, and a small group of "colored representatives."

The March 2 parade ended at the grounds of the new state capitol, where a ceremony took place during the laying of the cornerstone.

Local businessmen passed by on decorated horse-drawn wagons -- A home builder had doors, windows, sashes, and buckets of paint on his float; a baker featured cakes and pastries; the owner of a tack and saddle shop had a float displaying "full cowboy outfits" as well as his best horse gear; and the list went on. At the back of the parade were the owners of the Iron Front Saloon – who'd been sampling their own wares – and they waved signs advertising their drink specials and casino games.

After the last float passed, the party moved to the capitol grounds, where a half-dozen construction rigs rose high into the air. Suspended from the one in front was the cornerstone. Inside this block was a zinc box containing over 200 mementos and items donated by Austin residents, like photographs, drawings, Bibles, artificial teeth from the State Dental Association, and much more. Mayor Roberston placed several reports inside the box detailing Austin's excellent state of affairs, a directory of citizens, and the roster of children attending Austin's public schools.

Following a speech by Governor Ireland and a 49-gun salute from the Travis Light Artillery, the cornerstone was sealed and, to the accompaniment of cheers and applause from the crowd, was lowered into the ground.

And then, one week later, a young servant woman woke up in the middle of the night and found a mysterious man standing next to her bed.

THE YOUNG WOMAN WAS A RECENT IMMIGRANT from Germany who lived in a one-room servants' quarters behind the kitchen of a large home on Hickory Street.

Yes, almost the same living situation as Mollie Smith.

She later told the police that the man just stood there for a moment, mostly hidden in the darkness, and then he suddenly said, "Your money or your life!"

The young woman screamed, and the man struck her over the head with some unknown hard object, splitting open her scalp.

Hearing the screams, the house owner ran from his bedroom to the young woman's quarters in the back. By the time he got there, though, the man was gone.

FOUR NIGHTS LATER, A BLACK COOK who worked for a local doctor was awakened by what she described as "a violent shaking" at the locked door to her private quarters. When she looked out the window, no one was there.

An hour later, in a nearby neighborhood, two young black women were also awakened by the rattling of a locked doorknob. The door led into their quarters, which were located behind a mansion belonging to their employer, Major Joseph Stewart, a former Confederate officer who spent most of his time touring the state, performing a lengthy poem that he'd written about the glories of the Old South.

One of the women opened the door and stepped outside to see who was there, then suddenly felt herself grabbed roughly from behind. She screamed for help, and her attacker, whom she never saw, released her and ran away.

Too terrified to be alone, the two women spent the rest of the night in the kitchen. But when they returned to their room the next morning, they discovered a lamp – which had not been lit when they left – somehow burning. They also found their bedding and clothing thrown into a pile in the middle of the room. Apparently, whoever had been trying to get into the room earlier had returned while they were in the kitchen.

TWO NIGHTS AFTER THE INCIDENT AT MAJOR Stewart's home, an intruder slipped into the servants' quarters at the rear of a home house belonging to Abe Williams, owner of a shop that sold fine suits and dresses.

In the darkness, the intruder attacked the Williams housekeeper, tearing the covers from her bed and brutally striking her several times on the head and face. She was still screaming when the man disappeared.

THE ATTACKS STOPPED FOR A FEW DAYS, but then, on March 19, someone started tapping on the window of the servants' quarters behind the home of Colonel J.H. Pope, a cotton planter who owned a large farm outside of town. Pope's two servant girls – Swedish immigrant teenagers named Christine and Clara – froze in their beds, too terrified to move.

Then, the tapping stopped, and there was the sound of a pistol shot. The bullet passed through the window and lodged in a wall. Screaming, the girls slammed the door open to the outside and raced toward the main house. One of the girls, Clara, was grabbed from behind but was unable to turn around and look at her assailant. She did keep screaming, though, and that brought Colonel Pope and his sons outside with guns. At the sight of the armed men, the attacker released Clara and ran into the darkness.

The two teenagers returned to their room and locked and barricaded the door. Within minutes, though, another shot was fired through the window. The bullet struck Christine in the back, between her shoulder blade and spine, knocking her to the ground. Luckily, it had missed her vital organs, and she survived.

IN THE DAYS THAT FOLLOWED EACH ATTACK, stories appeared in the newspaper, but little thought was given to them. No one – at that time, at least – connected them with the murder of Mollie Smith, and no one would consider the implications of a mysterious man breaking into the rooms of servant girls until later when girls began to die.

Like many other growing cities, Austin had its share of petty crime. Thieves broke into homes and stole valuables and unattended purses. Chickens disappeared from backyards, and men who traveled the country by freight train sometimes jumped off in Austin and wandered the town for a few days, looking for things to steal.

The attacks on local servant girls were perplexing, mostly because whomever the man who was breaking into their quarters wasn't looking for anything to steal. He seemed more interested in hurting or frightening them, a crime no one could wrap their heads around. So, they did what people in the South had been doing for years – they blamed the attacks on the "colored folk."

White Austin residents assumed the "invasions," as one reporter called them, were carried out by black men. A writer for the *Daily Statesman* put it, "Bad blacks! It seems from the sameness of the deviltry and its constant repetition that there must be a regular gang of these brutes who perambulate the city at the small hours of the night to do their unholy work."

In 1885, about 3,500 African Americans lived in Austin, making up approximately 20 percent of the population. Many lived in servants' quarters in their employers' backyards. Others lived in small apartments above the stores or restaurants where they worked. Still others resided in small, all-black neighborhoods on the edge of the city.

One of the black neighborhoods, called Clarksville, had been started on several acres of land that former governor Elisha Pease had given to his emancipated slaves at the end of the Civil War. The typical Clarksville house consisted of three rooms, laid out in a "shotgun-style," with one room directly behind another. Sometimes, as many as a dozen family members lived in one house. The front doors were small and the ceilings low, so almost every occupant had to bend forward to avoid hitting their heads. The roofs leaked, the thin walls were drafty, and a creek carrying sewage would often flood the homes.

And Clarksville was the "nice" black neighborhood.

Austin's poorest black neighborhood was only a dozen wooden shanties next to the city dump. On windy days, trash blew into the houses. Residents of the neighborhood frequently searched the dump, gathering rotten fruit, potatoes, and dog-chewed bones for their meals.

Most of Austin's black adults were uneducated and unable to read and write. For work, they had the lowest-paying jobs in one of two fields – common labor or domestic service. The men usually worked as janitors, barbers, porters, carriage drivers, waitstaff, and bellhops. They shoveled coal for the railroads, worked at sawmills, factories, and brickyards, and picked cotton on farms outside town. It was essentially the work that no one else wanted to do.

A white Austin family posed with their black servants.

The black women were mostly servants. Their days started as early as 4:00 A.M. They'd wash with rags dipped in water buckets, eat a breakfast of cornmeal and molasses, and go to the kitchen of the main house, where they removed the ashes from the previous day's fire and carry in wood for a new fire. The rest of their day would be filled with dozens of duties – cooking, cleaning, mopping, scrubbing, emptying chamber pots, hauling trash, and doing all the laundry, which was a massive task that required an endless cycle of soaking, rinsing, scrubbing, starching, drying clothes on outdoor lines, and ironing with a hot piece of metal that had been heated on the stove.

Finally, after serving dinner and cleaning the kitchen, they would eat the leftovers provided for them and return to their quarters to sleep, get up early, and start the whole thing again the next day. They usually received one day off each week –

Inside the Black Elephant, Austin's African American saloon in the 1880s.

Sunday so that they could attend one of the black churches in town.

Compared to the years of slavery and post-Civil War Reconstruction -- when African Americans deemed troublemakers were viciously beaten or hanged in a grove of oaks on the east side – life had improved in black Austin.

In their segregated neighborhoods, black residents opened shops and owned their own businesses. One of those businessmen, a formerly enslaved person named Thomas Hill, ran a grocery and unofficial bank, loaning money to other black residents from the back of his store. There was also a weekly black newspaper, the *Austin Citizen*, a few restaurants, a blacksmith shop, a dress shop for women, and the Black Elephant, an African American saloon.

On weekends, black residents entertained themselves with horse races, baseball games, and dances at Sand Hill. A group of men formed the Austin Cadet Band, and another group started a fraternal society called the Dark Rising Sons of Liberty. Black traveling acts often came to town, offering music and shows, including a cowboy who called himself "Dick the Demon Negro." He specialized in wrestling steers to the ground, holding on to them with just his teeth.

The most exciting news for black parents was the chance for their children to be educated. In 1885, three state-funded "colored schools" opened in Austin, serving up to 400 students. Older students could attend Tillotson College and Normal Institute, which had been opened on the city's east side by the American Missionary Association, an all-white Christian organization based in upstate New York dedicated to opening black colleges in the South. The school offered basic education courses and practical training in carpentry, home building, farming, canning, cooking, sewing, bookkeeping, and teaching.

One white teacher even offered a course in public speaking, which he claimed was designed to eliminate his students' "old-time thick and indistinct plantation pronunciation."

This calls to mind the adage about the road to hell being paved with good intentions.

Black families in Austin were thrilled to have the chance to allow "colored" children to be educated.

Many of Austin's white citizens also had good intentions regarding "accommodating" Austin's black residents. Julia Pease, the former governor's daughter, hosted an annual Christmas party at the Pease estate for the residents of Clarksville, giving each child a bag of candy or a shiny new dime.

The German owner of Pressler's beer garden allowed African Americans to rent out his establishment to celebrate Juneteenth, their day of freedom. Texas enslaved people weren't freed until June 19, 1865, the day Union troops landed in Galveston and two months after the Confederacy had surrendered.

Some of the city's white business owners had started to allow blacks in their stores at specified times. A couple of white-owned saloons had created black areas at the end of their bars, and one had opened a blacks-only craps table in their gaming room.

The opera house owner, Charles Millett, periodically allowed blacks to buy tickets to sit

Pressler's Beer Garden was one of the businesses in Austin that allowed black residents for special occasions.

The grocery store owned by E.H. Carrington – an African American man – in Austin. On the right side in front are (left to right) E.H. Carrington, his brother Albert Carrington, and E. H. Carrington's son-in-law, L. D. Lyons. The store opened in 1872 and Albert was a blacksmith and worked out of the yard in the back of the store. He was a city alderman from 1883 until 1885.

in the upper balcony for some of his shows – although never for operas. He believed those performances were too artistic for black tastes.

In 1883, Austin city leaders had even allowed a black man named Albert Carrington, who owned a blacksmith shop, to be elected as a city alderman, representing the mostly African American Seventh Ward on the east side.

But no white leader – no matter how progressive – was ever heard promoting equal rights for the city's black residents. In Austin – as well as the rest of the United States at the time – the prevailing belief among white men and women was that blacks were intellectually and morally inferior. Doctors and anthropologists of the nineteenth century published papers in medical journals claiming that blacks had smaller brains than whites and that the shape of their bodies was conclusive proof they had developed from a "primitive species." Newspapers didn't hesitate to refer to

African Americans as "coons," "Sons of Ham," "dusky denizens," and even worse.

In Austin, old newspapers are filled with letters from residents complaining about the city's black residents. They were angry about things like "raucous noises" that blacks made at their Sunday church services and about how they "loitered" on downtown street corners.

There were also constant complaints about Austin's younger black men. Unlike the older African Americans who had been raised in slavery, the whites stated that the new generation didn't seem to be as "deferential" or "respectful." Thanks to this, young black men were continuously blamed for all sorts of crimes. An editorial in the *Daily Statesman* noted, "Idleness and drink will lead off these ignorant creatures, and there is no telling, if they are permitted to idle about a town of this size, what they will do finally. There is no doubt, but they will resort to theft, and then it is but a small step to murder."

None of the servant girls assaulted in March 1885 had been able to get a good look at their attacker. A couple of them told the police they believed black men had attacked them, but they weren't sure. One of the women said the man who tried to break into her quarters was possibly "yellow." Another said her assailant had painted his face coal black, like a performer in a minstrel show. The servant girl from Germany said she thought the man who showed up next to her bed and struck her in the head was white.

Nevertheless, Austin's white residents couldn't imagine that white men would want to terrorize harmless servant girls for no reason. They were convinced that the German girl, overcome with fright, had been mistaken about the skin color of the man she'd seen. The strange attacks were undoubtedly the work of rowdy young black men.

One man was so sure of it – and so angry about it – that he proposed that the Austin police department round up all the known black criminals, take them outside of town, whip them to within an inch of their lives, and tell them never to return.

Another man sent a letter to the newspaper editor encouraging all homeowners to shoot first and ask questions later when they spotted a black man snooping around a servant's quarters. An editor at the *Daily Statesman* – obviously an advocate of "responsible journalism" -- recommended the same thing, writing that "the killing of one or two of these characters cannot help but have a wholesome effect on the remainder of these night hawks. The first citizen who plants a charge of buckshot where it will do the most good in the carcass of one of these 'toughs' should be voted a gold medal and the thanks of the community."

A few older citizens in town didn't think whippings and buckshot sent a strong enough message. They recommended forming "vigilance committees" – a.k.a. lynching parties – just like the ones formed back in the old days to patrol the city. In a letter to the editor, one man wrote, "And if one of the scoundrels who have been out scaring and shooting our servant girls can be caught, let him be strung up to a limb or lamp post without mercy or delay."

EVEN THOUGH AUSTIN'S WHITE RESIDENTS were convinced they could get to the bottom of the story about the weird break-ins by stringing up some young black men, reporters in town were hoping for some actual information. They went looking for that information from Marshal H. Grooms Lee, who had recovered from his bout with the flu.

Tall and lean with a narrow face and long arms and legs, Lee was only 29 years old. He had been appointed marshal by a vote of the mayor and aldermen in December 1883, just a year and three months earlier. Before his appointment, he'd spent six months with the Texas Rangers and been a deputy sheriff for three years. He'd never seen much action. In the past, his job had mostly consisted of moving cattlemen who were grazing herds on land that didn't belong to them.

So, how did the young man end up with the top law enforcement job in one of Texas' fastest-growing cities? It was a combination of things – one of which was nepotism, and the other was because he was so polite and boring.

Austin's past marshals had been swaggering men who weren't afraid of using a gun. The most famous, elected in 1880 and just before Lee, had been Ben Thompson, an English-born gambler and deadeye pistoleer. He was the master of the spin move, able to whip on his heels while drawing his Colt at the same time, cocking the hammer, and firing away at his adversary. Western lawman

Bat Masterson later wrote of Thompson, "It is doubtful there was another man who equaled him with a pistol."

The problem was that after a few drinks, Thompson liked to engage in what the newspapers called "promiscuous shooting." One evening, he drunkenly stood up from his seat at Millett's Opera House and shot off his pistol because he believed the show was poorly staged. In 1882, a year after he was elected, he was forced to resign after he killed a San Antonio politician in a shootout. In 1884, he was shot to death in another San Antonio gunfight.

After that, the city aldermen decided they needed a marshal who wouldn't pull the kind of stunts that Thompson had. Lee seemed to be the perfect man for the job. He was a polite, quiet teetotaler whose father just happened to be one of the city's senior statesmen, Joseph Lee, a lawyer and former judge who'd been in Austin since the place was still called Waterloo. The elder Lee had lobbied for the University of Texas and helped plan the creation of the new state capitol building. The city needed a new marshal, and the aldermen were happy to do Judge Lee a favor. Like that, Grooms Lee had the job.

Austin's flashy – and dangerous – former marshal, Ben Thompson.

In one of his first acts as marshal, he purchased new uniforms and badges for his officers. He also took down a shaggy buffalo head – a police department mascot, by the way – and replaced its spot on the wall with solemn portraits of past Austin mayors. When he appeared at city council meetings to discuss police business, he presented formal speeches.

Needless to say, Lee was not exactly Wyatt Earp, but he was efficient, mild-mannered, and got the job done in a town that saw less than a half dozen murders each year. Besides that, the mayor and most of the aldermen believed that if they had reliable Sergeant Chenneville around, they wouldn't have anything to worry about. They even gave Chenneville a raise soon after Lee was appointed to the marshal's post, paying him $1,500 a year – almost as much as Lee made – to ensure he didn't leave.

Besides, as city officials were starting to realize, Austin no longer needed an old-fashioned gunslinger marshal who could hold his own against outlaws in the street. Most of the old outlaws that once terrorized Austin were gone – shot dead, hanged, or sitting in prison. There were still outlaws, but they rarely came to cities like Austin. They had a better chance at surviving away from the cities that didn't have ordinances against firearms, like the one Austin had recently passed. It levied a $25 fine on anyone carrying a firearm in public without a license.

The new marshal, everyone was convinced, would do just fine.

When reporters came to see Lee about the break-ins of the servants' quarters, he had no new information to give them. He just wanted to ensure they printed that he said more police officers were needed to keep up with Austin's growth.

It was something that a politician would have said, but in this case, he was right. The department's 12-man roster included day clerk Bart DeLong; night clerk Henry Brown; and "Uncle" Dick Boyse, the elderly boss of the chain gang who took prisoners out of jail every morning to shovel horse manure off the streets.

Another officer, Fred Senter, took an extended leave of absence every June so he could work as a cowboy on one of the few remaining cattle drives out of Texas. This earned him the nickname of "Hit the Trail Fred."

Two black men, Lewis Morris and Henry Madison, worked part-time with the department. They were allowed to arrest and interrogate black citizens only. They could wear uniforms but were not permitted to carry guns.

On most nights, only four officers worked the streets and mostly stayed downtown -- where most of the trouble was – leaving the rest of the city unattended and without police patrols.

But Mayor Robertson and the city aldermen rolled their eyes at Lee's proposal to triple the department's size. If they did that, the city's budget would be decimated, and they'd have to raise taxes. If that happened, the voters would throw them out of office during the next elections.

At a city council meeting after the March break-ins, one alderman, James Odell, who managed the Singer Sewing Machine office, suggested that instead of hiring more police officers, the city could offer a $500 reward to anyone who shot a black man invading a servants' quarters. Alderman Radcliff Platt, who ran a livery, feed, and seed company, said that the reward should instead go to the first servant girl who "plugged" her assailant with buckshot.

Platt's suggestion was met with laughter – everyone knew girls couldn't shoot.

More ideas were thrown around. An alderman who owned a lumber company, Lou Crooker, proposed the concept of "special policemen" – temporarily deputizing white men in the community and directing them to patrol the white neighborhoods like night watchmen. This would only be until the police apprehended the culprit, of course.

Alderman Max Maas seconded the plan but suggested that no announcements be made about the special police officers. That way, the "bad blacks" wouldn't know a manhunt was going on. Alderman George Brush, who made his living selling flush toilets and gas stoves at his hardware store, disagreed. The "class of people committing these crimes," he said, "are unable to read."

When the meeting wrapped, the aldermen agreed to pay about a dozen men $2 a night to keep watch in the white neighborhoods. The men they hired were friends and acquaintances of city officials who needed extra spending money or wanted to get away from their wives for a few nights. It wasn't exactly a force to be reckoned with.

By the last week of March, the special police officers were walking the streets and alleys while Chenneville and his officers were busy arresting a couple of black men who seemed good for the crime. One of them, a laborer named Gus Johnson, was charged with breaking into the quarters of a servant girl, and another, Abe Pearson, who worked in a barber shop, was also accused of a break-in, but the police claimed he raped the woman, too.

Both men proclaimed their innocence, but after their arrests, the break-ins, attacks, and window tapping suddenly stopped.

The only reported incident involving the use of a gun on an intruder involved, of all people, Chenneville's wife, Ellen. Late one night, while her husband was working, she heard a noise in the front yard, saw the outline of a man, and started shooting.

The bullets narrowly missed a neighbor who'd been visiting a downtown saloon and was so drunk that he had no idea he'd stumbled into the Chennevilles' yard instead of his own.

6. THE MURDER OF ELIZA SHELLEY

A WEEK PASSED WITHOUT ANY BREAK-INS, AND THEN, another. By mid-April, most special police officers were so bored that they were abandoning their patrols and sneaking off to spend their $2 at a saloon or a brothel.

Despite this, Mayor Robertson and the other city officials decided to keep the temporary officers on the clock until at least April 21, which had been deemed "Texas Day" by the organizers of the World's Industrial and Cotton Centennial Exposition in New Orleans. It was a sort of world's fair that had opened in December and was expected to draw as many as four million visitors from around the country and Europe before it closed in June.

Texas had never participated in any kind of expositions, which were taking place every few years in different American cities. The state skipped the 1876 Philadelphia Centennial Exposition, which celebrated the hundredth anniversary of the signing of the Declaration of Independence, another one in Atlanta in 1881, and another in New Orleans two years later. So, Governor Ireland declared that Texas would not miss the 1885 event. It was the moment for the state to show the rest of the country that Texas was no second-rate state filled with gun-toting outlaws and wild Indians.

It would also be – he usually neglected to mention – his chance to introduce himself to voters from other states in case he someday decided to run for president, as some of his supporters were urging him to do.

Ireland's staff had rented nearly a half-acre of space on the main floor of the U.S. Government and State Exhibits Hall building at the exposition. The hall was 33 acres in size and was the largest roofed structure in the world at the time. Five thousand electric lights illuminated it, and it was the centerpiece of the fair, which had been built on a former plantation between downtown and the Mississippi River in New Orleans.

The Texas section was the largest area for any state in the hall. Spelled out in bales of cotton at the entrance were the words "LONE STAR," and spelled out in sacks of grain was "WELCOME TO TEXAS." There were giant billboards advertising everything Texas was famous for – including cotton, grain, livestock, timber, coal, scenery, and so on – and to make sure visitors got the point, there was a marble globe that showed Texas to be bigger in size than the United States and all the countries of Europe combined. Not exactly to scale, but it helped to get the state's most famous motto into wide circulation – "Everything is Bigger in Texas."

THE MAIN BUILDING.

Thousands of people from all over the world visited the exhibit, and when it came time for Governor Ireland to give his speech on Texas Day on April 21, at least 10,000 people – twice the expected number – purchased tickets for the event. Seated on the front platform, the size of a horse corral, were around 800 Texas dignitaries, ranging from University of Texas professors to wealthy socialites from every city.

Ireland spoke about Texas' new prosperity and lack of crime and invited all who were listening to come and visit – or better yet, move their families to his great state.

The applause that followed was deafening, and a little girl approached the stage to bring flowers to the governor. When he took them, he kissed her on the cheek. She was followed by a young woman who also presented Ireland with a bouquet. According to newspaper reports, the crowd cheered, hoping the governor would kiss her, too. Ireland hesitated and glanced over at his wife, seated on the platform. Mrs. Ireland was a very proper woman who believed dancing was so sinful that she refused to attend her husband's inaugural balls. She glared at him, and rather than kissing, Ireland offered the young woman a deep bow, much to the audience's dismay.

But they applauded him anyway – they'd loved his speech – and when the ceremony ended, hundreds crowded around to offer their congratulations. A champagne lunch followed, and the party lasted long into the night. When the guests finally left, it looked like the middle of the day outside. Throughout the exposition grounds were massive towers that held giant, newly invented electric "arc lamps," which lit up the fairgrounds like the midnight sun.

The many visitors from Austin who had come for Texas Day were undoubtedly impressed, but many wondered how the bright lights could ever be considered a useful invention.

Why would anyone want to light up a city all night long? What possible purpose would that have?

BY THE TIME THE POLITICIANS, CITY OFFICIALS, and exposition attendees returned to Austin, the spring temperatures made everyone forget about the harsh winter chill at the start of the new year. The downtown sidewalks were crowded with shoppers, homes were being built, gardens and farm fields were being turned over for planting, and new arrivals were coming to Austin every week. All the predictions Mayor Robertson had made about the city's prosperity seemed to be coming true.

Things were going so well that Mayor Robertson and the city alderman disbanded the special policeman program on April 27.

It was almost as if the "phantom attacker" who had been preying on local servant girls was waiting for the program to end.

On that very night, a man entered the servants' quarters of a home on Mulberry Street. The cook who lived there was gone, but a female friend was sleeping in the bed. The man grabbed her throat with one hand, pressed a razor against her throat with the other, and promised to kill her if she screamed.

At that moment, the cook and another woman came into the backyard. When they saw the door to the cook's room was standing open, they called out to the woman inside. A man suddenly crashed through the open door and ran off into the darkness.

THE NEXT NIGHT, SOMEONE HURLED A LARGE stone into a servant girl's cabin in the backyard of a home on Rio Grande Street. A neighbor heard the woman's screams, ran outside, and fired a shot at a fleeing man. He missed, and the man kept running.

AN HOUR LATER, J.M. BRACKENRIDGE, PRESIDENT of the City National Bank, was awakened by a noise in his backyard. He looked out the window and saw his cook, an elderly black woman, struggling with a man. Brackenridge shouted out the window, and the man ran away. A few hours later, the man – or someone else – returned and pelted the house with rocks.

OVER THE NEXT FEW DAYS, CHENNEVILLE AND his men arrested three more black men – Andrew Jackson, Newt Harper, and Henry Wallace – whom the newspaper described as "hard-looking Negroes." They also arrested a janitor from the Variety Theatre named Jack Ross and an elderly black man who was known around town simply as "Old John."

Old John had spent some time over the past year as an inmate at the State Lunatic Asylum. He was locked up after he was heard telling people he was worth $260 million in gold, and he'd buried it next to the Colorado River.

Apparently, things like that could get you committed to an asylum in the 1880s.

He was recently released by Dr. Denton, who was convinced he was harmless. But now, reported the *Daily Statesman*, it was thought he had been the man who attacked the cook on Mulberry Street and "that he had a hand in the outrageous attacks made a few weeks ago."

In truth, neither the newspaper nor the police knew if Old John or any other men they arrested had anything to do with the attacks. Hoping to get a confession out of someone, they chained the men to iron rings cemented to the floor of the jail and subjected them to brutal interrogations.

And yet, no one confessed to anything. The suspects swore they'd never broken into any servants' quarters and had no desire to harm any woman.

But maybe the arrests frightened the attacker into seclusion again because the assaults stopped again. Nothing would happen now for almost a week.

THE FIRST WEEK OF MAY BROUGHT MILD temperatures but light rain almost daily. On the afternoon of May 6, there was another rain shower, followed by a spectacular sunset.

On the city's east side, some of the black residents went to the Baptist church for the wedding of Lucie A. Lomax, the daughter of a shopkeeper, to H.G. Grant, a young schoolteacher.

A 31-year-old servant named Eliza Shelley didn't attend the wedding and wasn't on the east side. She was working at the home of her employer, Dr. Lucian Johnson, a medical doctor and former state legislator. The Johnsons lived in a fine house at the corner of San Jacinto and Cypress Streets.

Servant's quarters behind a home in Austin. Most of these cabins and shacks were typical of this one – small, cramped, and without most comforts.

That evening, Eliza made dinner for the Johnson family. After her own meal, she cleaned the kitchen, polished the stove and silverware, and then went to her small cabin in the Johnsons' backyard – a cabin so small that she had to duck to keep from knocking her head when she went in the door. Her three young boys were waiting for her there. She made them supper from the leftovers collected from the Johnsons' dinner table. Soon, Eliza and the children put out the light and climbed into bed.

Eliza and the two smallest boys were at the head of the bed. Her oldest, who was seven, was across the end. Her husband, William, was not there. He'd been sent for a five-year stay at the state penitentiary for stealing a horse in 1884.

Early the next morning, Dr. Johnson was up and left to go to the market and buy some groceries for the family. While he was away, his wife heard screams coming from Eliza's cabin. She sent her niece, who was barely a teenager, to see what was happening, and when she peered into a window, she began screaming. She was too terrified to go into the cabin, and when she returned to her aunt, she collapsed into her arms, unable to speak about what she'd seen.

When Dr. Johnson arrived back home, he was apprised of the situation and realized he'd better have a look for himself. He walked out to the cabin in the backyard, opened the door, and stepped inside. The first thing he saw was Eliza's boys huddled in a corner, weeping and crying. On the floor next to the bed, wrapped in a quilt, was Eliza. She had been hit with an ax so hard above her right eye that parts of her brain were oozing out of the wound, mixing with the blood that covered her face.

Like Mollie Smith, Eliza had been slaughtered by a madman.

Dr. Lucian Johnson, medical doctor and state legislator

WHEN SERGEANT CHENNEVILLE STOMPED into Eliza's cabin, he noticed that both of her trunks had been broken open and her garments scattered across the floor. He ordered that the woman's body be taken out into the backyard, where there was sunlight. When officers removed the quilt from over her body, they found she had also been wrapped in a sheet from the bed. They carried everything outside and removed the wrappings, giving those who were gathered in the yard a clear view of Eliza's wounds.

Besides the ax wound to her head – which likely caused immediate death – the killer had mutilated her body. Eliza had a deep, round hole between her eyes that looked as if it was possibly made by a thin iron rod. There was another one over her ear. Knife wounds were found up and down her body, and some of them were very deep. The knife's blade had been rammed straight down into her flesh, then pulled directly out, causing muscle tissue damage and heavy bleeding.

The men standing in the yard gazed down at the wrecked, savaged body and tried to keep from being sick. All of them were recalling the terrible condition of Mollie Smith's body several months earlier, but none of them wanted to say what he was thinking – that the same killer had struck again.

When reporters arrived on the scene, Chenneville was already untying his bloodhounds to see if they could pick up a scent. The barking, drooling dogs circled Eliza's body, sniffing and shoving their noses against her motionless, bloodied form. They poked around what were described as "large, broad, barefoot tracks" that had been found around the cabin, and the bloodhounds seemed to follow a trail of some sort toward the alley. But then they stopped. Once again, the police were out of luck with the dogs.

But, this time, there had been a witness to the murder.

Chenneville went to speak to Eliza's seven-year-old son. The boy said he'd been awakened in the night by a man with a white cloth sack over his head with two holes cut out for the eyes. He couldn't tell if the man was black or white. The man asked him where his mother kept her money, but the boy said he didn't know. The man told him to put his head under a pillow and not look out again. If he did, he'd kill him. The man told him he'd be on his way to St. Louis on the first train the next morning.

Afterward, the boy went back to sleep, unaware that anything had happened to his mother until daylight. It was his screams – and those of his brother's -- that attracted the attention of Mrs. Johnson and led to the discovery of Eliza's butchered body.

Of course, the boy's story sounded preposterous. A man in a mask had broken into the cabin, slammed an ax into Eliza's school, pulled her from the bed, jammed an iron rod into her skull two times, stabbed her repeatedly with a knife, wrapped her in a sheet and a quilt and then woke up a little boy to ask where his mother's money was? And then, as a bonus, told him he was taking a train to St. Louis?

Was the boy in shock? Did he have a wild imagination? Or was he just telling the story in a way that made sense to a seven-year-old who just woke up to find his mother was brutally murdered in a single room that he shared with her and his little brothers?

Maybe it was all of the above, but whatever it was, after Chenneville finished his questions, a reporter for the *San Antonio Express* sat down with the boy and asked him to tell his story again – and he did, in the exact same way. He didn't "vary it at all," the newsman later wrote.

Dr. Johnson, clearly upset by the murder, came outside and told reporters that Eliza was "an excellent woman." She was hard-working, reliable, and honest – so wonderful that he, his wife, and children treated her more like a "lesser member of the family than a servant."

Of course, then he added that it made no sense that someone would want to kill Eliza for her money since she had "only a few paltry cents to her name." I'm sure he didn't realize he was telling everyone how poorly he'd paid her for her work.

Johnson was asked if he knew of Eliza having any enemies, and he said he didn't know anyone who disliked her or any men she was romantically involved with. He said she seemed devoted to her husband and was patiently waiting for him to finish his time in prison. She didn't deserve to die in such a way, Dr. Johnso said, regardless of her race.

ONCE AGAIN, THE POLICE FIRST THEORIZED that the murder was the result of a domestic dispute, but the statements from Dr. Johnson and the absence of Eliza's husband seemed to rule that out. With no other clues but the footprints outside the cabin, Chenneville went looking for a barefoot black man – and it appeared that pretty much any barefoot black man would do.

Two hours later, the police arrested a shoeless teenager named Andrew Williams, who lived near the Johnson residence. He was described as a "half-witted colored boy" by those who lived in the neighborhood. He was brought in for questioning but soon released when it was discovered that his feet were not the same size as those left at the scene.

An inquest was convened, and it was ruled that Eliza Shelley had met death "at the hands of a person or persons unknown." The same undertaker who retrieved her body carried her first to the hospital for an autopsy and then to the Colored Ground, where she was buried only yards away from the grave of Mollie Smith.

Mr. Nitschke, the old cemetery caretaker, added Eliza's name to the list of those interred on the grounds, but he was, once again, reluctant to detail what had happened to her. This time, he simply wrote that Eliza Shelley's death was caused by a "wound to the throat."

7. THE "SERVANT GIRL ANNIHILATOR"

THE CEMETERY CARETAKER DIDN'T WANT TO draw attention to the manner of Eliza's death, but the newspapers didn't feel the same way. The papers in Austin, Fort Worth, and San Antonio printed screaming headlines the next day that read things like:

"INHABITANTS OF THE CAPITAL CITY AGAIN SHOCKED BY A BLOOD-CURDLING MURDER," "A MOTHER BUTCHERED IN THE PRESENCE OF HER CHILDREN, and my favorite, which uses the lengthy, lurid prose of the era – "THE FOUL FIENDS KEEP UP THEIR WICKED WORK – ANOTHER WOMAN CRUELLY MURDERED AT DEAD OF NIGHT BY SOME UNKNOWN ASSASSIN, BENT ON PLUNDER! ANOTHER DEED OF DEVILTRY IN THE CRIMSON CATALOGUE OF CRIME!"

A story in the *Daily Statesman* claimed that "clear-headed conservative men" were gathering on street corners along Congress Avenue to discuss the attacks on the city's servant girls. Some theorized that there must be some black gang – "a band of colored fiends" – behind the assaults and murders. One popular rumor said the gang worked for a black labor union that had been trying to recruit the city's servant girls to join and

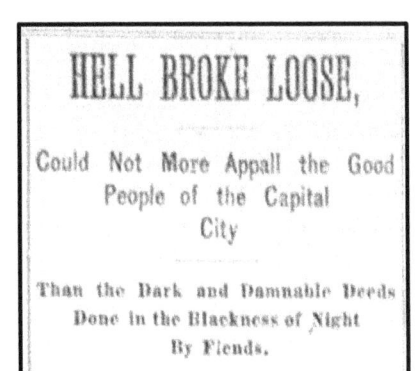

> HELL BROKE LOOSE,
>
> Could Not More Appall the Good People of the Capital City
>
> Than the Dark and Damnable Deeds Done in the Blackness of Night By Fiends.

demand high wages from their white employers. The gang attacked the women who refused to join.

William Sidney Porter, the drugstore clerk who'd grow up to be the writer, O. Henry, came up with a nickname for the gang. After Eliza's murder, he wrote to a friend who had recently moved to Colorado that life in Austin had been "fearfully dull, except for the frequent raids of the Servant Girl Annihilators, who make things lively in the dead hours of the night."

Of course, that nickname would later be applied in the singular when it began to be suspected that the attacks were the work of one man.

The idea of a marauding gang of black ruffians came from the fevered imaginations of Austin's white residents after Eliza's murder – not from the city's African American inhabitants. They weren't talking about a gang. Many black residents believed that a "demon" or someone with an "evil eye" had come to Austin.

Many in the city, especially the older folks, believed wholeheartedly in the practice of Hoodoo, a form of American folk magic that was based on African religions brought to the country by enslaved people and then mixed with the traditions of Native Americans, European immigrants, and enslaved people. Hoodoo was practiced for healing, attracting good luck, love, and money, and for protection against evil.

Hoodoo was very popular after the Civil War, including in Austin. It would later spread throughout the United States as African Americans left the South during what became known as the Great Migration. Just as Delta blues singers went north to Memphis, St. Louis, and Chicago and traded their acoustic guitars for electric instruments, conjurers took Hoodoo to communities in the North.

In Austin in 1885, though, Hoodoo workers were selling special powders to servant girls to scatter around their doorways to keep them safe. They made specially brewed tonics for the women to drink and made "gris-gris" and "mojo" bags – leather pouches containing magical herbs, roots, coins, bones, and other things -- to carry for protection.

But whether they believed in Hoodoo or not. No servant girl was feeling safe in Austin that summer. They stacked furniture against the doors at night and nailed the windows closed, even on the hottest nights.

MEANWHILE, SERGEANT CHENNEVILLE was busy meeting with his various informants and tasking the department's two black officers to find out what they could from the African American community. All of them came back to Chenneville with no information at all. People were scared, they said. Aside from that, they had nothing to report.

Chenneville got into the habit of riding his large bay horse through the black neighborhoods, intently eyeballing every black man that crossed his path. His rides usually took him to the Black Elephant saloon – typically a good place to "round up the usual suspects" – but he found no leads worth following.

On May 10, five days after Eliza Shelley's murder, Chenneville believed he'd caught a break. A man named Andrew Rogers came into the police department and announced that he knew who'd murdered Eliza.

Rogers said that one of his neighbors, a young black man named Ike Plummer, had been involved in a brief romance with Eliza earlier that year after her husband went to prison. He claimed that a few weeks before her murder, he'd seen Eliza arguing with him. Plummer was angry at her because she wouldn't loan him any money. And then, Rogers added, he'd walked by Dr. Johnson's house on the day of the murder, and he'd seen them arguing again.

According to Roger's story, Plummer again demanded money. "I have none for you," Eliza replied. "What little I have is for my children, and I don't want you around me."

When Plummer walked away angrily, he said threateningly to Eliza, "I'll see you again!"

Rogers said he thought he'd seen a hammer or a hatchet sticking out of Plummer's back pocket when he hurried off down the street.

But that wasn't all. Rogers also said that later that night – probably about 1:00 in the morning – he was awakened by a noise outside and looked out to see Plummer entering his house, which was just next door.

After hearing this account, Chenneville had one of his black officers, Lewis Morris, go to Plummer's shack and arrest him on a charge of "suspicion of murder." The sergeant later explained that he didn't go himself because he feared Plummer might run if he saw the big man coming.

Reporters who got a look at Plummer after he'd been locked up in the jail described him as a "tall, ungainly, ill-kempt Negro" with a "half imbecile grin." It was suggested that Plummer was not only uneducated but might be mentally disabled, as well. Plummer did have a minor criminal record after being arrested a couple of times for vagrancy, but he had never been charged with a violent crime. A farmer who had hired Plummer to pick cotton for him told a reporter, "There was nothing of a vicious disposition about him."

There also wasn't any physical evidence that linked Plummer to the crime – or any other crime, for that matter. There was no blood on his clothing, and his footprints didn't match those around the front door of the cabin. Even though they tried, officers could not find anyone who could corroborate the story that Andrew Rogers spun for the police.

Reporters also poked holes in Rogers' story, speculating that he made up the story to put Plummer behind bars because of a feud or disagreement. They found it hard to believe the mild-mannered man now sitting in jail would have killed Eliza over such a small amount of money. And if he did, he was well-known to Eliza's son, and the boy would have recognized him – at least his voice – even if he was wearing a mask.

The Austin correspondent for the *San Antonio Express* stated that he didn't believe Plummer would ever be convicted, and he also predicted that it would only be a matter of time before another attack took place.

His prediction came true just two weeks later.

ON THE EVENING OF MAY 22, A SHOEMAKER named Robert Weyermann, who lived with his family just east of downtown and across the street from a popular German-owned beer hall called the *Scholz Garten*, heard a noise coming from his backyard. It sounded like a low, painful moan that suddenly turned into a loud, piercing scream.

Robert and several other family members ran outside and found Irene Cross, their black cook, lying on the ground. Her right arm had been struck by some sharp object so hard that it was nearly severed in two. A long, horizontal cut extended halfway around her head, from her right eye to her ear. It looked as though someone had attempted to scalp her.

Irene tried to speak, but blood was running from the gash in her head, streaming down her face and into her mouth. More blood was spurting from her half-severed arm.

Robert had her carried to a spare bedroom in his home, trying to make her comfortable. This was something considered a very generous act by a white man at the time – letting a black servant bleed to death in one of his beds.

The popular beer hall, Scholz Garten, was across the street from the site of the brutal attack on Irene Cross.

A bandage was wrapped around her head to try and stop the bleeding, and another was applied to her arm. Neither did much good. The blood continued to flow, staining the sheets and blankets and soaking through to the mattress underneath her.

"Who was it?" someone cried. "Who did this to you?"

Irene looked up, her eyes going in all directions as her skin paled to a sickly gray. She tried to speak again, but then an expression of confusion came across her face, and no words came out.

The Weyermanns feared she'd never last the night.

But she did. By sunrise, a steady parade of people came to the Weyermanns' home to glimpse Irene through the window. Somehow, she was still alive. A reporter from the *Daily Statesman* was allowed to enter the house and talk to her. He later wrote that he was "horrified by the ghastly object" he saw on the bed. He bent down and asked Irene if she could identify her attacker, but she only managed to let out a faint groan.

A police investigation had been launched as soon as word was sent to headquarters that another attack had occurred. Of course, the investigation only consisted of bringing Chenneville's bloodhounds to the Weyermanns' yard so they could fail for the third time in a row to pick up the killer's scent. The men there watching, leaning against the fence, just shook their heads and chuckled.

As with the case of Eliza Shelley's murder, all the police had as far as eyewitness testimony went was the story of another child – Irene's 12-year-old nephew who lived with her in a two-room cabin behind the Weyermanns' house. The boy said he'd been sleeping and had opened his eyes to see the figure of a man coming through the outer door and into his room. He described the man as a "big, chunky Negro" wearing a brown wide-brimmed cloth hat, ragged coat, blue shirt, and black pants rolled up over his bare feet and ankles.

Oh, and he was carrying a very large knife.

When the boy started to cry out, the man quietly told the boy that he wasn't there to hurt him and ordered him to keep quiet. The man then walked into Irene's room, which contained two single beds – one for her and one for her 17-year-old son, who wasn't there. He worked nights as a porter in one of the city's saloons. The nephew said the man stayed in the back bedroom for only a few minutes and then ran out the door into the backyard.

Moments later, Irene stumbled out after him. She was bleeding badly, went out the door, and fell in the yard. Her screams had alerted Robert Weyermann.

When newspaper reporters interviewed the nephew, they thought his statement was baffling. They found it hard to believe, in the darkness of the cabin, that he could get such a good look at the man, especially since he'd only been there for a matter of seconds. Had the boy, in his excitement, gotten carried away and invented parts of the story to please the police, as they believed their other young witness had when his mother was slain a few weeks earlier?

Irene managed to hang on for one more day and, after considerable suffering, finally died during the early morning hours of May 25. Before she slipped away, she mumbled something, but no one could understand her. Whatever she had been trying to say, she took to her grave.

A familiar series of events followed – an autopsy, an inquest that ruled Irene had been killed by "a person or persons unknown," and a swift burial in the Colored Ground.

The caretaker once again opened his ledger to mark the woman's passing. This time, under the listing for the cause of Irene's death, he wrote, "wounds."

BY NOW, IT WAS BECOMING OBVIOUS IN THE CITY that the same slayer had taken the lives of all three women recently killed – and likely attacked the ones that survived. However, most of Austin's "clear-headed conservative businessmen" had a hard time accepting that a lone black man could outwit the police. Rumors spread of a murderous "Negro gang" that was at work. One man even speculated that they lived like a band of outlaws in one of the caves or cliffs along the Colorado River outside of town. They swooped into the city at night and did their killings, some said, which is why Sergeant Chenneville had not been able to find them.

Others insisted the gang consisted of "escaped convicts" who had vowed to slay servant women in Austin because the gang's leader had caught a venereal disease – or it maybe it was tuberculosis – from a servant girl.

Still, others claimed the gang was a "secret, oath-bound association" made up of fanatically religious black men who disapproved of any African American who had sex with men who weren't their husbands. Their goal was to stamp out "Negro prostitution" and "compel the members of the Negro race to live in the bonds of matrimony."

And best of all was the story that some mystical "killing mania" was sweeping through Austin's black neighborhoods. Advocates of this far-fetched theory said that the murder of Mollie Smith had inflamed the blood instincts of young black men, leading them to murder other black women they didn't like.

As you can see, panic – edged with hysteria – occurred in the city. The African American population lived in fear, while the white residents speculated about what was happening. They weren't worried about themselves, in any case. The victims of the killer were black, so white people had nothing to fear.

It was a nuisance, though, that whoever this killer was, he was shrinking the number of servant girls in Austin. Who was going to do all the cooking, cleaning, and laundry if black girls were too afraid to go to work?

THE POLICE, MEANWHILE, WERE DOING THEIR BEST.

Marshall Lee was trying to reassure everyone that nothing was amiss, and that Sergeant Chenneville and his men were pursuing many good leads.

But then, on June 2, someone stuck a pistol into a partially opened window of the servant's quarters that adjoined the home of Henri Tallichet, the professor of modern languages at the University of Texas. The shadowy figure pulled the trigger and fired a .42-caliber bullet into the arm of the professor's young black maid. When he heard the shot, Professor Tallichet grabbed his own pistol and rushed into the kitchen. Just as he pushed open the door to the servants' quarters, a second shot rang out, and the bullet whizzed past his head. Whoever the man was, he fled before Tallichet had the chance to return fire or get a look at him.

That same night, an intruder visited the house of Major Joseph Stewart – the same Major Stewart whose two servant women had been attacked back in March – and threw a large stone through the window of the servants' quarters. However, the women who stayed there had asked one of the grooms who also worked for the major to bunk down in an extra room as protection. When the rock shattered the window, he was immediately on his feet, pistol in hand. He ran outside after the rock thrower and fired several shots at him. But the intruder quickly disappeared down an alley, leaving his identity a mystery.

With more attacks occurring, Chenneville and his officers did the only thing they could do – arrest more black men. They locked them up on vagrancy charges for disturbing the peace, public intoxication, or anything they could come up with. They hoped that one of them, during his uncomfortable stay in jail, would confess that he knew something about the murders.

It was a stupid plan that resulted in zero leads. Or perhaps I should say it was a plan that defined "insanity" – doing the same thing over and over again but expecting a different result.

But Chenneville had one man – a black man, of course -- that he wanted to track down and interrogate. His name was Oliver Townsend, and he was a suspected chicken thief. That might not sound like much of a career, but he was a larger-than-life figure in Austin's black neighborhoods. According to the legends, he could slip into a white man's chicken coop "as noiselessly as a cat," grab some sleeping birds, snap their necks, and vanish with them into the darkness. He was long gone before the other chickens could wake up and raise a ruckus. The *Daily Statesman* called Townsend "the great and bloodthirsty robber of the hen-roost who has figured in several daring midnight hen murders."

Townsend was so good at his job that during the previous Christmas season, an Austin homeowner had paid two nightwatchmen to keep an eye on his chicken coop, which was filled with fattened turkeys and chickens for holiday dinners. On Christmas morning, the guards discovered six missing birds – vanished right under their noses. It was assumed that only Oliver Townsend was good enough to have pulled that off.

For some reason, Chenneville got it into his head that if anyone could get in and out of a servants' quarters without being seen, it was Townsend. He ignored the fact that killing black servant women was much different than wringing the necks of some stolen birds.

On June 6, two officers found Townsend at the Black Elephant, cuffed him, and hauled him off to jail. It was said they were "forced to listen to some ugly cuss words that the prisoner used in giving vent to his opinion regarding them. In the choice slang of the day, Mr. Townsend is a tough, and though he may be proof against bullets, is liable to have a hard time with hemp."

A HARD CASE.

A COLORED CROOK'S ESCAPE FROM A LEADEN MESSENGER.

The first head line is said to fit Mr. Oliver Townsend (colored) "like the paper on the wall." Oliver has been so often written up in the local papers that any further biographical sketch of him would be almost superfluous. He is perhaps the most expert chicken thief in America, but it was not on account of the feathered tribe that he got into fresh trouble yesterday.

It seems that he and a Dago were quarreling in front of French & Weed's livery stable. Both were under the ardent. A deputy sheriff, named Crenshaw, undertook to effect the arrest of the enemy of fowls. Oliver "sassed" him and refused to be arrested. He had a horse hitched near by and getting on him started to depart when a deputy sheriff named Crenshaw fired at him. The chicken lifter took not a particle of notice of the bullet, though it grazed his head, and rode down to one of his Pecan street resorts, where Officers Peck and Robinson came up on him and carried him to the jug. They had to "pack" him the entire way, and were also forced to listen to some ugly cuss words that the prisoner used in giving vent to his opinion regarding them.

In the choice slang of the day, Mr. Townsend is a tough, and though he may be proof against bullets, is liable to have a hard time with hemp some of these days.

Oliver Townsend's reputation in Austin was questionable long before the murders began.

The implication of those words was clear – Townsend may have eluded a few angry chicken owners who fired a shot at him in the past, but if he'd committed the murders, he'd certainly hang.

However, like every other man the police had arrested and interrogated since Mollie Smith's murder, Townsend swore he'd never attacked any of the women, and he didn't know anyone who had. Chained to the iron ring on the floor of the cell, he was beaten and questioned endlessly, but he confessed to nothing.

Eventually, Townsend was also released, and the police returned to the streets, looking for more black men to harass and arrest. Things became so worrisome that African American men who spotted an officer would hold their hands out in front of them to show they weren't carrying a knife or an ax. Others – fearing Chenneville's search dogs – applied asafetida to their legs and feet. This strong-smelling salve made from old tree roots, rotten vegetables, herbs, and spices had been used since the days of slavery to confuse bloodhounds.

None one wanted to find themselves chained to the iron ring at the jail.

By this time, many servant women weren't just locking their doors. They were quitting their jobs and leaving town to live with relatives in other cities. Others were allowed to spend the night inside their employers' homes, lying on pallets on kitchen floors. Some held onto their mojo bags or quietly sang and prayed for at least a few hours of sleep before their workday began again.

Many others asked God for protection, but it seemed the Devil had come to Austin, and there was only so much that God could do.

8. "AUSTIN IS ONCE MORE SERENE"

BY MID-JUNE, THE ATTACKS HAD STOPPED once more. Not even a rock was thrown anywhere in the city. White residents speculated that the "bad Negros" had been scared off by the police department's brutal interrogation tactics or by the frightened homeowners who had been shooting freely at anyone who came too close to their servants' quarters.

They may not have caught the killer, but at least they'd frightened him off to become someone else's problem.

The rest of June was so quiet in Austin – mostly free of crime – that the *Daily Statesman* wrote, "Austin is once more serene."

Usually, that's what people say right before something terrible happens, but not in this case. Austin really was peaceful from the date of the last attack through July 4. But even when things got noisy again, it was for a good reason.

Independence Day saw Austin's various kinds of entertainment back in full swing. There were boat races on the Colorado River and games and contests in Central Park. Families swam in Barton

The new Driskill Hotel, the "most sophisticated hotel west of St. Louis."

Creek and had picnics on the riverbanks. The creek offered a "ladies only" section, where a few daring young women jumped into the water wearing bathing dresses that revealed their lower legs. Men pitched horseshoes and played baseball. Children competed to catch a greased pig. There was food, fun, and frivolity everywhere.

At sunset, nearly 6,000 people gathered along Pecan Street downtown to celebrate laying the cornerstone of the new hotel that wealthy cattleman Colonel Jesse Driskill was constructing. He planned to spend $400,000 to build what he bragged would be "the most sophisticated hotel west of St. Louis." The hotel would be four stories high, with hydraulic elevators and flush toilets on the top floor. The blueprints called for a large saloon, billiards room, and barbershop on the first floor. The second floor would offer a dining room, bridal apartment, parlors, and ladies' dressing rooms. The hotel's 60 rooms would be on the top two floors, and each would have a chandelier, large couch, rocker, four-poster bed, private balcony, and an electric bell with which to ring for a porter. The 12 corner rooms would have private bathrooms, an unheard-of luxury for any hotel in Texas.

Driskill had also ordered that enormous stone busts of himself and his two sons, Tobe and Bud, be carved into the exterior of the hotel because he wanted future generations of Austin residents to be able to look up and see his family. As evidence of his continued loyalty to the Confederacy – he'd made his fortune selling the Confederate government beef during the Civil War – Driskill ordered that his bust be facing south.

Of course, that meant he was looking toward Mexico, but I'm sure he meant this as a symbolic gesture.

For the ceremony, scores of small incandescent lights were strung over Pecan Street in front of the hotel. Both a brass band and a string band performed. As the crowd roared in approval, fireworks were launched into the night sky, and showers of red, white, and blue fire fell like stars and exploded.

When it was over, hundreds lingered on the streets, heading into saloons or stopping in restaurants for late-night dinners. A group of businessmen and politicians gathered at the Pearl House, just across the street from the railroad depot, for a dinner in honor of Colonel Driskill. Seated at one long table, they drank champagne and ate a lavish eight-course meal. As the night neared its end, they made inebriated toasts under a cloud of cigar smoke to the colonel, the city of Austin, and the state of Texas.

Mayor Robertson made the last toast, raising a glass to the capital city and declaring, "No city has the promise of a more healthful prosperity."

Amidst all the celebration that occurred that day, none of the white residents of Austin spoke about – or likely gave any thought to – the black servant girls who had been attacked and murdered over the last six months.

Out of sight was truly out of mind.

LATER IN JULY, MAYOR ROBERTSON HOSTED a meeting of the Texas Semi-Centennial Organizing Committee, which was in charge of planning the celebration of 50 years of Texas Independence. It would be held in Austin in March 1886, seven months away. Although the mayor wasn't sure how they'd top the parade and cornerstone ceremony from the previous march, he vowed that the upcoming celebration would "eclipse anything ever attempted in Texas."

In early August, Robertson hosted an important visitor to Austin, J.W. Olds, whom the mayor greeted at the railroad depot when he arrived from San Francisco. Olds was a researcher and ghostwriter for Hubert Howe Bancroft, one of the most popular American historians of the day. For the last several years, Bancroft had been working on a massive, 39-volume project that collected the history of the western half of the continent, from Central America to Alaska. He had recently decided to devote one entire volume to Texas, so he had sent Olds to Austin to collect material about Texas history, starting with the first white settlers in the 1520s and concluding in the 1880s, with Austin and the rest of the state at the start of the modern age.

Historian Hubert Howe Bancroft sent his researcher J.W. Olds to Austin during the time of the murders.

Roberston wanted to make sure that Olds saw the best of Austin. It was arranged for him and his wife to stay in a suite of rooms at the city's finest boardinghouse. Dinners were thrown in his honor. He met with Governor Ireland and William Swain, the comptroller already campaigning to be the next Texas governor.

As part of his research, Olds visited shops and restaurants on Congress Avenue, spoke with the professors and administrators of the new University of Texas, and even visited the State Lunatic Asylum, where Dr. Denton showed off the freshly landscaped grounds, renovated dormitories, and the chapel where his daughter and son-in-law Dr. Given had been married.

He also toured the new state capitol building, which was still under construction – and, by all accounts, the biggest and most expensive construction project in America. Over 500 workers were spread throughout the 22-acre grounds, putting up iron girders and pillars, excavating the basement, building foundation walls, and installing water pipes, ventilation shafts, and gas and electrical fixtures. Each afternoon, a locomotive called *The Lone*

Star pulled flatbed cars laden with red granite straight from a nearby quarry using a narrow-gauge railroad track built for the construction. Cranes unloaded the granite, which was then carved into perfect rectangular blocks by trained stonemasons "imported" from England and Scotland. Olds was so impressed by the building that he wrote that, when completed, it would "rival in dimensions and magnificence any other edifice of its kind in the United States."

But Olds was not impressed with everything he experienced in Austin. He was almost certainly told about the attacks on the city's black servant women, but he had little sympathy for them. In his notes, he wrote that white citizens periodically had to endure the behavior of "debased Negros" who "engaged in frays among themselves, which generally terminated in bloodshed."

He made it clear that the "frays" were of little significance to white residents and officials in the city.

DURING THE MONTH OF AUGUST, MANY residents left the city for summer vacations, some traveling to other parts of the South and others taking the train to Galveston to enjoy time along the Gulf of Mexico. Sergeant Chenneville even took a few days off because there was little to do. Wrote a reporter, "If something doesn't turn up soon, Austin's police force will probably adjourn for a fishing frolic."

For those who remained in Austin, the last week of the month turned brutal. Temperatures soared, with thermometers topping out in the triple digits. A crew of men with a water wagon traveled back and forth along downtown's sunbaked streets, spraying them with water to keep down the dust.

On August 29, a few hundred people braved the heat to troop out to the fairgrounds to watch the Austin baseball team face off against the neighboring Georgetowns for the regional championship – proving that it wasn't just the team from the capital city with an unimaginative name. The Austins – so hot that their sweat soaked through their gray flannel uniforms – won by a score of 19-10 to advance to the state playoffs.

The downtown streets were filled with their usual activity that night – couples dined in restaurants and stopped at the "air-cooled" ice cream parlor. At the saloons, men gathered to drink and play cards. Women were not allowed inside, so servers were

Fulton's Ice Cream Parlor in Austin – the perfect place to spend a late August evening in 1885.

stationed on the sidewalk to bring refreshments outside to the ladies who wanted them.

As the evening air cooled a little, people began strolling toward home. Even with all the windows open, the houses were stifling in the late summer heat. The temperatures were only manageable inside after the sun had long disappeared over the horizon and a breeze could be coaxed inside. Most believed another peaceful night lay ahead for the city of Austin.

But they were wrong.

Just after midnight, a man slipped through the shadows just southeast of downtown. His journey took him past a few stables and homes, and then he turned down an alley that ran behind the home of Valentine Osborn Weed.

The "Servant Girl Annihilator" had returned.

9. THE YOUNGEST VICTIM

VALENTINE WEED LIVING IN A LARGE, TWO-STORY Queen Anne-style home just a block away from Dr. Lucian Johnson's house, where Eliza Shelly had been murdered in May. It was a grand house, and Weed had worked hard to afford it. He was still relatively young but had started a livery stable downtown from which he earned a hefty income leasing horses, wagons, and carriages.

More compassionate than many other white employers in the city, he had moved his servants into his home after the attacks began. They were too afraid to sleep in their separate quarters out back, and Valentine had no desire for his cook and maid to leave her job and possibly the city.

On that night, a pallet in his kitchen served as a bed for his servant, Rebecca Ramey, and her 11-year-old daughter, Mary. Rebecca was about 40 and a large woman, likely weighing nearly 200 pounds. She was well-known in the black community because her brother was Albert Carrington, Austin's only black alderman. Rebecca had

The home of the Valentine Weed family.

formerly worked at the Austin Steam Laundry and had been married to a man who was a bellhop at the popular Avenue Hotel. But when he disappeared from Austin a few years earlier – the rumor was he ran off with another woman – Rebecca had started working for the Weed family so she could have her daughter, Mary, close to her side.

Mary spent her mornings at the all-black Central Grammar School, and in the afternoons, she helped her mother. She ironed clothes, made beds, chopped wood, carried in water, built fires, cleaned, and cooked – anything Rebecca needed her to do. The Weeds loved both Ramey women and treated them well. They encouraged Mary to keep up with her education so she could someday enroll at the Tillotson College and Normal Institute and become a teacher. The Weeds and Mary's mother believed the young woman had a bright future ahead of her.

Mary Ramey

But no one had any idea a man was lurking outside.

He opened the back gate to the Weed property and likely paused before entering the backyard so that he didn't spook Tom Thumb, the miniature Shetland Pony that belonged to the Weed children that lived there.

The man crossed the backyard, somehow not making a sound as he walked through the dry oak leaves that had fallen from the trees. When he stepped onto the back porch, the boards creaked slightly, although they weren't loud enough to wake Rebecca, Mary, or the Weeds. Slowly and silently, he eased open the back door into the kitchen.

The man was carrying a wooden club when he entered the house. It was wrapped in buckskin, and the end of it was packed with several ounces of lead and sand. It was a formidable weapon. There was a leather thong that usually dangled from the end of the club, but the man had it wrapped around his wrist. He crossed the kitchen floor and loomed over Rebecca and Mary.

For some reason, Rebecca woke up. When she realized someone was standing and looking down at her and her daughter, she tried to focus her eyes to see who it was. However, the man was just a black shape in the darkness. Rebecca never had the chance to utter a sound before the man struck her savagely on the side of the head with the object he had in his hand. It hit her like a solid fist, and thanks to the sand that surrounded the lead weight, the sound of it striking her skull was nothing but a dull thunk.

The blinding pain from the attack was so sudden and paralyzing that Rebecca couldn't cry out. She saw a bright light and then nothing as she was knocked unconscious.

The last thing she saw was the man dropping the club and reaching for her daughter.

AT SOME POINT, DURING THE EARLY MORNING hours, Rebecca regained consciousness and began to groan. She wanted to call for help but could not form words and speak.

Her groans continued until 5:00 A.M. when they awakened Valentine Weed and his wife. Hearing the noise, he asked his wife what the sound was, and she said it sounded like a dog howling in the backyard. He disagreed – "It was an unnatural noise," he later said. He lit a small lantern, grabbed his pistol, and started across the back gallery toward the kitchen. His wife, in her nightgown, followed behind him.

Valentine Weed

The sound grew worse as they approached the kitchen, and Valentine pushed open the door.

He found Rebecca on the floor, on her hands and knees, trying to get up, but was unable to stand. Blood was flowing from her temple, puddling on the floor. Part of her forehead looked as though it was caved in, and the line of her jaw was crooked. Her pain was so great she could barely speak but managed to tell the

Weeds, "I'm sick." When they asked where Mary was, Rebecca could only shake her head.

Weed saw the club lying on the kitchen floor. Blood was smeared all over it, and he deduced that it had caused Rebecca's injuries. But where was Mary?

Gun in hand, he went outside and yelled toward the home of his next-door neighbor, Stephen Jacqua, who was one of the owners of a flour, feed, and hay supply store in town. The sun was starting to come up, so he knew that Jacqua was already awake. The back door of the neighboring house opened, and Jacqua came outside. He met Valentine at the fence and was told that someone had entered his house, attacked Rebecca, and took her daughter. He asked Jacqua to help him search for any clues in the backyard.

Together, they decided to check a small shed in the yard where tools were stored. Jacqua said during the inquest that followed, "I carried the light, and Mr. Weed pushed the door of the outhouse open with the barrel of his gun. We saw the girl lying on the floor, as I supposed, dead."

But Mary wasn't dead – not yet. Her eyes were partially open, and she was staring at the two men in a daze with no expression on her face at all. There was blood all over her lower face, coming from her nose, and more blood trickled from both of her ears. The men left the shed and returned to the yard to look around, expecting to be attacked. But they heard only the early morning sounds of the neighborhood waking up – the attacker was long gone.

Valentine told Jacqua to stay in the yard and not allow anyone inside the shed. He was smart enough to understand that the crime scene must be preserved until the police arrived – a realization it's unlikely the actual police would have had in Austin at the time.

He called out to his wife and sent her to Dr. Johnson's home so he could attend to Rebecca and Mary. Then, Weed ran to Sergeant Chenneville's home, only a few blocks away. He told him to come at once and bring his dogs.

When Dr. Johnson arrived, he examined Mary in the shed but knew he could do nothing for her. Whenever she took a breath, more blood poured out of her ears and puddled beneath her head. Another physician, Dr. Richard Swearingen, heard the commotion and went to the shed to see if he could help. Unfortunately, he agreed with his colleague – they could do nothing for the girl.

When Chenneville arrived with a cacophony of barking bloodhounds, he also came into the shed. Together, the men surmised that the intruder, after attacking Rebecca, had grabbed Mary, clamped a hand over her mouth so she couldn't make a sound, and carried her out to the shed.

Unlike the other attacks, Mary had been raped before the attacker had jammed some long iron rod – like the one used on Eliza Shelley – into Mary's ear, piercing one side of her brain. Then he had pulled out the rod and jammed it into the other ear – essentially lobotomizing her. Horribly, this would be her cause of death.

Dr. Johnson cradled Mary's head in his hands, trying his best to comfort her, but just as the sun started to rise, she made a tiny sobbing sound, and she died.

AS IF THE AUSTIN POLICE DIDN'T SEEM INCOMPENTENT enough already, Marshal Lee didn't arrive at the murder scene until seven hours after the Weeds had discovered Rebecca and Mary. Because it was Sunday – and his day off – he'd slept late at his father's house.

By all indications, Chenneville and his officers were fine with the marshal staying away. No one had called Lee, and no one had gone to his father's home to alert him to the new murder.

Lee spent a few minutes talking to Valentine Weed and inspected the backyard shed. A few minutes later, he left and went downtown to the police department to handle some paperwork. He certainly didn't have anything to offer the investigation.

Chenneville and the other officers did their best to get to the bottom of the mess. An officer found some footprints in the sandy soil next to the gate that led from the Weeds' backyard into the alley. Chenneville's bloodhounds sniffed around, and, for once, they caught a scent. They ran down the alley and came to a halt two blocks away at a stable, where a young black man named Tom Allen was found sleeping in the hayloft. Chenneville's dogs lunged at the young man, biting him on the hands, arms, and legs.

Tom, known around town as "River Bottom Tom," worked on the water cart that sprayed the downtown streets to keep down

TRAGEDY AT AUSTIN.

THE SERVANT GIRL AGAIN THE VICTIM.

An Eleven-Year Old Mulatto Girl Outraged and Murdered and Her Mother Left for Dead – Officers on the Trail.

[SPECIAL TO THE NEWS.]

AUSTIN, August 30.—Another one of those most horrible murders, for which Austin is becoming notorious, occurred last night, and again the servant girl is the victim. At 7 o'clock this morning Beckey Ramey, a mulatto cook, about forty years of age, and weighing about 200 pounds, was found lying on the floor, covered with blood. She had a deep wound in the temple, and had been beaten about the neck and face.

Mary Ramey, her 11 year old daughter, was found across the yard on the floor of a wash house, gasping for breath. She had been stabbed in both ears with some sharp instrument, supposed to be a file or screwdriver, and had also been ravished. At each gasp for breath the blood flowed from the wounds in her ears. She died shortly after being discovered, being unconscious from the time she was found till her death.

The tragedy took place on the premises of V. O. Weed, at 300 East Cedar street, he being of the firm of Weed & French, proprietors of the Girls' stables.

Mr. Weed's statement of the affair is to the effect that Beckey Rainey and her daughter were employed by him as servants; that they were good workers and of quiet habits, and had no male visitors whatever; that Beckey and her daughter slept on a pallet in the kitchen. About 4 o'clock this morning he heard groans. He awoke his wife and they got up and followed the sound to the kitchen, where they found Beckey. She was covered with blood and was trying to get up. On being asked what was the matter, she said she was very sick. She was evidently unconscious and has not spoken again. Her wounds are such as will likely prove fatal.

As the girl was not in the room search was at once made for her and she was found in a small room used as a wash room, situated in the yard, about thirty or forty feet from the house. There she lay on the floor, where the fiend had outraged her, with blood running from both ears where she had been stabbed. She was too far gone to speak and died without saying a word.

Mr. Weed at once sent for a doctor and Police Sergeant Chenneville and Officer Wilson arrived soon afterward and started to work with blood hounds. The dogs took a trail at once and ran down the street about two blocks to a stable and stopped. In this stable Henry Taylor, a negro, commonly known as River Bottom Tom, was found. He is employed by a man on whose premises he was employed to drive a watering cart, and has been rooming there. As the dogs refused to take any other trail the negro was arrested. He was taken to Mr. Weed's and his footprints compared with tracks that were found in the yard. They fitted exactly, it is stated, even to a peculiarly shaped toe. Sergeant Chenneville is almost positive that Taylor is the guilty party.

Dr. Sweaningen, who was summoned to attend the victims, thinks the women were struck while asleep with sand bags, and not afterward, as there were no screams or struggle heard.

Later—The woman is better, and has regained speech and consciousness, but gives no intelligible account

the dust. He was immediately arrested on a charge of "suspicion of murder" and taken to jail.

By this time, a crowd was gathering around the Weed home. Many of them were on their way to church when they heard the news about the murder and stood around gawking in their best clothes and Bibles tucked under their arms. They watched as Mary's body was taken from the shed and loaded onto the undertaker's wagon for the trip to the dead room at the City-County Hospital. They also saw Rebecca being loaded onto the wagon so she could be cared for in the hospital's "Negro Ward," a cramped, windowless room down the hall from the dead room that contained a few beds.

When the newspaper reporters gathered around Valentine Weed, he told them that Rebecca and Mary were "good workers of quiet habits." He added that Rebecca led an "orderly life" and was "a good and virtuous woman." He stated that he would gladly give money for a reward fund for the capture of Mary's killer.

The activity at the Weeds' home concealed the fact that the investigation into the attack was going nowhere. Although one police officer told a reporter that Tom Allen's feet perfectly matched the footprints found in the alley outside the Weeds' back gate – even to a "peculiarly-shaped toe" on one foot – the truth remained that it wasn't surprising that his footprints were in the alley since he lived nearby and often traveled that way.

In addition, the hay where Tom had been sleeping should have been coated with blood from the attack on Rebecca and Mary, and yet, not a drop of it was found in the hayloft.

After Tom was arrested, he was examined by Dr. William Burt, the staff physician from City-County Hospital. According to Dr. Burt, the exam proved conclusively in his mind that Tom was not the man who raped Mary. No other information was offered – and we have no idea what this examination consisted of -- but Dr. Burt was certain.

Chenneville also tried and failed to find anyone who had a story to tell about Tom having some grudge against Rebecca and Mary. He did what he could to get Tom to confess – even subjecting him to the usual brutal questioning – but like all the other African American men who had been dragged to jail and interrogated, Tom insisted he'd had nothing to with the attack on Rebecca and Mary or any of the other attacks.

Chenneville then received a fresh tip: another black man named Aleck Mack might be involved. Determined to make another arrest before the day was over, they went looking for Aleck, who had often been described in the newspaper as "a petty thief of a particularly quarrelsome nature," "a very impudent Negro," and a "notoriously bad darkie." Among the city's white residents, Mack was particularly notorious because he had once defiantly drunk from a "whites-only water bucket" at a construction site on a hot summer afternoon.

Although Aleck hadn't been seen around Austin in months, he had returned that summer, and when officers tracked him down on the east side, his legs and feet were covered with asafetida, which to Chenneville meant he was up to no good. And another black man was on his way to jail.

During the following interrogation, Aleck, like Tom Allen, claimed to be completely ignorant about the attacks on Rebecca and Mary. He said that he barely knew them. He later told a reporter who came to interview him in jail that he had used the asafetida on his feet and legs because he'd gotten word that the police were looking for him. He knew Chenneville would use his dogs, and Aleck said he was terrified of them.

Autopsy notes written by Dr. William Burt at the City-County Hospital.

But he swore he had nothing to do with the murders and attacks in Austin.

TWO DAYS LATER, MARY'S SMALL BODY WAS placed in a coffin and taken by the undertaker to the Colored Ground. Waiting by the front gate, as always, was Mr. Nitschke, the caretaker. He directed the undertaker's wagon and the mourners that followed it to an open grave under a live oak tree and then returned to his office to place her name in the ledger.

He'd finally realized there was no way to pretend the slayings weren't happening. In the column for cause of death, he carefully wrote, "Murdered."

The cemetery caretaker was not the only one who had stopped pretending the murders weren't happening. By now, all the newspapers in Texas were running stories about the murders and attacks – and most were criticizing Austin officials for their failure to find the "bad blacks."

Even the local *Daily Statesman* was losing patience with the police and the city government. An editor wrote: "We pay for protection, but why is there none – absolutely none? The citizens are overcome with terror, not now at the bold daring desperado in the open street, but at sneaking midnight prowlers, seeking an opportunity to outrage the unprotected and to shed the blood of the innocent."

In the saloons and on the street corners along Congress Avenue, there were more calls for full-time police officers who could be hired to work only at night. Other men continued to demand a vigilance committee to be formed – one that didn't answer to the police. One man told a reporter, "If such a step is taken, it will not only certainly put a stop to these nightly outrages, but it will be the means of ridding this city of a horde of loafing, shiftless, vagrant Negroes who have infested it for years."

Austin's black community was as vocal about the murders as they could be. Alderman Albert Carrington and businessman E.H. Carrington (seen here, far right) were brothers of Rebecca Ramey.

Austin's black community leaders took a much different view of things than the racists who wanted to put together lynching parties, but they were also demanding action from the police. Reverend Grant, Alderman Carrington, Dr. Quinton B. Neal – the city's only black physician, William Wilson – principal of the all-black public schools, and the publisher of Austin's black newspaper, Jeremiah Hamilton, decided to take their demands to city and county officials. The men bravely gathered at the county courthouse to ask that the city's black residents be given better police protection.

One of the men – the newspaper didn't record who it was – read a formal statement:

Whereas the city of Austin has been wronged, outraged, and thrown into the intensest excitement; and whereas, not one of the fiendish scoundrels has been caught and punished; therefore, be it resolved, that we, the colored citizens of Austin, pledge ourselves to use every lawful means to aid the civil authorities in arresting and punishing these villains to the fullest extent of the law." The statement ended with a request that city officials offer a "suitable reward for the arrest and punishment of the parties who committed the murder upon Mrs. Ramey's daughter last Sunday morning.

The group tried to meet with Governor Ireland and hand him the statement, but they were told that he was sick. He wasn't, of course, but he wasn't going to jeopardize his political career by getting involved with local murders.

Mayor Robertson didn't meet with the committee either. He didn't want the white residents of the city to think that he was listening to advice from black men.

But Robertson didn't need anyone to tell him that his political future was in trouble if the killings didn't stop. The city elections were scheduled for December, and a wealthy lumberman named Joseph Nalle – who'd lost to Robertson the last time – made it clear that he planned to challenge him for the mayor's office again.

Nalle had been born in Culpepper, Virginia, but came to Austin in 1870. He was the first man ever to ship a trainload of lumber to the city. By 1884, Nalle had lumberyards in Austin, Waco, Burnet, Stephenville, and Alexandria, Louisiana, and was well-known and well-liked in the city despite a deadly brush with the law that had happened a few years before.

In March 1878, Nalle was the city's Ninth Ward alderman, who had some political differences with a Fifth Ward alderman named Thomas J. Markley. They'd taken opposing sides on a proposition to appropriate money for building an additional city market house.

Joseph Nalle

At the council's March 11 meeting, things became heated. However, they really boiled over the next day when Nelle and Markley began exchanging words in the editorial office of the *Daily Statesman*. Nalle grabbed a heavy inkwell from a desk and hurled it at Markley. He also flung a pair of scissors at him and was going to attack him with a chair, but a reporter pulled it out of his hands. Another alderman threw a punch at Markley, leaving a mark on the other man's face, and Markley bloodied the man's nose. They quickly came to their senses and apologized, agreeing that there should be no bitterness between them since both were Freemasons.

Markley apologized to *Statesman* publisher John Cardwell, who had been in the room when the fracas began, and Cardwell said he hoped that friends could be made all around. Markley said that when he saw Nalle again, they would talk and reach an understanding. When he left the newspaper office, he stated he would "go down the street and shave and feel better."

At 2:00 P.M., Markley was reported outside the Crystal Saloon, speaking with a man named Gillebrand about what had happened that morning. Then, Markley turned his head and said, "There is Nalle now coming up."

Nalle was with a man named Odom, and they stopped where Markley was standing.

Markley asked him, "Are you as good a man as you was a while ago?"

"I am," Nalle replied.

Accounts vary as to which man moved toward the other first, but they clinched and began to struggle. While in that clench, Nalle removed a knife from his pants and stabbed Markley near the heart with it. His arm moved back and forth at least two more times as he stabbed Markley again. When the two men separated, Markley clutched his chest. Blood was seeping out between his fingers. He staggered backward into the saloon and collapsed. He was dead when he hit the floor.

Nalle wiped the blood off the knife on his pants, replaced it in his wristband, and gave himself up to the authorities. Markley had been unarmed. The coroner's inquest revealed that he'd been stabbed three times in the heart.

Excitement over the killing spread through the city, and it was said that if not for the intervention of a few influential men, Nalle might have been lynched.

As one of the richest men in Austin, Nalle hired a prominent attorney named William "Buck" Walton, who also represented wild card lawman Ben Thompson, who'd been involved in more than his share of questionable killings. As he'd often done for Thompson, Walton managed to get an acquittal for Nalle after obtaining a change of venue to friendlier Williamson County.

Years later, Nalle was in contention to take over Robertson's mayor job. He was already telling voters they wouldn't have to worry about their servant girls getting attacked if he was mayor. Austin wouldn't be overrun by black criminals, he said, because he'd ensure that a real marshal, not some rich man's son, was in charge of the police department.

And Nalle wasn't the only Austin resident pressuring Robertson to remove the polite and efficient Marshal Lee from duty. One man put it this way to a reporter, "The marshal is a good, honest, well-meaning man, but he is deficient in the ability which should characterize a man occupying the important position that he does. And if the chief of the police force is inefficient, the force is, too, no matter how capable the men comprising it may be. A change is imperatively demanded. The reputation of the city marred and blackened by a fearfully bloody record, demands it."

Robertson knew, though, that if he crossed Joseph Lee by firing his son, he'd never raise another dollar in Austin for future campaigns. So, he came up with a different idea – he'd do what the black committee asked and offer a reward for the arrest of the killer, which would bring detectives from all over the country to Austin. He'd also write to a friend who owned the Noble Commercial Detective Agency in Houston and ask him to send his best man to Austin.

Surely, between the Austin police department and the score of detectives who were about to descend on the city, they'd finally be able to catch the man who was attacking and slaying the servant girls in the city.

IT WAS NOT UNCOMMON DURING THE LATE nineteenth and early twentieth centuries for small-town police departments – or even those with little experience dealing with serious crimes – to turn to private detective agencies for assistance.

The leading agencies in most of the United States were the Pinkertons, Burns, and Kirk. They worked for wages and reward money. Some waited for calls while others took it upon themselves to work a case, hoping they might be hired or rewarded for the information they uncovered. Detectives of this sort were in great demand, and until state and local governments began training their own investigators, they were the closest thing to experts when it came to investigating crime scenes. Detectives, especially those from the major agencies, were given great respect by the public and police officers, but the quality of their skills varied widely. Some were good, some were bad, and many were downright corrupt. There were many accounts of private detectives railroading suspects, planting evidence, and inventing witness accounts.

There wasn't much that Mayor Robertson could do to stop freelance private detectives from coming to Austin to get involved in the investigation. However, he'd decided to stack the deck by contacting the Noble Agency in Houston.

Robertson could more easily have contacted Austin's detective agency, the Capital Detective Association, a three-person operation that opened in 1884. However, he knew they had less experience than his police department. The local detective agency was little more than a merchant police force, hired to watch over businesses at night, to recover stolen merchandise, or to track down employees who were stealing. These were things the police department didn't have the workforce to deal with. The agency wasn't going to be helpful in a murder case.

The Noble Commercial Detective Agency, though, was another story. The owners – former Houston sheriff C.M. Noble and John F. Morris, former marshal of the Houston Police Department – promoted themselves as the Texas version of the famous Pinkertons, taking out carefully worded advertisements in the state's newspaper that made it look as though they were an affiliate of the national company. One of them read: "We are prepared to furnish Detectives of unquestioned ability to perform all Railroad, Bank, Insurance, and all branches of Detective Work. We are in daily communications with the Pinkerton Agency, East and West."

The Pinkertons were undoubtedly famous. Founded by Allan Pinkerton in 1850, the agency quickly became one of the most important crime detection and law enforcement groups in the United States. While there were scores of other private police agencies in the country, none had the notoriety or success rates the Pinkerton Agency achieved. At a time when most police forces

The Pinkerton agency was the most famous detective force in America in the 1880s but, naturally, that wasn't who Mayor Robertson hired to investigate the murders.

lacked the workforce and resources needed for difficult investigations, the Pinkertons, with their famous "We Never Sleep" motto, became the best hope for bringing many criminals to justice.

By the 1880s, the exploits of the Pinkertons were the stuff of lurid newspaper stories and dime novels, offering details of their hunts for bank robbers, railroad bandits, swindlers, kidnappers, and outlaws like Jesse James.

A reader of any Texas newspaper could see that any of the six detectives who worked for the Noble Agency were just as brave and dedicated as the men who called themselves Pinkerton agents.

And maybe they were, but Noble and Morris had no connection to the Pinkertons. They just refused to let the truth get in the way of a good advertisement because their loose claims brought them a lot of business. After only one year in operation, they also opened offices in San Antonio and Dallas. They also gave frequent interviews that trumpeted the arrests made by their best detectives – especially those made by Mike Hennessey, a former New Orleans police captain.

Built like a boxer with broad shoulders and powerful arms, Hennessey was considered an expert manhunter, slipping into cities and small towns to search for criminals and witnesses that no one else could find. He had solved several notable crimes and brought more than one killer to justice. He was, according to every report, a relentless detective.

And this was why Mayor Robertson wanted him sent to Austin to help with the case. At this point, Robertson didn't need anyone to tell him that Marshal Lee was in way over his head. Even always reliable Sergeant Chenneville seemed to have no idea what to do beyond bringing in his bloodhounds and beating men half to death to get a confession. He was a good man, but he had all the intellectual depth of the billy club that he carried with him on patrol. Chenneville was a blunt weapon; as this case had already proven, something with a sharper edge was needed.

Robertson talked the city aldermen into paying for Hennessey's services -- $10 a day, plus expenses – and into allowing him to claim the reward if he caught the killer. There would be other competition for that reward if other detectives came to town, but Roberston was confident in the Noble Agency detective's abilities.

Finally, it seemed this investigation was getting somewhere.

HENNESSEY AND TWO ASSISTANTS – GEORGE Hannah and Ike Himmel – arrived in Austin on September 9. They checked into rooms at the Carrollton House, two quiet blocks off Congress Avenue, under false names. They also brought along their own bloodhound, which they tied up in the hotel's small backyard.

Their first stop was the police department, where they were brought up to date on all the known details of the various murder investigations.

And then they went to work.

Trying not to draw attention, and with their hats pulled down low, the trio casually walked to the houses where the murders had occurred. They met with some of the servant women who had survived attacks, questioning them about any details they didn't tell the police but had since recalled about the man they saw in their rooms – height, weight, hair, scars, anything at all.

In the evening, dressed in old, worn-out clothing, wigs, and false beards, the detectives drank in the saloons of the east side, covertly listening to conversations, hoping to overhear something they could use.

They returned to the hotel at the end of each night and scribbled detailed notes about everything they'd learned.

Unfortunately, their anonymity didn't last long. Austin was soon buzzing with news that Noble detectives were in town. Reporters began hanging out in hotel lobbies, hoping to land an interview with them. Women followed with the sole purpose of swooning over the handsome detective Hennessey. Things worsened once they learned the men were staying at the Carrollton House. Someone was always waiting for them in the lobby, so the detectives started slipping out the back door, only to find neighborhood kids petting the bloodhound they'd brought.

Although he offered the impression that he wasn't looking for it, Hennessey loved the attention. A few days after their identities had been discovered, he told a reporter that he and his men were already "drawing a net pretty closely around a number of suspicious characters." Hennessey assured newspaper readers that he and his men would find the killers. They just needed a little time.

The detectives prowled around the city for a few more days, and it wasn't long before some of the reporters trailing them began to get the sense that they had no better idea of how to catch the killers than Chenneville did. One wrote, "The detective force that has been trying to run down the murderers of the girl, Mary Ramey, reported some days since they had a clue to the fiends. They left the trail to go and inform newspaper reporters of the fact, and thereby lost it, which they have not been able to find since, even with the aid of their bloodhound."

When the story appeared, Hennessey assured reporters that he and his assistants were making progress. Good detective work requires a lot of patience, he explained. Sources had to be carefully cultivated, and physical evidence had to be collected, which took time. The key was to put together all the facts and then arrest the killers.

On the last weekend of September, Hennessey decided to take a short break and return to Houston to take care of some personal matters.

It was almost as if the "Servant Girl Annihilator" was waiting for him to go because as soon as he did, horror returned to Austin.

11. DOUBLE MURDER

ON SATURDAY NIGHT, SEPTEMBER 27, TWO servant women who lived in sparse quarters behind a home on Rio Grande Street heard a noise outside. One of them bravely cracked open the door and peered out into the gloomy evening.

There was a man standing inches away in the shadows. "I'll kill you if you open your mouth," he whispered at her.

But she screamed anyway, and the man fled. When Chenneville and other officers arrived a short time later, the maid could not describe the man except to say he was white.

THE NEXT NIGHT – SUNDAY, SEPTEMBER 28 – a cook who lived in servants' quarters behind the home of Dr. Wade A. Morris, just a few blocks west of the new state capitol, began screaming when she heard a noise at her window. It sounded like someone was trying to break inside. She caught a glimpse of the man but could not offer the police any solid description.

AN HOUR LATER, MAJOR W.B. DUNHAM, EDITOR of the *Texas Court Reporter*, was awakened by the sound of a muffled cry from the servants' quarters in the backyard of his home on Guadalupe Street.

Dunham's cook, a lovely young black woman named Gracie Vance, lived in the quarters with her boyfriend, Orange Washington, who worked at Butler's Brick Yard. Two other women who worked for local families – Patsy Gibson and Lucinda Boddy – were staying there, too. They were too scared to sleep alone in the quarters at the houses where they worked.

The two homes where attacks took place in late September were within just a few blocks of the new state capitol building.

Assuming that Gracie and Orange were arguing – a not uncommon thing – Dunham went to his back door and shouted for the couple to quiet down. After that, he closed the door, went back to bed, and was soon back to sleep.

But his sleep would soon be interrupted.

Several minutes later, he was startled awake by a loud groan. This time, he grabbed a pistol and hurried into the yard to see one of Gracie's visitors, Lucinda, staggering out of the small house. Her head was bloodied, and she was having trouble keeping her balance.

She turned and looked at Dunham and cried out, "Mr. Dunham, we are all dead!"

Dunham sent her to lie down on the back porch and started toward the servants' quarters. Just then, his next-door neighbor, Iron Front Saloon owner Harry Duff, hurried into the Dunham yard carrying a lantern. He said he'd heard the noises, too, and had called the police.

The two men went into the small house. Duff raised his lantern, and the men took in the blood-soaked scene before them. Patsy Gibson was barely alive. She was curled on her side, and blood was pouring from a wound in her head.

Orange was dead. He was lying facedown on the floor between the bed and the wall in a pool of his own blood. A bloodied ax was lying on the bed next to him.

Gracie was nowhere to be found.

The two men left the shack when they heard galloping hoofbeats on the road – Chenneville and another officer, James Connor, had arrived. The policemen dismounted and, holding lanterns, they followed a bloody trail that led away from the servants' quarters. They climbed over the backyard fence – which was nearly four feet high – and kept following the bloody trail into the yard of the Hotchkiss family, who lived next door to Major Dunham. The

> **Weekly News Summary.**
>
> **INTELLIGENCE FROM ALL PARTS.**
>
> **DOMESTIC.**
>
> ORANGE WASHINGTON (colored) and his wife were murdered in a cabin in North Austin, Tex., a few nights ago by unknown persons.

portion of the yard separated from Dunham's yard by the fence was a grassy area where they pastured their horses.

As Chenneville and Connor drew closer to the Hotchkiss stable, one of the men stumbled and fell. Under the pale yellow glow of their lanterns, they discovered what had caused the man's fall – it was the battered corpse of Gracie Vance.

Gracie's face had been beaten so badly that she was unrecognizable. Her features had been reduced to a mass of bone, skin, and blood. Her head was knocked off center as though it had come loose. Lying in the grass next to her was a brick, and it was covered with blood and bits of flesh and brain matter. This was apparently what the killer had used to bash in her skull.

Her hair and nightgown were saturated with blood. The only thing that wasn't bloodstained on her body was a small silver open-faced watch that was attached to a delicate chain around her wrist.

Robbery had certainly not been the motive for her murder.

As the two men studied the body, they suddenly heard a loud cry from the Hotchkiss house. Hanna Hotchkiss had seen someone – or thought she did – running toward the black neighborhood west of her home.

Even though they saw absolutely nothing, Chenneville and Connor drew their revolvers and fired blindly into the darkness. They fired eight times in all, hoping one of their bullets would hit whoever was supposedly running away from them.

I doubt they gave much thought to the bullets hitting innocent bystanders, drawn to the area by the excitement.

Leaving Gracie's body unattended, the two officers ran back to the Dunham house and jumped onto their horses. As they bolted down the dark street, the animals raised a cloud of dust. Both men still had their guns in hand, planning to shoot again, but there was no one to be seen. If someone had been there – which is unlikely – they had vanished.

More police officers soon arrived at the Dunham house, including the Travis County Sheriff W.W. Hornsby and some of his deputies. Marshall Lee also showed up – not taking seven hours to do so this time – but had little to add to the investigation.

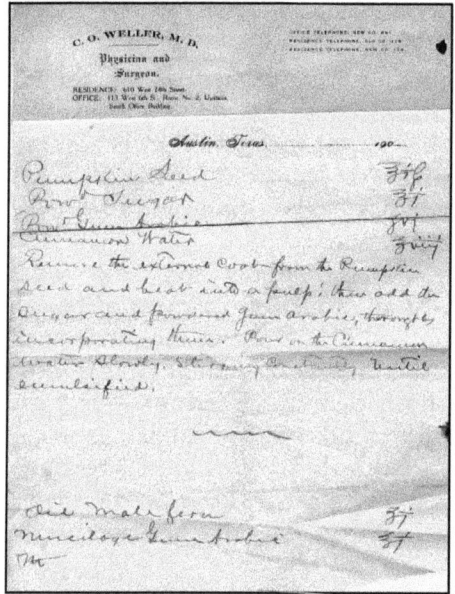

While Gracie's body was still lying out in the horse pasture, some of the officers began searching the nearby houses and servants' quarters, hoping for any lead. Other than Mrs. Hotchkiss, though, none of the neighbors had seen anything. Officers rode to the closest black neighborhood, hoping to find men awake and on the streets at that hour, but no one was out. The houses were dark and locked up tight.

Dr. C.O. Weller, who lived in the neighborhood, came over to the Dunhams and quickly examined Lucinda and Patsy, discovering that each of them had been hit one time in the head with a blunt object, likely the ax that was left at the scene. He also examined Orange's head, discovering he had been hit twice.

A prescription written by Dr. C.O. Weller, who examined the victims, listing his residence at 610 West 24th Street.

By now, the police had finally retrieved Gracie's corpse from the pasture next door. She was carried into the servants' quarters and placed on the bed. Dr. Weller leaned in close and examined her wounds. Like the others, she had been hit on the head – probably with the ax – but then, after being carried away from her house, she was hit at least a dozen times with the brick. One of the blows had landed on the bridge of her nose, shattering the bone, and the other blows had struck her temple, jaws, cheeks, and eyes. One reporter on the scene noted that Gracie's face looked "like jelly."

Chenneville and a few other officers crowded inside the shack as the doctor finished his examination. They smoked cigars to keep the coppery smell of blood out of their noses.

As they tried to reconstruct the crime, it was suggested that the killer had slipped into the shack around 1:00 A.M and quickly struck each of the four people sleeping there in the head. Perhaps because Orange continued to struggle, the attacker hit him again. The second blow had killed him. The intruder then picked up Gracie and carried her out of the house, lifted her over the fence, and took her into the Hotchkiss horse pasture, where he brutally beat her to death with a brick.

The entire attack, they guessed, had taken place in complete darkness in a matter of only a few minutes. The killer – whoever he was – seemed to be perfecting his methods of murder.

BY THE TIME THE SUN WAS UP, THE NEWS of the latest attacks had spread throughout the city. Crowds began arriving at the Dunham house, and a carnival-like atmosphere pervaded the surrounding streets. Streetcars began what reporters called "a thriving business," hauling sightseers from downtown to the scene of the two murders. Young men from the nearby University of Texas walked over, hoping to glimpse Orange Washington or one of the battered servant girls. By now, the dead had been moved from the servants' quarters to the main house, and people fought for the chance to peer into the windows at them.

Eventually, the path was cleared, and Gracie and Orange were taken away to the hospital's dead room. Lucinda and Pasty joined Rebecca Ramey in the Negro Ward down the hall.

At some point that morning, the police learned that Gracie had been recently pursued by a man named Dock Woods. Rumor had it that he was angry when Gracie turned him down in favor of Orange.

Excited to have the name of a black man they could pursue, the cops pounced on this new lead. Woods lived in a shanty on a cotton farm about eight miles south of Austin, so a posse of

HORRIBLE TRAGEDY.

Four Persons Foully Murdered by a Negro Man.

Special to the Light:

AUSTIN, September 28.—The most atrocious murder that has ever occurred in Austin, was committed this morning between 1 and 2 o'clock at the residence of Mr. Dunham, in this city, whereby four persons, one man and three women lost their lives. Mr. Dunham had in his employ a negro woman named Grace Vance, who occupied a room in the rear of the house with a man who she lived with; there were two girls visiting this woman and had a bed on the floor, making four persons who were in the room at the time the murderer entered. The first person who was struck down was Orange Washington, whose head was split open with a hatchet, with the same hatchet or ax the two girls were knocked senseless, and the woman Grace Vance was dragged out of the window, thrown over a fence and then dragged over a vacant lot fully a hundred yards from the cabin, where she was found lying in the weeds with a brick alongside of her all besmeared with blood. Blood stains could be seen on the window sill and fence, and the trail was plainly seen where the women had been dragged. Her head was literally covered with gashes inflicted with the brick, and she presented a horrible scene after death. Sergeant Cheyenville and posse gave chase to a negro soon after the murder had been committed, and in the direction the negro run. A horse, bridle and saddle were found hitched to a tree, which was taken possession of and has since been identified; the posse fired eight shots after the fiend but he made good his escape, but will doubtless be caught as he is known. Much excitement prevails throughout the city. The woman Vance, was the only one who was outraged.

officers, including Marshal Lee, rode to the farm and found him picking cotton in one of the fields. He was stunned to hear about the attack on Gracie. He had not left the farm the previous night – there were at least ten other men to vouch for him – but when someone spotted a little blood on the bottom of his shirt, he was immediately seized. Woods was arrested on "suspicion of murder" and taken to Austin.

As word spread about his arrest, a group of men who'd been drinking in a saloon since around sunrise came up with a plan to remove Woods from the jail and string him up on a light post along Congress Avenue. After hearing about the plan – I'm guessing he was in the saloon, too – a reporter from Fort Worth dashed to the telegraph office and sent a wire to his editor, insisting that Woods was about to be lynched by a group of white men. Just for good measure, he also invented a separate story that claimed "a large body of Negroes" was gathering to lynch Woods themselves if he turned out to be guilty. "The indignation of the Negroes is terrible," he claimed.

There were no lynching parties. The white men kept drinking, and the black lynching party never existed at all. That was fortunate because, within a few hours, the case against Dock Woods had fallen apart. A doctor who examined him found an open sore on his body, which was the source of the blood on his shirt. The white owner of the cotton farm told police that he had not only seen Woods on the evening of the murders at 10:00 P.M. but had also seen him the next morning at 4:00 A.M. when all the workers had been awakened to start work in the fields. Since Dock would've had to walk to Austin and back to have committed the murders, there was no way he could be the killer.

As police officials realized they would have to let Woods go, a dry goods store owner named John R. Robinson arrived at the police department with his Swedish servant girl. He said that since Mary Ramey had been murdered, the teenage maid had been sleeping in a bedroom in the main house, only going back to her quarters during the daylight hours to change clothes.

Robinson said that when the girl walked into her quarters that morning, she discovered someone had been there. Her dresses had been pulled from the closet and thrown on the floor, her clothing trunks had been emptied into a pile, and the sheets and blankets had been torn from the bed. The young woman had searched through her belongings, and only one thing was missing – a silver, open-faced watch attached to a delicate silver chain that could be worn around her wrist. She had received it as a gift from her father before she left Sweden.

One of the officers quickly retrieved the silver watch that had been found on Gracie's wrist and showed it to the girl. She gasped in surprise and then turned it over to show that her name was inscribed on the back. When asked if she knew how her watch had ended up on the wrist of a murdered black servant girl, she shook her head. She had no idea who Gracie was.

There was a stunned silence in the police department. The men were struggling to try and put things together. Why would someone break into the quarters of the Robinsons' servant girl, go to the Dunham home – with perhaps a stop at Dr. Morris' house on the way to frighten the cook – and then brutally assault the four people he found there? Why would he take Gracie away from the others, beat her to death with a brick, and then take the time to fasten the Swedish girl's silver watch around the dead girl's wrist before vanishing into the night?

As far as they could tell, the killer was purposely trying to make fools of them, showing the police there was nothing they could do to stop him.

No one knew what to think – or what to do next.

ON THE EVENING AFTER THE DOUBLE MURDER, Captain Mike Hennessey returned to Austin. He went straight to the police department to find out all he could about the attacks, and then he and his men hit the streets, talking to sources they'd been cultivating around town.

Two days later, he asked newspaper reporters to meet him on the front steps of the temporary state capitol. He called the press conference to announce that he and his men had made a break in the case.

As the reporters waited, pencils and notepads in hand, Hennessey said that come across a black teenager named Jonathan Trigg who had agreed to reveal some very important information.

According to Hennessey, Trigg claimed to be at the Black Elephant on August 29, the night Mary Ramey was murdered. He was standing near Oliver Townsend -- Austin's legendary chicken thief – and overheard him telling another of the saloon's patrons that he planned to murder little Mary. Trigg decided to follow Townsend when he left the saloon and witnessed him walking toward the Weed home, but he left and never actually saw him commit the murder.

When a few reporters gave skeptical glances to each other, Hennessey noticed and insisted there was more. Trigg claimed he ran into Townsend again on the night of September 28 – when Gracie, Orange, Lucinda, and Patsy were attacked. This time, he'd seen Townsend downtown, talking to another black man that Trigg didn't know.

As Trigg got closer, he heard the other man say to Townsend, "You'll be caught up with."

Townsend replied, "I have been killing them all, and I have not been caught up with yet."

Townsend then allegedly added that he was going to murder Gracie Vance that very night. He turned and started walking north along Congress Avenue. Trigg said he followed him to the Dunham house, where Townsend met another black man that he didn't know. Moments later, the two men walked toward the Dunhams' servants' quarters and went inside. Trigg said that when he heard a woman scream, "Please don't kill me!" he got scared and ran away.

Hennessey held up a typed piece of paper that he told the reporters was Trigg's statement, detailing what he saw and heard. They were Trigg's own words, stating that he heard everything Oliver Townsend said and had followed him to the locations of two of the murders, even though he didn't see the murders committed.

And the detective wasn't finished. He announced that he had also gone to the hospital to talk with Lucinda Boddy and Patsy Gibson, and Lucinda said that she had seen Dock Woods – Gracie's former suitor – standing at the window of Gracie's house just before the attacks occurred.

Hennessey was now convinced that Townsend and Woods were the perpetrators.

But what about the watch on Gracie's wrist? Hennessey had an answer for that, too. Woods must have snuck away from the cotton fields that afternoon, ridden into town on a stolen horse, and taken the watch from the Robinsons' servants' quarters because he wanted to give it to Gracie at the Sunday evening church service, thinking the gift might win her away from Orange Washington. Hennessey stated that the farm's owner must have been mistaken about seeing Woods. When Gracie refuses to accept the gift, Woods contacts Townsend, who helps him take revenge.

The reporters just stared at Hennessey in disbelief for a few moments before they started firing questions at him – they couldn't believe the famed detective could be so foolish.

Did Hennessey expect them to believe that this teenager just happened to be close enough to Townsend – a chicken thief with no history of violence – on two occasions to hear him talking about servant girls? And this same teenager followed Townsend to the scenes of two murders without being seen? And without actually seeing him murder anyone?

It wasn't long before reporters learned that Trigg worked as a waiter at the Carrollton House, the very hotel where Hennessey and his men were staying. Obviously, they surmised, the detectives had gotten to know Trigg and persuaded him – maybe even bribed him – to make up a story that fingered Townsend and Dock Woods. Was Hennessey unaware that Woods' employer had already provided him with a solid alibi for the day and evening of the murders?

To make matters worse for Hennessey, a reporter from the *Daily Statesman* had also visited the hospital's Negro Ward to speak with Lucinda Boddy. He wanted to see if she would verify that she'd seen Dock Woods. What he found, though, was that Lucinda and Patsy Gibson were in such extreme pain from the attack that neither could have a conversation. According to the reporter, Lucinda's "brain matter was oozing from wounds in her skull every few moments." He stated that Dr. Burt, the hospital's staff physician, was preparing to use trepanning – a medical operation in which a hole is drilled in the skull – in hopes of relieving the pressure on her brain. "There appears to be a chance for the loss of her mind," the reporter added.

Now trying to save face, Hennessey admitted that perhaps Lucinda, in her delirium, misidentified Dock Woods when he spoke with her. He also acknowledged that Trigg might have exaggerated parts of his story.

But he was certain of one thing --- Oliver Townsend was the leader of what he called "a gang of scoundrels" who were murdering Austin's servant girls. What's more, he said, he was already accumulating more information on other members of Townsend's gang and would soon be making arrests.

ONE WEEK AFTER THE DOUBLE MURDER, ON Saturday night, October 3, Hennessey let Marshal Lee know that he was ready to make an arrest. He told Lee that he had new evidence that linked Aleck Mack – the "impudent Negro" who had already been questioned and released – to the gang of black scoundrels.

Perhaps to keep an eye on Hennessey and his men, or maybe because he didn't want to be left out of another part of the investigation, Lee told him he would be coming along to make the arrest.

Significantly, Sergeant Chenneville wanted no part of it. He'd already lost all trust in the detectives.

Hennessey and two of his men, along with Lee and two police officers, went to the Black Elephant, where Mack was drinking. Hennessey asked Lee to go into the saloon and tell Mack he wanted him to answer some questions.

When Mack saw Lee, he just stared at him. He wasn't afraid of Lee, so he didn't try and run. He followed the marshal out the front door and into the street, where the detectives suddenly grabbed him. When Mack tried to fight back, they pounded him with their fists until he fell to the ground. After that, they kicked him until he surrendered. A white man who lived nearby, Press Hopkins, later said that Mack's screams woke up everyone in the neighborhood.

But the beating outside the Black Elephant became the least of the pain that Mack endured over the next few days.

He was dragged off to jail, thrown into a cell, and chained to the iron ring on the floor. For the next couple of days, Hennessey used every tactic he knew to try and get the man to confess. Mack was beaten, whipped, threatened, and starved, but he continued to say – as he'd already told Chenneville – that he was innocent.

When he was finally released, Mack went straight to the newspapers and told reporters about the days he'd spent being tortured by Hennessey and Marshal Lee. At one point, he said, they'd looped a rope around his neck as if to hang him – what they called a "nigger neck stretching."

Lee, of course, denied Mack's allegations, calling them "a malicious falsehood, concocted in the most damnable spirit. If Mack had any bruises or scars on his person, they are the result of his own desperate efforts to resist arrest and incarceration. I never struck him, nor saw anyone else strike him. He was not maltreated in any way, and one such force used as was absolutely necessary to conquer him."

Hennessey also claimed that he and his assistants had not physically abused Mack, but no one believed it. No one believed Lee either, but white residents weren't all that worried about what a black criminal like Aleck Mack had to say.

What they were concerned about, though, was how the detectives from the Noble Agency had turned out to be such a disappointment. No one else was tracking down the killer, but at least they weren't grandstanding in the press and making fools of themselves.

And then things got worse for the detectives. One of Henessey's men, Ike Himmel, supposedly spent an evening at a downtown saloon in hopes of picking up gossip about potential subjects. Instead, he ended up drinking too much, got into an argument with another customer, pulled out a pistol, and fired a bullet into the ceiling – a violation of a city ordinance.

One of the detectives was at the Two Brothers Saloon to gather information but ended up drinking too much and got into a fight. This was the last straw for city officials.

Less than a week later, Mayor Robertson and the city aldermen voted to cancel their contract with the Noble detective agency. One of the aldermen, Joseph Platt, complained that the only thing the detectives had done during their month-long stay in Austin was "stand on the capitol steps and with a great flourish of trumpets" announce the arrest of a black man who'd already been questioned and released by the police. The aldermen voted to increase the reward offered in hopes that other detectives – the ones they weren't footing the bill for – might have better luck.

An indignant Hennessey packed up and left for Houston with his bloodhound, who'd never left the hotel's backyard.

Inspired by the reward, freelance detectives and Austin residents began showing up at the police department to offer the names of black men they thought were responsible for the attacks.

Based on these tips, the police did make some arrests, one of whom was a black man named James Thompson, who was allegedly overheard in a saloon making a drunken confession about murdering one of the servant girls. There was also a 14-year-old boy who was arrested after he was seen carrying a knife. But after a brief series of questions, both were released.

Acting on another tip, officers spent a few days following a man known as "Maurice," an immigrant from Malaysia. Maurice was a cook at the Pearl House, and he lived in a boardinghouse not far from the Weeds' home, where Mary Ramey had been killed. It was said that Maurice would get "beastly drunk" after work and wander the city at night. In addition, "fresh blood" was supposedly found in a pool of water not far from Maurice's boardinghouse on the day Mary was killed.

However, when the police were watching him, Maurice didn't do anything out of the ordinary. He went to work each night, did his cooking without complaint, and returned home to his room at the boardinghouse.

Maurice – unlike all the other suspects targeted by the police – wasn't black, but he wasn't white either. He was the "other," and in that place and time, he was a suspect, whether he'd done anything wrong or not.

BY HALLOWEEN, THE NEWSPAPERS WERE widely reporting that the Austin police had run out of steam – and ideas. "It is beginning to be believed that the detection of the Austin servant girl murderers is as far off as ever," noted the *Galveston Daily News*.

Other papers went after the city's leaders for failing to find the killer or killers. A reporter for the *Fort Worth Gazette* wrote, "If a radical change is not made in the government of the city so that crimes may be prevented and glaring vices suppressed, it will be far better for Texas to closer her university and cast the keys into the sea. A city incapable of governing itself is not a place for building up a university of a first class."

In Austin itself, worried homeowners stocked up on guns and ammunition. Some men even took their servants into the backyard, gave them pistols, and taught them to shoot bottles off fence posts. Even so, more and more domestic workers were leaving Austin every day.

A writer for the Dallas Daily Herald noted, "The servant girl will soon become one of the rarest and costliest of capital luxuries."

ON NOVEMBER 10, MAYOR ROBERTSON finally decided to include something about the murders in his formal State of the City address. He spent days working on it, knowing it needed to be perfect. His election opponent, Joseph Nalle, was gaining support among voters, and the vote seemed too close for comfort.

Predictably, Robertson began his speech with good news about the city's finances, bridges, streets, and a new hospital wing, but then he got to the murders:

> During the last year, a number of the most dastardly crimes known to the law have been committed in this city. These crimes have been of the most revolting character, attended with evidences of the grossest brutality, and perpetrated at the dead hours of the night, in nearly every instance upon unprotected colored females.
>
> Much has been said and written about these crimes, and the city government has been subjected to severe criticism, sometimes unfriendly and sometimes bordering on malicious. I undertake to say that the city authorities, ably aided by the state and county officers, have faithfully and earnestly labored to detect the perpetrators of these crimes and to bring them to punishment, but they have failed at success.
>
> I employed detectives who came with the highest endorsements as honest and skillful men. They, too, have failed to detect the guilty parties. Great vigilance and energy have been displayed by private citizens, who have devoted much time and labor to bring to light the real criminals. They have accomplished nothing.
>
> The crimes still remain a mystery. They are abnormal and unnatural, as compared with ordinary crimes among men. No one, not even an expert, skilled in the detection of crime, can find a plausible motive. The mutilated bodies of the victims are always found in parts of the city where crime is not expected or anticipated, and beyond the fact of the murders we have never been able to penetrate.

Robertson did his best to reassure the audience in the silent chamber that the killings would soon come to an end. He told the crowd firmly, "I have faith to believe that the authors of these crimes will yet be discovered. No human is strong enough to hold such a secret. Some guilty conscience will unburden itself sooner or later."

He closed the speech by trying to raise everyone's spirits by crowing about the city's great future, its location, picturesque surroundings, and healthy climate.

But those who had come to hear the speech were not reassured. They walked out of city hall deep in thought.

Did Robertson truly believe that the murders would only stop when one of the killers confessed? Did that mean there was nothing more anyone could do to stop them?

If that was the case, many of those who'd been in attendance mused, then the city of Austin was truly at the mercy of the unknown killer.

12. GRAND JURY

WHILE NOT EVERYONE AGREED WITH MAYOR Robertson's thoughts about the murders, they could agree on one thing he said – the murders were certainly "abnormal and unnatural."

By the late fall of 1885, four servant women and one servant's daughter had been killed with axes, knives, iron rods, and a brick. It wasn't clear if any of the women had been raped, but the fact that many of them were half-naked and their organs exposed suggested some twisted sex was involved. Stranger still, two of the women had been "decorated" in a way after their deaths – Eliza when she was wrapped tightly in her quilt and bedsheet and Gracie with the stolen silver watch.

The victims had all been left on display, in full view for everyone to see. None had been hidden in secrecy, like in the woods outside town or tossed in the Colorado River. It was as though the killer wanted his crimes discovered to get attention for his deeds.

And there was another puzzling detail about the cases – a potential witness was left alive at the scene of each murder. Whoever slaughtered Mollie Smith allowed her boyfriend, Walter Spencer, to live. When Eliza Shelley was murdered, the intruder didn't touch her three boys. Whoever killed Irene Cross didn't harm her nephew. When Mary Ramey was slain, the killer only struck her mother with a club, hard enough to make her unconscious but not hard enough to kill her. When Gracie Vance was dragged away and murdered, her friends were only struck one time to get them out of the way. It was true that two blows to the head killed Orange Washington, but the doctors and police believed his death was an accident. He likely tried to stop the attack, and the killer had hit him a second time. It was that blow that turned fatal.

By this time, Austin residents were finally starting to talk openly about the fact that the murders – with all their strange and gruesome elements – were not the work of "ordinary black criminals." The murders, it was now being said, were well-planned, carefully worked out, and "intelligently consummated."

The Austin-based reporter for the *San Antonio Express* suggested a name for the killer that was embraced before the "Servant Girl Annihilator." He called him the "Midnight Assassin" – a killer, he wrote, who "strides at will over Austin's sacred soil." The reporter explained:

The fact that this series of crimes is composed of some of the boldest, most startling flagrations in criminal annals, that they have extended over a period of many months, and that the perpetrator has, so far, not only accomplished his ends but successfully escaped and blinded the police, would seem to indicate that he is a criminal of no mean ability, but one of the most remarkable ghouls known to the death history of any section of the country."

A century later, the reporter wouldn't need to explain what he was talking about – everyone would already know that a depraved but brilliant serial killer was at work in Austin. There would be a police task force to investigate each case, a forensic team would go over each crime scene carefully, and the FBI would offer profilers advice about the main suspect.

But this was nineteenth-century America. Not only were there no task forces, forensics, or an FBI, the term "serial killer" didn't even exist. There were occasionally people who were called "multiple murderers," though. Periodically, there would be "maniacs" who, in the grip of some psychotic rage, would go on a killing spree.

The people of Austin had read about such people in the newspapers of the day or in the "penny dreadful" type books that were printed to entertain the readers with violence and blood.

They read about a respected sexton named Thomas W. Piper -- the "Belfry Butcher" -- who stunned parishioners at the Warren Avenue Baptist Church in Boston after he confessed to the rape and beatings of four victims after a body of a little girl was found in the belfry of the church.

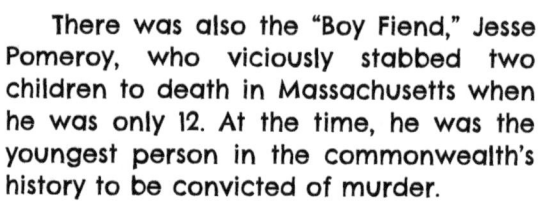

There was also the "Boy Fiend," Jesse Pomeroy, who viciously stabbed two children to death in Massachusetts when he was only 12. At the time, he was the youngest person in the commonwealth's history to be convicted of murder.

And they read about Joseph LaPage, a French-Canadian trapper who confessed to the rape, mutilation, and murder of schoolteacher Marietta Ball in St. Albans, Vermont. His arrest revealed other victims and even the missing head of a young woman named Josie Langmaid in Pembroke, New Hampshire.

The people of Austin knew there were monsters among them, but they never expected one in the city. Besides that, the maniacs that littered the pages of newspapers and cheap books looked and acted insane and were almost immediately identified by the police and arrested because they rarely tried to cover their tracks.

They had no idea how to deal with an anonymous killer who set out to slaughter women, one after another, in a ritualistic fashion to satisfy some private need or a pathological hatred. Even the writers of fiction had not yet created such a character. The closest that any writer had come – assuming the residents of Austin in the 1880s read Edgar Allan Poe – was the murders at the start of his story "The Murders in the Rue Morgue," when a mother and daughter are ripped apart in a

The "Boy Fiend" Jesse Pomeroy

The Edgar Allan Poe story "Murders in the Rue Morgue" was one of the most violent things most people in Austin had read before the murders appeared in the newspapers.

bedroom in Paris. However, the killer in Poe's story was an escaped orangutan, not a human being.

It was still thought that a human would never do such a thing. And yet, it was happening right there in Austin.

It still made the concept of a serial killer for Austin residents almost impossible to grasp. It seemed far-fetched that a man could act perfectly normal during the day, not attracting any attention, and then commit murders by night that were beyond comprehension. How could a crazed, bloodthirsty killer like that go unnoticed in their small city?

In 1886, Austin residents would wonder if the answer to their killer's identity could be found in another work of fiction – *The Strange Case of Dr. Jekyll and Mr. Hyde.*

A year later, a writer provided what might have been the answer to the question that so many people were asking. It was in 1886 that Robert Louis Stevenson wrote *The Strange Case of Dr. Jekyll and Mr. Hyde*, a story about the duality of good and evil in man's nature and how the mild-mannered doctor manages to unleash his inner persona – the loathsome and malevolent Mr. Hyde.

But that was in the future – and a work of fiction. It offered no suggestions for the people of Austin in late 1885 when it came to dealing with their resident monster.

THE AVERAGE RESIDENT OF AUSTIN CONTINUED TO be baffled by the idea of a "Midnight Assassin," and so was the Travis County grand jury, which handed out its most recent list of indictments just two weeks after Mayor Robertson's speech.

Toward the bottom of the page was the name "Walter Spencer" – the boyfriend of Mollie Smith, who'd been murdered during the early morning hours of New Year's Eve 1884. The grand jurors had decided that when Walter broke into the Hall home that morning, frantically crying that Mollie was missing, he was only pretending to be innocent.

They claimed that enough evidence existed that proved Walter was Mollie's killer, and they wanted to put him on trial for first-degree murder.

It was the grand jury's version of the Austin police departments rounding up the "usual suspects" for each murder – in other words, the closest black men they could find.

THE MAN WHO HAD PRESENTED THE MURDER case against Walter to the grand jury was the county's 31-year-old district attorney, James Robertson, the younger brother of Austin's mayor. In the mid-1870s, James followed his brother to the city from their family home in Tennessee, studied law at his brother's firm, passed the bar exam, and moved to Round Rock, just north of Austin. He married, started a family, and opened a law practice. In 1884, he had campaigned for and won the office of district attorney.

District Attorney – and brother of the mayor – James Robertson.

He had been in office for less than a year but had successfully prosecuted a handful of felony cases and had won convictions for a few routine killings. During the servant girl murders, though, he'd never pushed for indictments against any of the black men who'd been arrested, correctly believing that there was no evidence to take their cases to trial.

Why his opinion had changed with Walter Spencer remains a mystery. No documentation explains Walter's indictment. It's possible some new evidence was unearthed, but more likely, Mayor Robertson, knowing his political future was on the line, came to his brother and asked for help. Or it's possible that the district attorney took it upon himself to help his brother by securing an indictment against one of the murder suspects. The city elections were just weeks away by that time.

Whatever occurred, the grand jury's announcement undoubtedly pleased Mayor Robertson. He was now able to say that justice was in the process of being served – which he likely repeated as he was out shaking hands with voters on Election Day, December 8.

Joseph Nalle was also out on the streets looking for votes that day, and conspiracy rumors quickly spread. There were allegations that Nalle had brought it more than 100 men from out of town, paying them to cast "illegal votes." But if he did, he could have used a few dozen more. By the end of the day, Robertson was narrowly reelected by just 53 votes.

As a side note, Albert Carrington, the city's only black alderman, lost his reelection bid to Dennis Corwin, a white surveyor who'd been a captain in the Confederate army. Many of Austin's white residents had organized an "Anti-Colored Movement" to try and prevent Carrington's reelection. To them, the servant girl murders proved that the black race could not be trusted with civic responsibility.

It also didn't help that newspapers widely reported that the Carrington family believed the servant girls were being murdered by a white man.

Later that night – after the votes had been counted and recounted – Robertson's supporters gathered outside his home and called him to come out. The mayor and his wife, a socialite and descendant of Stephen F. Austin, stood on the porch and waved.

Then, the mayor offered another of his speeches about the future of Austin. Things, he said, had never looked better.

ONE WEEK AFTER THE ELECTION, THE TRIAL of Walter Spencer began. District Attorney Robertson told the jury that Spencer had likely caught Mollie with another man and decided to get even. During the argument that occurred between the couple, either Mollie had hit him with the blunt side of the ax before he grabbed it away and started attacking her, or he had hit himself on the head with it after he murdered Mollie. He was trying to make himself look like a victim, not the killer.

When the prosecution's opening statement sounds like a lot of "likely," "maybe," and "either-or" to you – you'd be correct. It was all guesswork and supposition. And what followed was no better because it soon became clear there was no evidence pointing to

Walter's guilt. Robertson didn't even have a witness who could testify to seeing Walter and Mollie argue. All Robertson could do was try and assure the jury that Lem Brooks – Mollie's ex-boyfriend, who'd been initially arrested – had such a good alibi that the only person left in Austin with a reason to kill Mollie was Walter Spencer.

But what was that reason? The D.A. didn't have an answer for that.

After just one day of testimony, the prosecution rested its case. Walter's court-appointed lawyer called a few witnesses who testified to Walter's peaceful relationship with Mollie, how much he cared for her, and how grief-stricken he'd been since she'd died. After Mollie's murder, Walter moved in with his mother on the east side of town. Although he still suffered terrible headaches from the attack, he still worked at the brick factory. He'd also joined an all-black baseball team that played against teams from other towns. He'd been living a very quiet life, avoiding trouble with the police, so he'd been very surprised to be arrested and put on trial.

The trial was a farce, but even so, there was still a good chance that Walter would be convicted. He was a poor, young black man facing an entirely white jury, and if they returned a guilty verdict, it would be the first time in months that Austin residents could be reassured that the "bad blacks" were being taken off the streets.

But the jury – one of whom was J.B. Blocker, a successful cattleman who routinely hired black cowhands for his trail drives – was suspicious of the prosecutor's case from the start. They stayed in the jury room for a few minutes and, after one vote, returned to announce a "not guilty" verdict. Walter Spencer walked out of the courthouse a free man.

Robertson, humiliated by the verdict, refused to comment to reporters when the case ended. His brother, the mayor, was also silent. But to show the citizens that he was still taking action to keep them safe, the mayor called the aldermen to city hall and proposed that a search begin immediately to replace Marshal Grooms Lee when his term ended on December 22.

13. ONE KILLER, ONE RANGER

WITH THE ELECTION OVER, MAYOR Robertson had less to fear if he angered Lee's father, so he had a decision to make about the beleaguered marshal.

By all accounts, it had been a tough autumn for Lee. Residents were still talking about how he'd overslept on the morning of Mary Ramey's murder and how his attempt to team up with Hennessey and his detectives to arrest Aleck Mack had ended in embarrassment.

Lee had tried to defend himself and his office, issuing a report that noted that his officers had collected more than $9,000 in misdemeanor fines over the last 15 months and stepping up patrols around downtown businesses. It was too little, too late, though, and city officials were ready to see him go. He spent his last days in his office, doing paperwork. He told friends that when his term expired, he was getting out of law enforcement and returning to work as a surveyor. It was a job he'd had before, and it seemed to suit his temperament better.

Twelve men submitted their names to be Lee's replacement, including a deputy U.S. marshal, a former county sheriff who was now running a feed store, an attorney, and the owner of the Proper Star Saloon. Chenneville added his name to the list, but he likely knew that the mayor and the aldermen were happier with him as a sergeant, running things from behind the scenes.

Lee's replacement was James Lucy, a captain with the Texas Rangers, the famous statewide law enforcement organization. Stephen F. Austin had unofficially established the Rangers in a call-to-arms written in 1823. Over a decade later, in 1835, Daniel Parker

Austin's new marshal, James Lucy, was chosen from the ranks of the Texas Rangers, the legendary law enforcement organization. The Rangers were often involved in murder cases around the state, especially the most baffling ones, so why were they never asked to investigate the murders taking place in the very town where their headquarters were located?

introduced a resolution to create a team of rangers to protect the Mexican border. However, the federal authorities dissolved it after the Civil War. Once Texas had its own government again, the Rangers were reformed.

With statewide jurisdiction, the Texas Rangers investigated crimes ranging from murder to political corruption. They protected the governor of Texas, tracked down fugitives, fought the last Native Americans in the state, tracked down – or shot down – outlaws, bandits, cattle rustlers, and horse thieves, and even ended riots – or so the story goes.

The most famous phrase associated with the Rangers wouldn't come into use until about a decade after the servant girl murders, but it's worth mentioning here.

That phrase was "One Riot, One Ranger."

It comes from a sensationalized story about Captain William "Bill" McDonald, who was sent to Dallas in 1896 to prevent an illegal heavyweight prize fight between Pete Maher and Bob Fitzsimmons.

Trouble was expected if the fight wasn't allowed to happen, so city officials contacted the Rangers.

According to the story, the mayor met McDonald's train at the station, asking him where all the other Rangers were. McDonald is said to have replied: "Hell! Ain't I enough? There's only one prize-fight!"

The Texas Rangers were headquartered in Austin, making their absence from the story of the "Servant Girl Annihilator" mysterious. The Rangers were often involved in murder cases around the state, especially the most baffling ones, so why were they never asked to investigate the murders taking place in the very town where their headquarters were located?

I have no idea and haven't found anything that answers that question.

James Lucy, however, had made a name for himself with the Rangers. He was fearless, good with his guns, and was part of the 1878 shootout between the Texas Rangers and outlaw Sam Bass and his gang in Round Rock.

Lucy also impressed city officials with his intelligence. He graduated from the University of Missouri, and when he came to Texas in 1873 to join the Rangers, he'd been assigned a series of complicated land fraud cases that resulted in at least a dozen convictions.

It was widely believed that if anyone could end the murders, it was James Lucy.

AFTER THE ANNOUNCEMENT OF LUCY'S appointment to the marshal's job, Austin had a sense of relief. The residents began to feel that life could return to normal, especially with the holiday season quickly approaching.

As Christmas drew near, shop owners decorated their windows with ornaments, red and green paper, and decorated trees. Christmas trees had long been part of winter celebrations in European countries like France and Germany. They had first gained popularity in America in the 1840s after Queen Victoria of England placed one in her home in honor of her devoted husband, Prince Albert, who was of German heritage. By 1885, everyone wanted one, and a quaint German tradition came to symbolize the holiday season.

And so had Santa Claus – the Americanized version of St. Nicholas, who brought gifts to good children on Christmas Eve. In Austin, Santa – who hadn't yet adopted the red, fur-lined suit we know today – was nevertheless portrayed by one of Austin's portlier citizens and could be found at Stacy and Baker's newsstand and tobacco shop, seated in a chair by the front door. The children who came to see him were all asked if they had been good that year.

The shop windows along Congress Avenue were lighted by strings of incandescent lightbulbs and filled with presents for children --- dolls, baseballs, musical instruments, tea sets, baseballs, and gloves – while other windows displayed silk gowns for Christmas balls and shawls, scarves, and handkerchiefs that would make the perfect gift for wives and daughters.

At the studio of Austin's best-known photographer, Samuel B. Hill, discounts were offered for holiday portraits. Some men brought their entire families to the studio, and standing before a painted backdrop, mothers urged their children to remain still while the negatives were exposed. Women came to have individual portraits made, which they planned to give to their husbands as Christmas gifts, or they brought their children for a portrait that would freeze

Family photograph from the studio of Samuel B. Hill.

time for just a moment and become a photograph in which the little ones remained forever young.

But not all were celebrating this holiday season. On the evening of December 22, after the 9:00 P.M. roll call at the police department, Grooms Lee handed over his badge to his replacement. He gave a small speech, thanking the men for their service and wishing them the best in the future before he slipped silently out the door into the night.

That night, Marshall Lucy helped Chenneville and the other officers patrol the streets. He was on duty the next day, December 23, and again on Christmas Eve, greeting people who came downtown to do their last-minute Christmas shopping.

Throughout December 24, people lined up at Bill Johnston's market to buy steaks, ham, and turkeys for the evening's dinners. Others went to Prade's ice cream parlor, where, according to their advertisements, they were selling fruit baskets, decorated cakes, and French candies. The baker, Charles Lundberg, in the spirit of goodwill, even provided a Christmas meal to all the prisoners at the county jail.

As the sun started to set, the gas lamps along the street were lit, and the owners of restaurants and saloons turned on their incandescent lights. Dr. J.J. Tobin, one of the city's pharmacists, invited friends to his home to watch fireworks. Children from the state's Asylum for the Blind held a concert, and at the Asylum for the Deaf and Dumb, another group of children gathered around a Christmas tree and decorated it with strings of candy and popcorn.

There was even a Christmas party at the State Lunatic Asylum. Dr. Denton had arranged for a select group of inmates to gather in the main day room, eat popcorn, sing Christmas carols, and stay up later than their usual bedtime so one of the employees could dress up as Santa Claus and hand out candy.

The shops and restaurants began to close as late afternoon turned into evening. The owners turned off the lights, locked the doors, and headed home. Families gathered all over the city to eat

Christmas Eve dinners and decorate their trees with ornaments, candles, and strings of berries and popcorn.

Eventually, children were put to bed, lights were turned out, and the city fell almost silent, except for the clock at city hall, which chimed loudly at midnight.

Marshal Lucy, Sergeant Chenneville, and several officers remained on duty, watching the streets downtown. A few officers checked the handful of saloons that were still open, looking for suspicious characters. Others walked the alleys behind the buildings along Congress Avenue, looking for tramps. They walked through the vice district, ensuring the men visiting the brothels behaved themselves.

And then came the sudden pounding of hoofbeats, shattering the quiet. A man on horseback rode onto Congress Avenue, coming from the south side. The rider was Alexander Wilkie, a nightwatchman for one of the local saloons.

He began to yell when he caught sight of the uniformed policemen. "A woman has been chopped to pieces!" he cried. "It's Mrs. Hancock, on Water Street!"

There would be no Christmas celebration for the police officers of Austin on this night.

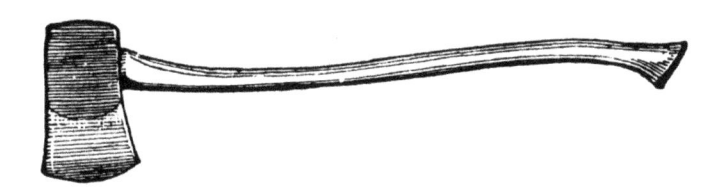

14. "THE DEMONS HAVE TRANSFERRED THEIR THIRST FOR BLOOD TO WHITE PEOPLE!"

SUSAN HANCOCK WAS THE 43-YEAR-OLD WIFE of Moses Hancock, a wealthy carpenter and the mother of two daughters. She was described in contemporary accounts as "a beautiful woman" who "bore an unblemished character," a tender mother and devoted wife," and a woman born and educated in the eastern states with much literary ability."

She was also, most importantly, white.

When they heard the news, the police officers mounted their horses and raced to the Hancock home at the southern end of downtown, near the river. The men who didn't have horses began running. Marshal Lucy and a reporter from the *Daily Statesman*, who happened to be chatting outside of Martin's Shoes and Boots, climbed into a carriage and whipped the horses into a frenzy as they flew down the street toward the scene.

When he arrived, Lucy found Moses Hancock in the parlor of his one-story home. He was wearing only his long underwear, and they were stained with blood. His wife was on the floor, lying on a quilt at his feet. There were deep gashes in her head – apparently made by an ax. One blow had struck her cheekbone, and the other, between her left eye and ear, had shattered her skull and pierced her brain. A trickle of blood ran from her right ear. It would turn out to have been pierced by a thin, iron rod – just as the bodies of some of the other victims had been.

This was obviously the work of the same killer that had been bedeviling Austin for the last year.

Mrs. Hancock was still alive but senseless. Her breath was choking gasps. According to the reporter who had arrived on the scene with the marshal, "cupfuls of blood" were coming from her mouth.

From a back bedroom, the men could hear the cries of the Hancocks' daughters – one was 15, and the other, 11. Their weeping was drowned out momentarily when the front door opened, and Dr. William Burt arrived, accompanied by another physician, Dr. R.S Graves. They worked quickly to try and save Susan's life, pressing bandages over her wounds to stop the bleeding, injecting her with morphine, and even pouring some brandy into her mouth to see if she could swallow it. She couldn't.

Marshal Lucy quickly took charge of the investigation, pulling aside Mose Hancock to ask him some questions. In what would later be described as a "distracted, disconnected narration," he told the marshal that his wife had spent the last afternoon shopping downtown. After she had come home, their daughters were escorted to a Christmas party by a neighbor, and he and Susan had spent a peaceful evening in front of the fireplace, reading and sharing a piece of cake. They had gone to bed between 10:00 and 11:00 P.M., sleeping in adjoining rooms as they always did. A gas lamp had been left burning by the door for their daughters.

The girls returned home from their party a little after 11:00 and went straight to bed. Moses, able to relax after he knew they were home safe, fell asleep.

Just before midnight, though, he was awakened by a noise. He entered his wife's bedroom and saw her sheets and blankets thrown into a pile on the floor. Her trunks had been opened, and all her clothes had been pulled out. The window of her room, which faced the backyard, was open, and when Moses walked over to it, he saw there was blood on the windowsill.

Worried, he hurried outside and went around the corner of the house to find his wife lying in a pool of blood. He heard a sound near the back fence as he bent over her. He looked up and saw a shadowy figure in dark clothing. The figure – he couldn't tell if he was black or white – jumped over the fence and ran down the alley. Moses cried out, grabbed a rock, and hurled it toward the fleeing man, but it bounced harmlessly into a neighbor's yard.

Hearing Moses' shouts, his next-door neighbor, Harvey Persinger, rushed into the yard, and he helped Moses lift Susan from the ground and carry her into the parlor. Persinger then ran for help and encountered Wilkie, the nightwatchman, who rode up Congress Avenue, bringing the news of the attack to the police.

Telephone calls were already being made across the city. Alerted by one of the calls, Mayor Robertson soon arrived at the Hancock home, as did his brother, the district attorney. Within minutes, more men arrived, and soon, the street and yard were filled with onlookers from around the neighborhood and the local saloons. Some men carried lanterns, which they held up as high as they could to cast light into the darkest corners of the backyard.

Dr. Burt's teenage son, Eugene, had arrived with his father, and he was the one who found a bloody ax about three feet away from Susan's window. He picked it up, waved it around, and carried it to Moses Hancock, who said it belonged to him and that he usually kept it on top of the woodpile by the back fence.

Soon, Chenneville's bloodhounds arrived. Another officer had retrieved them. The sergeant took them over to sniff around the ax, the woodpile, and where Susan had been found. But thanks to the fact that so many people had already tramped through the yard, there was no trail for them to follow. So, he took them out to the alley, and they started running westward alongside the Colorado River. Chenneville and some of his men chased after them, guns in hand in case they ran into someone they needed to shoot. But, as usual, the dogs lost whatever trail they'd been following.

Chenneville, the officers, and a handful of volunteers gave up the search and slowly walked back toward the Hancock house, where they could see the lanterns of those still searching the yard for clues.

As they approached the house, they heard a loud noise coming up the road – another horse riding hard in their direction.

The man on the horse was Henry Brown, the night clerk at the police department, and he was coming toward them at a full gallop. When he saw Marshal Lucy, he started yelling that a woman had been found on Hickory Street.

"It's Eula Phillips!" he shouted. "Her head's been chopped in two!"

Eula Phillips

ALL THE MEN GATHERED AT THE HANCOCK HOME, policemen and volunteers alike, simply stared at Brown. They were too shocked to do anything else.

Eula was the 17-year-old wife of Jimmy Phillips, the son of a very successful Austin architect and builder named James Phillips. The small, petite young woman was regarded as one of the most beautiful women in the city, with deep brown eyes, auburn hair, and delicate features. Whenever she walked along the sidewalks of Congress Avenue in her stylish dress, broad feathered hat, and slimming corset, all eyes – men and women alike – turned to stare.

"It's Eula!" Henry shouted again. "She's in the Phillips' backyard!"

Abandoning one crime scene for another, men began jumping onto horses and climbing into buggies as they raced back up Congress Avenue. Chenneville brought along his dogs, which could be heard baying as they, too, sprinted up the street.

The Phillips lived on Hickory Street, on the northwest side of downtown, just two blocks from city hall. It was one of the finer two-story residences in the city, built by James Phillips for his entire family, including his son and daughter-in-law.

The marshal and his officers were led into the backyard and taken to the outhouse. Next to it on the ground was Eula. She was on her back and lying in a pool of blood that was "warm and scarcely coagulated." Her nightgown had been pulled up to her neck, exposing her naked body. She had been struck directly above the nose with the blade of an ax – a solid, vertical blow that had split her forehead wide open. There was a second ax blow to the side of her head. Because her nightgown was twisted around her neck, the marshal speculated that the killer had used it like a rope to drag Eula across the yard.

And there was something new at this murder scene. Three small pieces of firewood had been placed carefully on Eula's body – two across her breasts and one across her stomach. Her arms had been outstretched, posed to look like a twisted version of Christ's crucifixion.

Marshal Lucy went into the house and was directed to the rooms in the back wing where Eula, Jimmy, and their 10-month-old baby, Tommy, lived. Jimmy was in bed, writhing in a stupor, and unable to communicate. The sheets were stained with blood. He had been struck one time with an ax, opening a large gash just above his ear. Dr. Joseph Cummings, who lived in the neighborhood, was already there, pressing a pillow against the wound. A bloody ax was propped up at the foot of the bed.

Since Jimmy couldn't talk, his mother, Sophie, told the marshal what had happened. She said that at some point after midnight – perhaps as late as 12:15 or even later – she'd been awakened by the sound of Tommy crying. She had walked into Jimmy and Eula's bedroom and nearly fainted when she saw Jimmy under bloody sheets and the baby, unharmed but upset, sitting in the bed holding an apple. The baby's nightclothes were also covered with blood.

Sophie ran back to the primary bedroom and woke up her husband. Using Jimmy's nickname, she screamed at him, "Bud is knocked in the head and Eula is gone!"

James bolted out of bed and went outside. With help from other men in the neighborhood, he eventually found Eula. Meanwhile, one of the neighbors had run to city hall and alerted the police department's night clerk about the attack.

When he was finished speaking to Sophie, Marshal Lucy was shown a bare, bloody footprint on the wooden floor outside Jimmy and Eula's bedroom, right next to the door that led into the backyard. He ordered the planks marked by the footprint to be cut from the floor and taken to the police department. He also directed one of his men to take the ax – which Sophie was certain had come from the woodpile behind the house – to the police department, too.

A BLOODY CHRISTMAS EVE.

SHOCKING BUTCHERIES AT AUSTIN.

Another Chapter of Crime From the State Capital That Makes the Blood Run Cold.

Special to The News.

AUSTIN, December 25.—Of all the murders that have been committed within the annals of Austin those of last night (Christmas eve) stand out in bold relief. Just one year ago this month the first of the series of murders was committed, and since that time the assassins have

STRUCK BLOW AFTER BLOW

with fatal result, and, although the mayor, police force and citizens at large have used every effort to put a stop to these bloody deeds, the perpetrators are still at large. Heretofore the fiends have been satisfied with murdering and raping colored servant girls, but last night, as though to start afresh, after twelve months of bloody work they murder and rape white women without apparent fear of detection. The fiends with evidently consummated plans went systematically to work at an hour when scarcely half of the population had retired. When people were passing to and fro, celebrating Christmas eve, they struck down one woman, and

MURDERED AND OUTRAGED

another, and inflicted a probably fatal wound on a man. At about 11.30 last night, M. H. Hancock, a carpenter residing at 203 East Water street, was awakened by groans. He was stopping, as was his custom, in a room occupied by him only. He arose, went into the next room in which his wife slept and found the room in disorder and his wife absent and blood on the bed and floor. Following a bloody trail, which led him out of the front door around the side of the house into the back yard, and there, lying in

Meanwhile, someone in the backyard spotted drops of blood on the top rail of the back fence. Chenneville's dogs were brought into the alley, and they headed off into the darkness, loudly barking as they ran. But soon, they came to a confused stop. It seemed that the scent – if there had been one – had just vanished.

A blanket was placed over Eula's body, and she was carried into the house. She had just been placed in the parlor when Jimmy, who had started to regain consciousness, muttered to Dr. Cummings, "Where's Eula?"

But the doctor kept silent. He later recalled that he didn't want to say anything that might cause Jimmy to go into shock and die.

SOON, NEWS OF THE DOUBLE MURDER was spreading all over town, burning up the telephone party lines and becoming the subject of gossip between neighbors. The names of both women were known to many in town, and while the loss of each was tragic, there was one thing about the murders that paralyzed Austin with terror – these victims were white.

As this new aspect of the murders started to sink in, white men throughout Austin reacted in different ways. Some loaded their guns, locked the doors, and refused to allow their wives and children out of their sight. Others believed that being at home was the worst place to be. They loaded their families onto carriages and wagons and hurried downtown. It wasn't long before several hundred people were standing under the gas lamps along Congress Avenue.

A reporter who worked as a freelancer for the Western Associated Press ran to the Western Union office and sent a telegram to his bosses in St. Louis. "The entire population is in the streets, excitedly conversing," he told them.

Telegrams to other newspapers soon followed. The Austin reporter for the *Fort Worth Gazette* wrote, "People tonight are in a state bordering on frenzy. Groups of excited men parade Congress Avenue and ask each other, with white lips, 'When will this damnable work end? Whose wife is safe as long as these bloodthirsty hell hounds can commit such crimes in the heart of the city?'"

It was a nice bit of writing for a telegram.

Before the night was over, things were going to become more frantic. Around 3:00 A.M., with even more people arriving downtown, a group of horses became spooked and tried to bolt. A carriage racing down the street went up on two wheels as it rounded a corner. Police officers blew whistles and tried to keep people calm, but it was useless. People were terrified. Men were standing guard on street corners, holding lanterns and torches, and weapons of every kind --- rifles, pistols, knives, hatchets, and clubs.

"Had a man with a speck of blood on his clothes appeared, he would have been rent to pieces," a *Houston Daily Post* reporter wrote.

To increase the amount of light on the street, shop owners turned on their incandescent lamps. With tears streaming down their faces, several women huddled in carriages outside Millett's Opera House because owner Charles Millett had fired up his "outdoor lamp," which was supposed to make his marquee announcing upcoming shows visible at night.

When the sun finally came up, church bells across the city began to ring, signifying the arrival of Christmas Day. But no one felt like celebrating. For all practical purposes, Christmas had been called off in Austin. Churches opened for Christmas services, but few parishioners showed up. Most churches went without music because no choir members came to sing.

By late morning, the newsboys for the *Daily Statesman* were on the street, waving copies of the Christmas edition, which had been printed overnight. The front-page headlines – the ink barely dry – screamed:

BLOOD! BLOOD! BLOOD!
LAST NIGHT'S HORRIBLE BUTCHERY!
THE DEMONS HAVE TRANSFERRED THEIR THIRST FOR BLOOD TO WHITE PEOPLE!

People read the story over and over again, unable to comprehend what they saw. Even those who already knew the details of the two murders were shaken by the description of the firewood that had been placed on Eula Phillips' book – "evidently used for the most hellish and damnable of purposes," a reporter claimed.

A steady stream of people walked back and forth that morning between the Hancock home and the Phillips home, trying to see where the women had been found. Questions were asked, but no one seemed to have the answers. Why did neither woman cry out when the ax struck them? And how did no one hear the attacks taking place? Both families lived in the middle of busy neighborhoods. When the attacks occurred, Christmas Eve revelers were still out and about. Why were there no eyewitnesses to the attacks? And why had the killer struck twice in a single night? Had he been frustrated by the sudden appearance of Moses Hancock, as some suggested, and claimed another victim for some sick and twisted reason?

At the police department, Marshal Lucy ordered Chenneville and his officers to round up the usual black suspects, including Oliver Townsend, Dock Woods, and Aleck Mack. Each man was dragged in and told to remove his shoes, place his bare feet in a bowl of ink, and step onto a white sheet of paper to see if his bare footprint matched the bloody print that had been cut from the floor outside Eula's bedroom.

None of them matched. And none of the men confessed to anything during his latest round of brutal interrogations. They insisted they had spent Christmas Eve at home or the Black Elephant and were innocent of the latest attacks – just as they were innocent of all the others.

THE TERROR THAT WAS SPREADING THROUGH THE city climbed the ranks to the highest officials. Around noon, Mayor Robertson called an emergency public meeting in the House of

Representatives chamber of the unfinished capitol building. Nearly 1,000 people packed into the massive room, shoving, jostling, and talking simultaneously. "It was an infuriated multitude, white with heat," wrote one reporter.

Mayor Robertson held an emergency meeting in the House of Representatives chamber at the state capitol, which was then unfinished.

Robertson banged a gavel on the podium, calling out for order. He shouted to make himself heard, "I have called you to assemble and adopt some measures that, if possible, will bring these men to justice. It is a matter involving the protection of life and property, as well as the name and fame of our capital city. Something must be done, and I ask you to consider and determine what expedient should be adopted."

Former Confederate General Nathan Shelley rose and demanded that armed men be stationed around the city limits that afternoon. He said he would have these men start moving forward, step by step, questioning every man in their path and asking about his whereabouts in the last hours of Christmas Eve. Shelley said that if a man's answers were inadequate, the armed men would be allowed to take "appropriate measures."

Former Confederate General Nathan Shelley

A land agent named Frank Maddox proposed that the city hire 100 secret agents, known only to the marshal, who would hunt down the killers. He also wanted a city ordinance passed requiring all the "lower-class saloons" – code for "black" – to be closed at 10:00 P.M. each night.

It was obvious, as far as he was concerned, that it was in these such places where the killers were gathering and plotting their crimes.

Ira Evans, President of the New York and Texas Land Company, said it wasn't just the saloons that needed to be closed. He wanted the city to shutter all of Austin's gambling houses, brothels, and "other means of dissipation which lead to greater crimes."

Quite a few of the men in the chambers called on Mayor Robertson to temporarily suspend normal criminal statutes and allow for "lynch law," which would give anyone the power to make a citizen's arrest of a murder suspect, do whatever he wanted to do to that suspect, and not suffer any legal consequences for his actions.

After this dangerous suggestion, longtime Austin attorney Alexander Terrell pushed to the front of his room, intent on being the voice of reason. He shouted down several others and begged everyone to let Marshal Lucy handle the investigation. "A vigilance committee means blood, and is likely to victimize the innocent," he said. "When it rules, reason is dethroned and ceases to act. It would be fruitless of results and bring about calamities you would deplore."

I think Terrell was giving most of these men too much credit, and he likely soon felt the same way. When someone else called for the "lynch law," he shouted, "You men can't find the killers marching around the city!"

Groups of them shouted back, saying they damn well could. One of them yelled that the killers, when caught, should be taken to the grounds of the new capitol building and hanged so that everyone in the city could witness their executions.

Alexander Terrell and anyone who supported his efforts found himself outnumbered and finally agreed by voice vote that a "Citizen's Committee of Safety" would be formed, comprised of four men from each of Austin's ten wards. The committee's task would be to raise money for a new reward fund and assist in the police department's investigation.

Or, if need be, conduct their own investigation.

The city was now under the control of vigilantes, who could take the law into their hands any time they wished. They could arrest suspects, raid homes, interrogate anyone they wanted to, and, if the mood suited them, hang someone from the nearest light post. And I'm sure that I don't need to add that, to these men, the only viable suspects were black.

The city was in an uproar. The murder had now been going on for almost an entire year, and yet, no one had reacted this way before. That was, of course, because none of the earlier victims had been white.

MAYOR ROBERTSON HAD GIVEN THEM WHAT they wanted. Now, he hoped he wouldn't regret that decision. He shuddered to think of vigilante mobs roaming the city, doing whatever they wanted. He needed to bring this mess to an end before things got further out of control.

After the public meeting adjourned, the mayor and the city aldermen went behind closed doors – where the real decisions were made. They quietly passed legislation that allowed Marshal Lucy to hire 20 additional police officers, which would give him 34 men in all. Ironically, it was the same number of new hires that Grooms Lee had requested months before.

They also passed an ordinance that required all saloons – not just the black ones – to close at midnight and not reopen until 5:00 A.M.

Finally, it was decided that Mayor Robertson could "employ the most skillful detective talent available for a period of ninety days or so long as in his judgment the present emergency may demand." The mayor announced he would not be hiring amateurs this time. When the meeting ended, he went straight to the Western Union office and fired off a telegram to the Pinkerton Agency in Chicago.

WHILE THE PUBLIC MEETING WAS TAKING PLACE, George Thompson arrived in Austin. Thompson was the "dog man" for the state prison in Huntsville, and he'd come to town with six of his best bloodhounds to see what he could find. His dogs were reputed to be the best trackers in the state – certainly better than Chenneville's slobbering beasts – and legend had it they could stay on an escaped prisoner's trail even if he took off his shoes, ran through water, jumped on a horse, and rode away.

One account claimed that his lead tracker – named Bob – was known for his "wicked but intelligent eye. There is only one thing he really enjoys better than beef steak and eggs and that is to get on the trail of some fellow free from obstacles and run him over hill and dale."

Bob and his pals were taken to the Hancocks' and Phillips' backyards, but they found no scents to follow. It had been 16 hours since the attacks, and both yards had been trampled by other men's boots.

But while at the Phillips' house, Bob did do something strange. He suddenly turned to the house, barking loudly, and went straight to Jimmy and Eula's bedroom. A reporter noted, "Although there were several persons in the room, he passed by them all, and approaching the bed, reared up on it and smelt Jimmy."

Bob then got down and went off toward the parlor, where Eula's body had been laid out near the family's Christmas tree. Bob started barking again, and Thompson, baffled by his dog's behavior, dragged him out of the house because he was frightening the ladies in the room.

THE DAY WAS OVER, AND THE SUN WAS GOING down again. As it did, a new ripple of fear spread through Austin. It was at night, in the darkness and shadows, that the killer would strike.

At the police department, Marshal Lucy was doing all he could to alleviate public fears. He'd spent the day hiring new officers, and after pinning badges on their coats, he sent them out on the street to work with Chenneville and the veteran cops. He ordered all the men to stop any strangers they saw, demand their names and addresses, and make them explain why they were out and about. If a stranger didn't have a suitable answer, the man would be brought to jail, interrogated, and kept behind bars until morning.

In addition to the Austin police, deputies from the county sheriff's office and the U.S. Marshal's office were out on the streets, helping patrol the neighborhoods. Members of the new vigilance committee left their homes to walk around their wards, armed and ready for trouble. Even Grooms Lee came to the police department to man the telephones while everyone else was out looking for the killers.

Austin was now, effectively, under martial law.

Despite this overwhelming official presence, though, few residents were feeling safe. Many refused to sleep. Furniture was pushed against doors inside homes, and wooden planks and blankets were nailed over windows. Men walked the floors, rifles in hand, pausing every few moments to listen for the sounds of an intruder. Those who owned telephones would pick them up every few minutes to hear if any new attacks were being reported on the party lines.

But there were no attacks.

No one tried to break into anyone's home.

There were no sightings of "strangers."

No one was taken into the police department for an interrogation.

Now, more than 24 hours after the Christmas Eve attacks, silence had descended on Austin. Everyone was waiting and watching for what was going to happen next.

15. CHAOS IN AUSTIN

BY DECEMBER 26, NEWSPAPERS ALL OVER THE COUNTRY were reporting the murders in Austin – well, the murders of the two white women, Susan Hancock and Eula Phillips.

The headline in the *San Francisco Examiner* read:

A GHASTLY TALE OF TERROR FROM AUSTIN!

The *Missouri Republican* in St. Louis trumpeted:

CITY CURSED WITH SECRET BAND OF WOMAN SLAYERS!

And even the famous *New York Times* got into the act with its own lurid headline:

TWO WOMEN DRAGGED FROM THEIR BEDS, MALTREATED AND MURDERED!

While the residents of Austin didn't have their fears stoked by newspapers on the far side of the country, the same couldn't be said for the newspapers in Texas. All of them devoted large sections of their front pages to the two Christmas Eve attacks, all the news fit to print under melodramatic headlines like:

ANOTHER CHAPTER OF CRIME FROM THE STATE CAPITAL THAT MAKES THE BLOOD RUN COLD!

HELL BROKE LOOSE! DARK AND DAMNABLE DEEDS DONE IN THE BLACKNESS BY FIENDS!

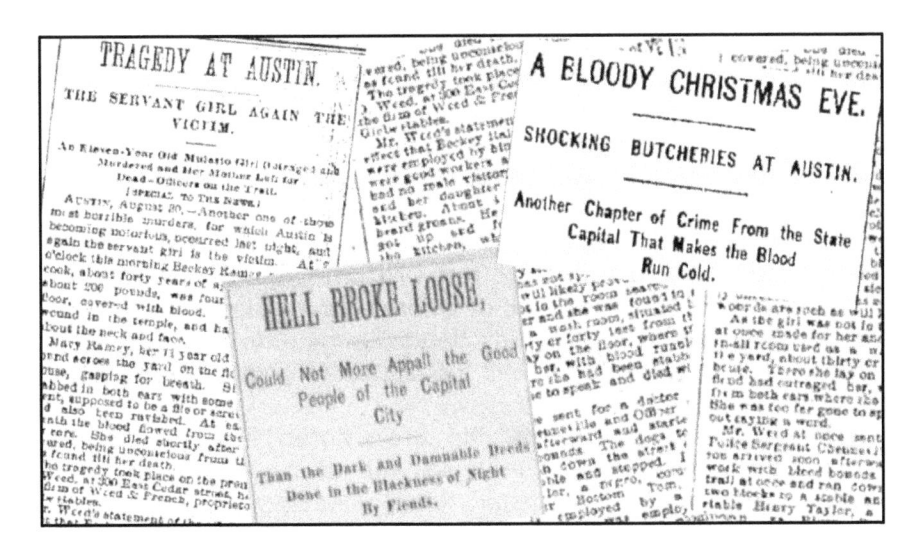

Every Texas editor knew this was their chance to sell more newspapers than at any other time in their history. It was one thing, after all, for a few black servant girls to be attacked, but something else entirely when the victims were proper white ladies.

Knowing this – plus, with most reporters being paid by the word in those days – the newsmen let loose with some of their careers' most florid and fanciful writing. They played up the social standing of both women, calling them "the wives of respectable citizens" and "the ornaments of highly respected homes." They described how the women were found in their backyards "bleeding and mangled," "weltering in blood," and with their limbs twisted "as in a dance of death." One reporter described Eula as "so beautiful, so frail, her face turned upward in the dim moonlight with the expression of agony that death could not erase."

But by describing the "murders," the reporters of late 1885 made the same mistake that I have in these pages. At that point, there had only been *one* Christmas Eve murder – unbelievably, Susan Hancock was still alive.

She had, somehow, survived her attack and, while unconscious, was at least still breathing. There was hope that she might revive or at least regain her senses long enough to give a statement to the police.

Eula, though, was very dead. Her body was left in the parlor of the Phillips' home. At the family's request, she wasn't moved to the dead room at the City-County Hospital. Dr. Cummings, the neighbor and family doctor, had performed her autopsy. He noted that Eula's "private parts" were "distended," which made him question whether she had engaged in sex before she was murdered – or if she was" outraged" by her attacker. He'd never get an answer to that question.

A justice of the peace and six inquest jurors came to the Phillips' house to hear testimony from Dr. Cummings, police officers, and members of the family, all of whom said they knew of no one who would want Eula or Jimmy dead. Jimmy didn't testify at the inquest. He was described as still too dazed "to give any intelligent account of the affair."

When the inquest was over, the jurors stated that Eula's death had resulted from "wounds inflicted with an ax in the hands of parties unknown."

Austin's most prominent undertaker, Monroe Miller, came to the house to prepare Eula for burial. He was assisted by one of the family's black servant women, Sallie Mack – who just happened to be the mother of "impudent Negro" Aleck Mack. Together, they removed Eula's bloody nightgown, washed her body, and slipped her into a simple white dress. Miller used cotton balls and putty to try and hide her head wounds and restore shape to her damaged face. After brushing her hair and applying makeup, he placed Eula into his finest casket, which was then carried outside to his hearse.

Eula's family and friends had now gathered – the men in black mourning suits and ties and the women in black dresses and hats with veils – and they followed the undertaker to the street. He climbed up onto the seat of the hearse, flicked the reins over the back of his black horses, and led the way toward the First Presbyterian Church with the cortege of mourners following behind.

Austin residents lined the streets as the procession passed by. Men snatched their hats from their heads, and women wept.

The drivers of the streetcars stopped their vehicles in their tracks as the hearse passed by.

When the funeral service was over, Eula's body was taken to Old Ground, the highest point in the cemetery, a fenced-in area reserved for Austin's most prominent families. As handfuls of dirt were tossed onto the casket lid and the minister recited a prayer, the mourners stared into the grave in stunned silence.

How could God, they asked themselves, take away a young woman with so much of her life still waiting to be lived?

God didn't answer.

THROUGHOUT THE REST OF THE DAY, hundreds of people remained on Congress Avenue as if befuddled and unsure of where to go. Those who were there with a purpose – men and women alike – lined up at J.C. Petmecky's hardware store to buy more guns and ammunition.

Sensing a business opportunity, a salesman showed up hawking "electric burglar alarm systems," which were electric bells placed on the doors of homes and servants' quarters that were guaranteed to ring whenever the doors were opened.

Another salesman offered Atwell's Patent Window Bolts, which he declared in an advertisement he took out in the *Daily Statesman*, "beyond all question the best invention for security against burglars and murderers ever offered for sale."

For the second night in a row, all of Austin's police officers patrolled the downtown area and the white neighborhoods, looking for strangers who acted suspiciously. But this did little to make residents feel safe. They stayed home, locked inside their houses. Restaurants closed early with no customers, but the saloons stayed open until their new early closing times. The men that gathered in them to drink were quiet, though, conversing in low voices.

They seemed to be waiting for something – like the sound of police whistles, running feet and cries that another murder had occurred.

But those sounds never came. The night was quiet, although the police did answer a few false reports of women who believed they saw a man standing outside their windows. Just before sunrise, a meat delivery man accidentally backed his wagon into the side of the kitchen of the Southern Hotel. The resounding thud woke the two black cooks who slept in an adjoining room. Both women sprang from their beds, screaming, "Murder! Murder!" One of the hotel guests threw open his window, pulled out a revolver, and began firing at the delivery wagon. Luckily, he missed the driver and his horse before policemen arrived at the scene.

The crowds returned to Congress Avenue on December 27, and later that morning, a rumor spread that an arrest had been made in the town of Belton, about 90 miles north of Austin. A policeman there had detained two men just as they stepped off a train that had arrived from the Austin depot. The officer had spotted blood on their clothing and was suspicious. He arrested them and took them to the Belton police department to talk to the marshal.

The suspects turned out to be poor, white, uneducated brothers in their early twenties named J.T. and J.P. Norwood. They worked on a farm south of Austin and told the marshal in Belton that they had gone to San Marcos that morning to board a train, started arguing, and had gotten into a fight. That was why they had blood on their clothes. They hadn't even been in Austin on Christmas Eve.

The marshal didn't believe a word of it. He was convinced the Norwoods had become infected by the same "killing mania" that was affecting Austin's black men. He called Marshal Lucy and told him that he'd captured the Christmas Eve killers and was sending them back to Austin on the next train with two officers as escorts.

Word of the arrest traveled up and down Congress Avenue that morning, and many of the men decided they wanted to get a look at the killers when they arrived on the train. They gathered at the depot but soon found the Norwood brothers weren't on the train that had just arrived. Lucy and Travis County Sheriff W.W. Hornsby – fearing the brothers would be dragged away, beaten, and maybe lynched – had stopped the train north of the city and had taken the Norwoods to the county jail, which was much heavier fortified than the Austin police department jail.

Tempers flared when it was discovered the brothers had been taken from the train, and the crowd marched back up Congress toward the jail. As they walked, more men joined with them. One reporter wrote, "They looked like a mob, their faces scowling and ugly."

At least one man yelled, "Bring us the Norwoods!"

Hornsby and his deputies met the crowd in front of the jail. The sheriff raised his hands and tried to quiet the crowd. Then he said the Norwoods had been "thoroughly investigated" and were "believed to be innocent." They had already been sent back to their farm. There was no reason for the two brothers to be harmed.

Hornsby's booming voice had done the trick. The mob slowly began to disperse. Some men returned to the sidewalks along Congress Avenue, while others went home.

For the third straight night, however, Austin was gripped by fear. An entire black neighborhood was awakened by the piercing screams of an older woman who thought she heard her doorknob being rattled.

At the Hancock home on Water Street, Susan finally took her last breath. She died in her bed, in the company of her husband, distraught daughters, and her doctors, who had been giving her morphine injections to ease her pain. She never regained consciousness to offer some clue as to the man who attacked her.

The inquest was held the next morning after breakfast, with jurors ruling that Susan's death was the result of "the

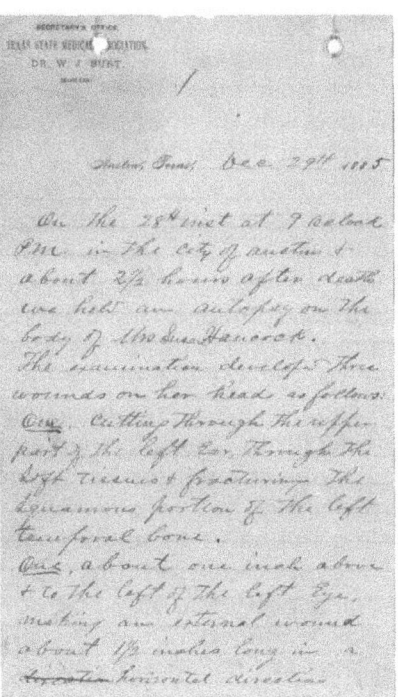

Dr. William Burt's notes from the autopsy of Susan Hancock

effects from a fracture of the skull and from a sharp pointed instrument being driven into the right ear, inflicted by the hand or hands of a person or persons unknown."

Undertaker Monroe Miller soon arrived and placed Susan's body in a casket. After her funeral at the Methodist Church, the casket was taken to the city cemetery, where Susan was buried on a hill between Eula's grave and the graves of the servant girls who preceded her in death.

SINCE THE CHRISTMAS EVE ATTACKS, MARSHAL Lucy had been holding on to the slim hope that Susan Hancock would regain consciousness – even for a few minutes – and tell him who had attacked her. Now that she was also dead, the investigation was back to square one. Austin's residents seemed to sense it – lines grew at the hardware store to buy guns and bullets, and the hardware store had also run out of locks and chains. A reporter for the *Houston Daily Post* noted, "If this thing is not stopped soon, several corpses will be swinging from tree limbs."

The police may have been short of clues, but they were being deluged with ideas of how to catch the killer. Someone suggested that all Austin women be given guard dogs. Another proposed sending mounted officers out to scour the countryside for six miles on every side of the city to search for suspects. When he met with the vigilance committee, Governor Ireland came up with his own – very strange – idea. He said that whenever the next attack occurred, someone who lived nearby should run to the closest city fire alarm and set it off. As soon as Austin's men heard the alarm, they should run out of their homes with their guns, head in the direction of the alarm, and stop anyone passing by who wasn't a "good citizen." The men would then escort the "suspects" to the police department for further questioning. He didn't make it clear how the men would know who wasn't a "good citizen," but I'd be willing to bet it had something to do with the color of their skin.

Mayor Robertson was a little more down-to-earth. He was begging people to stay calm and be patient. There was an army of police officers out on the streets, he said, keeping the killer at bay. He also had good news to announce – the Pinkertons were on their way to Austin and would be arriving soon. Soon, the killer would be caught!

Roberston asked his constituents to go on with their lives. He encouraged everyone to return to work, shop at the stores, dine at the restaurants, and see a show at the opera house. Just that night, Millett's would be presenting New York diva Emma Abbott, who was touring with the Grand English Opera Company. Millett had scheduled the show months before, paying top dollar for talent and $1,500 on new props for the performance. After that investment, he was not about to cancel the show. And to ensure that Emma Abbott wasn't scared of it, he'd arranged for an off-duty police officer to serve as her bodyguard, meeting her at the train station in San Antonio and escorting her to Austin.

New York opera diva Emma Abbott

Emma was happy to have the bodyguard because she felt the dread that pervaded the city when she arrived in Austin. As she and members of her company were taken to waiting carriages, newspaper boys waved copies of the *Daily Statesman* above their heads and shouted about the Christmas Eve murders.

Two performances went on that night without a hitch, although the theater wasn't as full as it normally was. At the end of the second show, most audience members didn't stick around for Emma's encore. They were too determined to be back in their homes – with their doors locked – before the clock struck midnight.

When the shows were over, Emma and her fellow singers rose in carriages to their hotel, escorted by the bodyguard. And then, like everyone else in Austin, they locked their doors and waited for the sun to rise.

ON DECEMBER 29, EMMA ABBOTT AND THE opera company boarded a train and left Austin. The always hopeful Charles Millett changed his marquee to advertise his next show – English actor Frederick Wade, who was touring the country with his

Shakespearean troupe and scheduled to be in Austin for Julius Caesar over New Year's weekend.

But few in town bought tickets – no one wanted to see a tragedy where the title character was stabbed to death right now. They were much too worried about being murdered themselves.

Instead, people gathered on Congress Avenue for the fifth day in a row and complained about the inactivity of the police. A group of businessmen passed around a petition that demanded that city officials close all "bawdy houses, disorderly drinking saloons, and gambling halls," which were, of course, "murdering grounds of virtue and innocence." In any case, that wasn't a plan that most men could get behind. The majority had availed themselves of at least one of those vices at one time or another.

However, the other idea that began floating around found a much more receptive audience. The idea, which came from a group of progressive citizens, was startling – illuminating the entire city at night using powerful electric lamps, perhaps like the high-powered incandescent ones that lit up the grounds of the 1885 New Orleans Exposition. Such lights would remove the shadows on every street and back alley in Austin.

As one man wrote to the editor of the *Daily Statesman*, "Their recent crimes, which have so lately horrified all lovers of peace and personal safety, would, no doubt, have been averted had there been sufficient light to prevent the fiend from finding easy hiding places."

It was a rather quirky idea – and a costly one. It would cost thousands of dollars for the city to erect electric lights, but if they could save Austin from future murders, it just might be worth it.

But before the idea could be pursued any further, a train arrived at the depot, and from out of the passenger car stepped several men in suits carrying suitcases. Word quickly spread through downtown – the Pinkertons had arrived.

Well, sort of.

Once again, Austin was going to be very disappointed.

WHEN THE MEN IN SUITS STEPPED OFF THE TRAIN, they were whisked off to City Hall to meet with Mayor Robertson, who had eagerly awaited them to arrive. He handed them a contract that guaranteed a $3,000 payment for 90 days of work.

No one knows what happened next, but there were likely cigars and perhaps a glass of whiskey to celebrate the deal and the fine job the mayor knew he could count on from Pinkerton agents. He probably asked the men about their famous bosses, Allan and William Pinkerton.

I'm willing to bet he didn't like their answer.

The detectives didn't work for the Pinkertons – well, not the real Pinkertons. They worked for Matt Pinkerton.

Who?

When Mayor Robertson sent his Christmas Day telegram to the "Pinkerton Agency" in Chicago, he naturally assumed it would be delivered to the offices of the famous Pinkerton National Detective Agency. However, Robertson hadn't written out the entire name of the agency on the telegram. As a result, the delivery boy had mistakenly – or was it a mistake? This is Chicago, after all – dropped off the telegram at the Pinkerton & Co. United States Detective Agency – another Chicago detective outfit that the mayor didn't even know existed.

Pinkerton & Co. was owned and operated by 32-year-old Matt Pinkerton, a balding, thickset man who was not related in any way to Allan and William Pinkerton. He had briefly worked as a nightwatchman for their company but was fired in 1882 for incompetence. So, he decided to cash in on the coincidence of his name and start his own agency, advertising himself – just like the agency in Houston had done – as an offshoot of the real Pinkertons. He even called himself one of their best men in his advertising literature and billed himself as "the author of several brilliant captures." He claimed to possess "such a remarkable tact for detective work" that "the most difficult operations of that agency" were often placed in his hands.

Matthew Pinkerton of the Pinkerton & Co. detective agency – just not the right Pinkerton detective agency.

Livid, the real Pinkertons told the Chicago newspapers that Matt Pinkerton was a con man who was capitalizing on his last name, but if someone didn't happen to see that interview, there was no way for them to know. Using the confusion to his benefit, Matt somehow stayed in business. He gave speeches about crime and the "homicidal impulse" to civic groups and organizations – who believed he was part of the Pinkerton agency – and event wrote a book that he self-importantly titled:

Murder in All Ages: Being a History of Homicide from the Earliest Times, with the Most Celebrated Murder Cases Faithfully Reported, Arranged Under Controlling Motives and Utilized to Support the Theory of the Homicidal Impulse.

Matt Pinkerton's wildly overwrought book about the many cases he'd allegedly worked on.

I'm not joking. That's the actual title.

But despite the grandiose nature of his book and the money he spent on advertising, neither Matt nor any of the "detectives" who worked for him had ever investigated a murder. They were mostly hired to investigate divorce claims and small financial frauds. They'd also tracked down people who embezzled from businesses where they worked and once had provided security for a mill in Michigan during a labor strike.

But now, Matt Pinkerton's detective agency had hit the jackpot. They were being asked to investigate what was, at the time, the most highly publicized series of murders in the country.

Of course, they'd been hired by accident.

There is no record indicating who Matt Pinkerton sent to Austin. His men could have been graduates of his "detective correspondence school." For a fee, you received a booklet that taught you how to stalk and interrogate suspects, and those who completed the course were sent a "certificate of membership," a "Pinkerton badge," and a credential letter from Matt Pinkerton himself. None of those things, naturally, were worth the paper they were printed on.

There is also no record of Mayor Robertson's reaction when he discovered he'd hired the wrong Pinkerton. However, he must have realized that if the word got out that he'd wasted the city's money on the wrong detectives – just like he'd done back in September – his political career was over.

So, he decided to say nothing about the mistake. Apparently, he also got the detectives to keep their mouths shut about who they actually worked for, too. Quietly, the mayor introduced the agents to Marshal Lucy and Sergeant Chenneville, who updated them on the Christmas Eve attacks and what had happened since. The detectives studied the bloody axes found at the Hancock and Phillips homes and examined the footprint left on the wood floor outside Eula's room. They did their best to act like they knew what they were doing, referring to the Pinkerton correspondence school materials to find what questions to ask.

The detectives then left to begin their investigation, but it soon became clear they would not be making an arrest any time soon. They walked through the backyards of the two homes where the attacks occurred and interviewed the same people the police had already spoken with. They also wandered up and down Congress Avenue, hoping to pick up some gossip, and then stopped in for dinner at the finest restaurants in the city, using the expense accounts the mayor provided for them.

Alexander Woolridge, president of the City National Bank and the head of the vigilance committee, quickly realized the Pinkertons had no idea of how to solve the killings any more than anyone else. He called a meeting and proposed that the committee offer a large reward – the biggest in Texas history at the time – for information leading to the arrest of the killers. If the reward was large enough, he believed, there was no way the murderers could remain hidden for long.

By the end of the meeting, every member of the committee agreed to offer $1,000 to the person who provided information that led to the capture of the killer of Susan Hancock or Eula Phillips.

They even agreed to an additional $1,000 for the name of the killer of the five black servant girls. With $3,000 on the line, they were convinced that someone would come forward.

The committee printed a circular with the headline, "REWARD-- $3,000!" and copies were hung all over downtown and printed in the *Daily Statesman*. The circular made it clear that "Every good citizen ought to be zealous in the aid of the committee."

Not wanting to appear cheap, Governor Ireland announced that he would also offer a reward from his own pocket -- $300 for anyone who provided information that led to the arrest of the killer of Susan Hancock and Eula Phillips. The governor didn't include the servant girls in the publicity about his reward.

Added together, it was a tremendous sum of money for the time – over $104,000 today – and it would have allowed a man to buy a nice home or farm and have enough left over for a new set of clothes, a fancy dinner, and two tickets to see a show at Millett's Opera House. So, not surprisingly, the police did start receiving a lot of new tips. Although almost all the potential suspects were African American, one man excitedly called the department and said he'd seen a white man washing bloody clothes in a creek next to a lime kiln a couple of miles from Austin. Lucy quickly sent officers to the kiln, and they arrived just in time to grab a poor white wood hauler named J.D. Echols. It turned out that the clothes he'd been washing had been stained reddish-brown from pecan stains, not blood.

Another anonymous tipster was convinced that a Mexican was the Christmas Eve killer. He suggested the police investigate Anastazio Martinez, a middle-aged man who lived in a shack next to the city dump. He spent his days picking rags, pieces of tin, scraps of iron, and anything else that interested him from the debris. The caller claimed he'd seen Martinez on Christmas Day carrying a bundle of women's clothing and suggested he'd broken into the Hancock and Phillips homes to kill the women and steal their clothes.

Two officers reluctantly rode to Martinez's shack, where they did indeed discover pieces of women's clothes. They also found an old, rusted six-shooter, seven butcher knives, a small ice pick, and a long iron rod, "such as might have been driven into the ears of Becky Ramey and Mrs. Hancock." The officers quickly brought

Martinez back to the department, along with two barrels filled with suspicious items that Martinez had in his home.

During the interrogations that followed, Martinez seemed disoriented and rambling. What he said didn't make much sense. He launched into a bizarre story in Spanish about being "told and ordered by the Almighty to go out at night and draw blood."

Or at least that's what the police officers who didn't speak Spanish claimed that he said.

But it turned out that none of the clothing in the bundle Martinez had been carrying belonged to Susan or Eula. He also didn't own a horse. It was hard to imagine that he could have had the strength and endurance to break into a house, murder a woman, carry her into the backyard, and then run uptown and do the same thing all over again just a short time later.

Obviously, the clothing and all the other "suspicious" items found in his shack had come from picking in the city dump. The scrawny, half-starved man didn't seem to be a threat to anyone.

Because Martinez was so befuddled, the police took him to the State Lunatic Asylum, and Dr. Denton gladly took him in. The asylum likely offered him his first warm bed and decent meal in years.

THE REST OF THE TIPS THAT CAME INTO the police department were just as worthless. Each was investigated, but each led nowhere.

Not sure what else to do, Marshal Lucy announced that they would round up all the city's vagrants and take them out to the city limits sign – or better yet, load them into a boxcar on the first freight train heading out of Austin. All the men would be told never to return. As one reporter noted, Lucy was essentially "cleaning out" Austin and getting rid of anyone who might be a potential killer.

However, Lucy's "round-up" didn't make anyone feel safer.

There were very few parties in the city on New Year's Eve. It was certainly nothing like the previous year when the news of the first murder had not yet spread throughout Austin. Most people stayed home that night – no masquerade ball at the Brunswick Hotel, no roller skating at Turner Hall, no fireworks, and no toasts to the city's future.

On New Year's Day 1886, Colonel Driskill did host a "calling party" at his mansion north of the university, and Dr. Johnson –

whose servant girl Eliza Shelley had been murdered in front of her children back in May – hosted one at his home, too. Governor Ireland threw his annual open house at the Governor's Mansion. One reporter estimated 300 men and women were in attendance, and another wrote that Charles Millett – likely hoping to boost his ticket sales – had brought along Frederick Wade, the actor performing at the opera house.

Everyone had a smile on their face, but they weren't happy. At every party, there was little celebration. People huddled together and discussed the murders. There was a dark cloud that loomed over the entire community. Even at the grand opening of the newly built Firemen's Hall -- the downtown station where fire wagons, hoses, and ladders would be stored – there was little in the way of goodwill and cheer. Mayor Robertson was on hand with another of his "future of Austin" speeches, but he was careful not to mention the murders.

When a small band played after the speech, couples danced on the new hall floor, but the party ended early. Everyone just wanted to go home and hide behind their locked doors until the sun came up the next day.

ONE THING THAT HAD BEEN ACCOMPLISHED since the Christmas Eve murders was that the authorities had finally started to realize that the murders had probably been committed by one man – the "Midnight Assassin," as some reporters were calling him. The "Servant Girl Annihilator" moniker would come into use later.

Some were speculating that the killer might be some deranged "maniac," and where would such a man be coming from? The State Lunatic Asylum, of course. It was suggested that perhaps some madman was slipping out at night, which wouldn't be hard to do since Dr. Denton – trying to make the asylum into some kind of utopia for the insane – had taken down the fences. Could one of the inmates be sneaking into Austin, murdering random women, washing up in the creek, and then returning to the asylum without anyone ever seeing them?

Checking the calendar, it was noted that all the murders had occurred either right before, right after, or during a full moon. Everyone knew in those days that too much exposure to moonlight could cause a person to behave in bizarre ways. It was right there in the name! "Lunatic" comes from *luna*, which means "moon," and *tic*, which means "struck" – so, moonstruck. Gossips around town asked if it was possible that someone – maybe not even an inmate at the asylum – was transforming into some kind of monster because of the full moon.

One hilarious suggestion by a reporter from the *Fort Worth Gazette* was that Austin was being terrorized by a real-life version of Frankenstein's monster, assembled from the parts of the dead as in Mary Shelley's 1823 novel. The reporter had obviously never read the book since this idea makes no sense – and because he spelled the name of the doctor who created the monster as "Frank Einstein."

There was also a theory from an out-of-town reporter for the *New York World*, which had sent an unnamed correspondent to Austin to chronicle a lurid crime story like the ones the *World* was most famous for. The reporter filed three stories from Austin, running under the headline:

THOSE EXTRAORDINARY AND SIMILAR ASSASSINATIONS OF WOMEN AT AUSTIN, FACTS AS MARVELOUS AS THE MOST EXTRAVAGANT FICTION.

The stories are actually a fascinating read, detailing the murders from an outsider's viewpoint, and he made note of the fact that none of the women had cried out before they were attacked. "Death came always swiftly, silently, and certainly," he wrote. Although police officers and private detectives had "sifted to the bottom of every fact connected with the appalling deeds, the clues, seemingly fresh at the start, rapidly have drifted away into a mist of uncertainty and finally disappeared altogether," he continued. "Numerous arrests have been made from time to time but not one has been productive."

What intrigued the reporter most was that there seemed to be no motive for the murders. In the past, he wrote, violent murders of women "have love, passion, ambition, or the supernatural for a background... But here in the city of Austin in the nineteenth century, these crimes seem to have nothing to palliate their naked brutality and gaping wounds. As yet, the ablest detectives can advance no satisfactory theory to account for their commission."

The *World* correspondent made it clear that he didn't believe an "organized gang of Negroes" did the killings. He also didn't think that the killers were hardened criminals with prison records or drunks in saloons with violent streaks. He pointed out that "all the worst characters in town" had been kept under watch by the police since the murder of Mary Ramey back in August. If men like that had been responsible for the murders, "they would have betrayed themselves long ago."

The reporter believed that the only logical conclusion he could reach was that the killer was a "cunning maniac of great strength, fleetness of foot, and a superior intellect." The man could "plot these crimes and carry them out in every particular without a mistake" and then "disappear into thin air almost immediately." He suggested that the man had a "secret hiding place" where he went after each murder so that he could wash off the victim's blood, change his clothing, and then return to the streets to look like just one more man in the crowd.

He was, the reporter proposed, hiding in plain sight.

He did not believe this man was emotionally out of control. He did not go around wanting to kill every woman he met. "This man is frugal," he wrote. "He kills only when necessary." He was not committing just a different kind of murder – he had a different way of thinking. He added, "I do not believe any man figures in the world's history with such a terrible and horrifying distinction from the rest of humanity. He may well give to history a new story of crime – the first instance of a man who killed to gratify his passion."

The unnamed *World* correspondent was more of a prophet than he ever imagined. Austin's monster had already created a place for himself in American history as our first documented serial killer.

THE *WORLD* ARTICLES WERE TELEGRAPHED to Texas from New York, and the *Dallas Morning News* reprinted it in its entirety. The paper was sold on Austin newsstands, and it's too bad the local police didn't read it. In just a short time in the city, the reporter – likely a veteran of covering crime in the much larger city of New York – had deduced more about the murders than the Austin police department had been able to do in a year.

Naturally, the *Daily Statesman* didn't reprint any of the material. That would have made too much sense. However, the newspaper started printing letters from citizens who likely had read the World articles and were starting to insist that a devious killer was on the loose. One resident suggested the police stop worrying about "tramps" and instead keep an eye on "the upper crust, which may be found, after all, to be the author of these terrible crimes."

Another writer -- who had either read Robert Louis Stevenson's recent book, *The Strange Case of Dr. Jekyll and Mr. Hyde* or noted the way the murdered women had been cut apart -- suggested the police look for a "practicing physician" who might be using his medical instruments to rip apart his victims.

As attention toward the murders peaked, it created more unease and paranoia in the city. Some men decided the best way to keep their wives alive was to move out of Austin altogether. They joined the steady stream of black residents who had already made that decision.

At the same time, newspapers across the state advised their readers to cancel any upcoming trips to Austin. A couple of editors recommended that parents who had daughters attending the University of Texas write letters to the university's president and tell him the young ladies would be staying home until the killer was caught.

The *Laredo Times*, the newspaper for the small, dusty little town on the Texas-Mexico border, even launched a promotional campaign to try and get Austin residents to move to their city. One of the selling points was that even though Laredo had a blood and violent past, it was now relatively peaceful and could offer Austin folks "a safe and quiet breathing spell from murder."

In early 1886, everyone seemed to be taking potshots at Austin. The *San Antonio Times* called it "a dark and bloody ground," the same description used for Civil War battlefields just two decades before. The *Dallas Daily Herald* called Austin "the Criminal City." And under a headline that read WORSE THAN BABEL, the *Fort Worth Gazette* said that Austin, "which once had been held up to the world as the Athens of the South, a shining example of virtue," was now a place of "lawlessness of the most repulsive type."

There were calls by these and other newspapers for Austin residents to find new city leaders, saying they should impeach city officials "from the mayor on down." The editor of the *Temple Times* wrote, "The city is a wealthy community, and there is no lack of money. But nothing worth of its name has been done to ferret out the hellhounds who, with periodical regularity, have butchered citizens without hindrance. Austin's citizens should let the mayor know that if this thing is not stopped, he will be swung by the neck."

That seems a bit extreme, but people were upset.

Mayor Robertson likely wasn't worried about being hanged, but he was undoubtedly feeling desperate. Everything he had done to try and stop the murders had failed. If something wasn't done about the killer soon, he was going to earn a place in Texas history as the man in charge of the capital city's downfall.

But something did change. It wasn't a solution to the mystery of the killer, but it was just the distraction that the people of Austin seemed to need.

16. EULA AND JIMMY

SHORTLY AFTER THE NEW YEAR, A MAN NAMED Thomas Bailes walked into the Austin police department and announced that he had some shocking and significant news about Eula Phillips, one of the women murdered on Christmas Eve.

According to his story, in the weeks before her murder, Eula had been living a secret, double life. He believed that this had been the cause of her murder.

EULA PHILLIPS WAS, AS ALREADY ESTABLISHED, well-known in Austin. She was descended from one of the state's first families – her grandfather had helped finance the Texas army during the war for independence – and her father, Thomas Burditt, had been a decorated Confederate officer and was now a prosperous farmer living just outside town. Her mother, Alice Missouri Eanes, was a member of a prominent Austin family. But in 1880, Thomas and Alice divorced for reasons never revealed, and Alice moved to Austin to live with Eula and Eula's older sister, Alma, a plain, quiet, and reserved young woman.

Eula was none of those things. She was outspoken, beautiful, and outgoing and had already made a splash in local society.

The young men of Austin were in love with her and competed for her attention, but no one was more smitten with Eula than Jimmy Phillips, whose father had gotten rich building the finest homes and buildings in the city over the last 30 years. Jimmy was described as "a fine-looking young man" who was "rather portly" and had "blue eyes and light hair." He wore a handlebar mustache and dressed like a dandy in the finest clothes sold in the men's shops of Austin.

But Jimmy had little, if any, ambition. He worked occasionally as a carpenter for his father, but he mostly spent the old man's money and was content to live in the back wing of his parents' mansion. He spent most of his time drinking in local taverns and playing the fiddle for a friend's band.

Somehow, though, he won Eula over, and soon, they were taking long buggy rides. Not long after that, Eula became pregnant. A hastily arranged wedding followed, and then she moved in with Jimmy in the back wing of the Phillips home.

Eula's father had done well, but what he had in the bank was nothing compared to the wealth of the Phillips family. Overnight, Eula began living a life of privilege. She attended ladies' teas and church socials. She dined in the finest restaurants and attended performances at Millett's Opera House. She bought all the dresses she wanted from downtown shops, ate frozen treats from the ice cream parlor, and was photographed at the famous studio along Congress Avenue.

In the spring of 1884, she gave birth to a son named Thomas, after Eula's father. Her friends came to the Phillips home with gifts, and Eula laughed and chatted with everyone while she held little Tom in her arms.

No one could have imagined from the smile on her face how desperately unhappy she was.

The problem was, not surprisingly, her husband, Jimmy. He had become a heavy drinker, and when he came home from the saloons at night, he was often violent and abusive. Later, a friend would recall seeing Jimmy hurl a cup of coffee at Eula. Her sister, Alma, had seen Jimmy throw a glass of milk at her. One night, Jimmy stumbled home from a saloon and started shouting at his wife and his sister, Adelia. Terrified, they ran to another room and locked the door, but Jimmy began to kick it in. The two young women opened a window and ran out of the house toward the police department, crying for an officer to protect them.

Jimmy's parents did their best to keep him out of the taverns and, in January 1885, even sent Jimmy, Eula, and the baby to live with a family friend on a farm near Georgetown, which was north of Austin.

It wasn't clear to anyone aware of what was happening behind the closed doors of the Phillips house why Jimmy was mistreating his wife. He had actively pursued her at one time. Perhaps he was like the "dog who caught the car" – now that he had her, he was angry that he'd had to give up his bachelor life, get married, and raise a son. These were responsibilities he was obviously not ready for.

Whatever the reason, Jimmy was never arrested or even warned by the police. What happened between a man and his wife was no one else's business in those days. A man could beat his wife all he wanted, and his wife – even one from a socially prominent family – was expected to endure almost any kind of domestic unhappiness, even if it included violence.

And Eula stuck to that. She refused to complain – at least not too loudly. Eula, Alma said, always acted "lady-like." But now, Thomas Bailes had shown up at the police department to talk about a different side to Eula – one that was not lady-like at all.

Bailes was a former assistant U.S. marshal who had started working for Austin's small Capital Detective Association in 1884. He was clearly a man with ambition – he'd put his name in the hat to replace Grooms Lee but hadn't been picked – and was tired of a job that was mostly collecting unpaid bills for local merchants. His desperate need for importance makes me wonder how far he'd gone to obtain it – and how many lies he could tell and still walk away with his honor.

Bailes talked his way into a closed-door meeting with Mayor Robertson, his brother, the district attorney, Marshal Lucy, and the top men for the Citizen's Committee of Safety. He explained to them that he'd learned that in the last months of 1885, Eula had regularly been taking a cab to a rundown neighborhood at the end of Congress Avenue near the Colorado River. She had gone there in disguise, wearing a shawl or veil, but he was sure it was her. When she arrived, she went quickly into a boardinghouse that was owned by a woman named Mae Tobin.

The men in the meeting all knew Mae Tobin. She was an elderly woman who wore only black dresses and was known around Austin as the "bawdy housekeeper" because her boardinghouse was actually a "house of assignation." It wasn't a brothel but a sort of discreet hotel where married businesspeople rented rooms to meet their mistresses or high-priced prostitutes. Rooms could be rented by the hour or the night, and there was a front and back entrance in case escape was necessary.

Bailes said that he had recently met with Mae Tobin, and she had admitted that Eula had come to her house on several

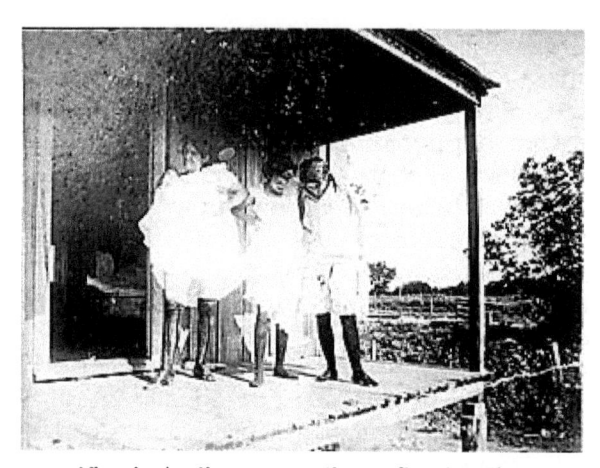

Vice in Austin was mostly confined to the segregated red light district that had been dubbed "Guy Town." But Mae Tobin wasn't offering a brothel. Her house was a discreet hotel that could be rented for "assignations" between unmarried couples.

occasions. Each time, she went into a back bedroom, where a man was waiting for her.

And then Bailes got to the really good part.

Sometime after 11:00 P.M. on Christmas Eve, Eula arrived at the house and asked for an available room. Mae Tobin told her the house was full, so Eula returned to a carriage waiting for her and disappeared into the night. An hour later, she was dead.

After Bailes finished his story, an officer was sent to find Mae Tobin and bring her to the station. She soon arrived but came with her attorney, W.W. Woods. She had plenty of experience with being asked to go to the police station for some questions. A deal was struck that required Mae to "reveal, make known, and tell all she knew as to the murder of Eula Phillips, or information of any kind that she might give, so as to show up the guilty person or persons and convict them." In return, the cops would live her "house of assignation" operation alone.

So, keep in mind, she had an incentive to tell the police exactly what they wanted to hear – and she did.

Mae acknowledged that Eula had come to her house several times during the weeks before her death. She came sometimes in the afternoon and sometimes at night. And it wasn't just to meet one man, she said. She had three lovers who met up with her at different times, but Mae noted that none of the men had ever told her their names.

When asked about Christmas Eve, she also admitted that Eula did some to the house, but she was turned away. All the rooms were filled. She wasn't sure if Eula was alone or if there had been a man in the carriage with her.

After Mae left, Bailes presented to the others what he believed had taken place. In his opinion, Jimmy had been out that night, had gotten drunk as usual, returned home, and passed out in bed. Eula had snuck out of the house and either had taken a cab to the boarding house or had been picked up by one of her lovers in his carriage.

When she returned home, Jimmy was awake, stewing silently while she changed into her nightgown and climbed into bed. Once he was sure she was asleep, he went outside, grabbed an ax from the woodpile, came back into the room, hit her twice with it, and then dragged her outside to the backyard, where he placed the pieces of wood on her body to make it look like she had been killed by one of the crazed black men who had been killing servant girls.

Once his wife was dead, Jimmy returned to the bedroom and hit himself with the blunt side of the ax so that the police would think he'd been attacked, too.

Bailes' possible version of events left the men stunned. They told him they needed to talk things over and that they would contact him soon. If this turned out to be true, Bailes was undoubtedly deserving of the reward that had been offered for the capture of Eula's killer.

But the question was – could it be true? It was a bit far-fetched, but it wasn't any more outlandish than some other theories going around town. Could Bailes – with help from Mae Tobin – have made up the story to get the reward money, though? Could Bailes just be pushing Jimmy's arrest so he could achieve the local fame that he'd always wanted?

Then, one of the men reminded the others of the strange behavior of Bob, the bloodhound, at the Phillips house on Christmas Day. After sniffing around the backyard where Eula had been found, Bob had gone straight into the house to where Jimmy was lying in bed. The dog's odd behavior finally seemed to make sense. Bob hadn't run off down the alley following the killer's trail because there was no trail to follow. The dog had pointed out the killer – the police just hadn't known it at the time.

Eula, they were now starting to believe, had not been murdered by the midnight killer – it had been nothing more than an uncomplicated domestic killing.

A hearing was convened before Justice of the Peace William Von Rosenberg, with Thomas Bailes as the star witness. An arrest warrant was promptly issued for Jimmy Phillips. He was charged with murdering his wife, a hanging offense.

Jimmy was "arrested" by an officer stationed in the hall outside his bedroom door. But even without the cop on duty, Jimmy was in no shape to try and escape. Thanks to his wounds, he couldn't walk and could barely speak.

Jimmy Phillips wasn't going anywhere.

WHEN NEWS BROKE OF THIS NEW DEVELOPMENT, Austin's shocked residents began gossiping about everything they knew about Jimmy and Eula. In those days – when even a whisper of sexual indiscretion could ruin a married woman for the rest of her life – it was impossible for most people to understand why a young wife from such high social standing would even go to a sorted place like Mae Tobin's house of assignation, let alone meet a man there who wasn't her husband.

Why would Eula have done it?

Was it because she wanted revenge against Jimmy for how he treated her? Had she taken money from her lovers and hidden it away, planning to use it when she left her husband for good? Or was it because of something no one in those days could understand – that a few minutes of intimacy with another man was her only way of finding pleasure and a little happiness in her unhappy life?

According to the newspapers, people all over town tossed out the names of Eula's suspected lovers. The names were of men who were "both young and middle-aged." Some guessed they were probably "gentlemen" or were among the young, rich bachelors in town who loved having a good time with pretty women.

In an interview with the *Daily Statesman*, James Phillips did his best to defend his son and daughter-in-law. He stated that Eula had never snuck out of the house to meet other men. He did admit that Jimmy had gone on a "drinking spree" a few weeks before Christmas, which led Eula to leave and stay with relatives, but he insisted she had come back in a few days. Jimmy had promised to straighten up and go to work – which he did. He helped build the new Fireman's Hall and even gave his paychecks to Eula to keep him from spending them in saloons.

James insisted the couple had been completely reconciled by Christmas Eve. Jimmy had gone out that afternoon to buy presents, including gifts for his son. He had also visited Booth and Sons, a store on Pecan Street, to make a payment on new furniture he'd bought for his and Eula's rooms. When his wife had gone to Jimmy and Eula's room that night at 10:00 P.M. to give them some cookies, Jimmy rested his head in Eula's lap. "They were as happy as any young couple I know of," he said. He added that his son's arrest was "a grievous outrage perpetrated without the shadow of evidence."

And James was certainly right about that – there was no physical evidence that linked Jimmy to his wife's murder. The behavior of a dog was not evidence. Bob, the bloodhound, could have followed the trail of Eula's blood and not any scent left by Jimmy. There was also the statement of Dr. Cummings, who had treated Jimmy that night. He said, "No one could administer to himself the sort of ax blow that he received to the head. Nor was Eula – who weighed just 100 pounds – strong enough to injure him so severely. The blows had to come from someone else.

Several newspaper reporters were also outspoken about their skepticism toward the evidence against Jimmy. A newsman for the *Fort Worth Mail* wrote, "The charge that Phillips, Jr. murdered his wife in the city of Austin on Christmas morning is declared to be an outrage of the deepest dye. The only charge that can be alleged against Phillips is that he would get on a spree occasionally. And if all men who are guilty of that charge had to be hanged, a thousand women would be forced to cling to one man's coattail, at least until another generation of men could be raised."

Misogynistic? Definitely. But he made a good point.

City leaders, though, were not backing down. Chairman Woolridge of the vigilance committee announced that they would raise funds to hire Taylor Moore, a well-regarded Austin lawyer and former district attorney himself, to "assist" District Attorney Robertson – you know, the prosecutor who tried to railroad poor Walter Spencer – at Jimmy's trial.

Interestingly, a few days after the Christmas Eve attacks, Taylor Moore had given an interview to the *St. Louis Republican* and said that he, too, suspected the murders were the work of a lone "maniac who at regular intervals feels an uncontrollable urge to outrage and murder women." But I guess after being offered a big fee from the citizen's committee to prosecute Jimmy Phillips, he'd apparently changed his mind.

He was now telling reporters that he and D.A. Robertson were already "up to their armpits" putting together a solid case against Jimmy. He had several people who'd known Jimmy and Eula ready to testify that Jimmy had made threats to kill his wife if he ever found out she was cheating on him. One man who he planned to put on the stand recalled an afternoon in November 1885 when Jimmy, with a pocketknife in his hand, angrily asked him if he knew where Eula was.

It all seemed a little too convenient to most Austin residents, and besides that, if Jimmy had killed his wife, then who had killed Susan Hancock?

Believe it or not, that question was soon answered. A couple of weeks after Jimmy's arrest, Justice of the Peace Von Rosenberg held another closed-door hearing in his courtroom. When it was over, he announced that Thomas Bailes —the same Thomas Bailes who had come up with "evidence" to charge Jimmy Phillips – now had "new evidence" about the Hancock case. That evidence had convinced Von Rosenberg to issue an arrest warrant charging another Austin man with murder.

That man, he said, was none other than Susan's husband, Moses Hancock.

17. SUSAN AND MOSES

IF IT WAS POSSIBLE FOR THE PEOPLE OF AUSTIN to still be shocked by anything, they were definitely shocked by the news that Moses Hancock was being accused of killing his wife – just minutes before Jimmy Phillips had also killed his wife. Moses dragged Susan into the backyard, the police claimed, just like Jimmy did.

Was it a coincidence that both men had staged the murder scenes to make it look as though their wives had been killed by the black men who were attacking servant girls?

Or were the accusations against Moses just as ridiculous as the ones against Jimmy – a desperate attempt by the police and Thomas Bailes to make it look like an actual investigation was taking place?

Almost everyone shook their heads in disbelief. At least Jimmy had a motive to kill his wife if she was unfaithful, that is. But Susan Hancock had been a quiet, kind woman, with nothing about her that could offense. She spent most other days at home, reading novels and writing letters. She was loved by her daughters and, most assumed, by her husband.

It was believed that she and Moses had a fine marriage. There were no outward signs of problems. The idea that this 55-year-old carpenter would suddenly decide to slaughter his wife on Christmas Eve seemed ludicrous.

An editor at the *Daily Statesman* was so baffled by Moses' arrest that he wrote that testimony from Thomas Bailes "will need to be as strong as the Holy Writ to convince the people of this murder-ridden community that Mr. Hancock – whatever motives might have existed – was the author of the damnable and hellish crime that sent his wife to the grave."

A reporter stated that Bailes and the prosecution had better explain why Hancock and Phillips – two men who didn't even know each other – would "transform themselves at the same hour into infernal fiends."

It turned out that an important figure in the Hancock case was Susan's sister, Mary Falwell, who lived in Waco. After reading about Jimmy Phillips' arrest, she paid a visit to the marshal in Waco and told him that she suspected that Moses Hancock had also committed murder. She claimed that life at the Hancock home was not peaceful, and that Susan had grown "nervous" and "uneasy" about her husband's increasing fondness for alcohol. When he drank, he shouted and cursed until Susan was in tears. He had once even kicked the family dog, she said. Mary believed the Hancocks hadn't been happily married for at least two or three years.

And then she dropped another bombshell on the marshal. She claimed that Susan had planned to "secretly move" with her two daughters to Waco. As proof, Mary produced a letter she said she'd found when cleaning up the Hancock house after her sister's murder. The letter, which had apparently been written in November or December 1885, read:

Dear Husband:
I have lived with you eighteen years and have always tried to make you a good wife and help you all I could. I have loved you and followed you day and night. But you won't quit whiskey, and I am so nervous I can't stand it. It almost kills me for you to drink, and Lena is almost crazy and will lose her mind. If I was to do anything to disgrace you and our children, you would have quit me long ago. Take good care of yourself. Write to me in Waco, and I will answer every letter.

Your wife until death,
Sue Hancock

Lena, by the way, was the Hancocks' oldest daughter.

But this letter is not exactly what Mary Falwell was claiming. Yes, Susan was upset by her husband's drinking, but it didn't seem like she wanted to leave him – she just wanted to get him to stop drinking. And perhaps they had patched things up since the letter

The Travis County Courthouse, where evidence against Jimmy Phillips and Moses Hancock was heard – and where their trials would take place.

was written between two and six weeks earlier – and Susan was still at home, sharing cake with her husband on Christmas Eve.

To the marshal, though – who likely hoped to get some of the reward money for himself – this letter was a "smoking gun." He contacted Thomas Bailes in Austin, who paid another visit to Justice of the Peace Von Rosenberg and claimed that Hancock had read his wife's letter, had undoubtedly gotten angry, and decided to kill her before she left for Waco and took their daughters with her.

Bailes admitted that it was a coincidence that Hancock, like Jimmy Phillips, not only chose to murder his wife on Christmas Eve but had deliberately made the murder look like it had been carried out by one of the servant girl annihilators.

But hey, coincidences happen, right?

And which scenario seemed more unlikely in Austin in 1886 – that two women were killed at the same time by their unhappy husbands who decided to copycat black killers, or that one mysterious man, for unknown reasons, had killed one white woman he didn't know and then raced across town to kill another one, all within the span of an hour?

AFTER HEARING WHAT BAILES SAID IN Von Rosenberg's courtroom, at least a few residents thought Hancock's arrest made sense. One man told a reporter that Susan's letter, combined with her sister's stories, was "of such character as to cast very grave suspicions" on Moses Hancock.

But that's just it – the letter could mean anything. Mary's stories were biased secondhand tales, and Bailes had devised a theory without evidence. Just as it was with Jimmy Phillips, there was no actual evidence that Moses killed his wife.

But, of course, that didn't stop rumors from spreading. One story making the rounds allegedly occurred in the 1870s when Moses had supposedly tried to attack his wife, but she had saved herself by "fleeing from the premises and taking refuge with a neighbor." Susan also allegedly once told a church pastor in San Antonio that she was worried her husband might get drunk someday and kill her.

More stories – still no evidence.

A *Daily Statesman* reporter went to see Moses at the county jail. He described him as handsome, with thick, swept-back hair and light-colored eyes, but on this day, looked "haggard and careworn." At first, he refused to talk, saying that the newspapers "have lied enough about me already, and I don't desire to have anything to do with them." But when the reporter asked if he had ever read the letter from his wife telling him she was leaving for Waco, he insisted he knew nothing about it.

When he was asked if he had a drinking problem, Moses said that he'd been on a few "sprees," but none of them lasted more than a few days.

"Is it not possible, Mr. Hancock, that at such times you abused your wife?" the reporter asked.

"I don't think I ever did," Moses replied.

"Mr. Hancock, can you prove by anyone that at one time, while drunk, you did not abuse your wife and threaten to kill her and that she went to a neighbor's house for fear you would?"

Moses told him that nothing like that had ever happened, and he referred the reporter to more than a dozen people in Austin who would say he and his wife had always gotten along well.

Those were stories, too – still no evidence.

As far as many were concerned, Moses wasn't offering much of a defense for himself. Even so, a much greater number of Austin residents were still unconvinced that Moses and Jimmy Phillips were killers.

They believed it was someone else, and Austin's white women, especially, were terrified that more murders were coming. They locked themselves in their homes at night, and while walking down the street, even in broad daylight, they would become unnerved by the sound of footsteps on the sidewalk behind them. One evening, a young single mother who heard a noise behind her was found by police crouched against a wall with her daughter, both "half dead with fright."

The hardware stores were still doing a brisk business selling guns and ammunition, burglar alarm systems, and window bolts. Druggists were offering sleeping potions and tonics guaranteed to "calm women's nerves."

Marshal Lucy did what he could to soothe the city's nerves. He continued having his men patrol the neighborhoods at night, looking for any sign of trouble. Sergeant Chenneville had also purchased two more bloodhounds, which the seller guaranteed were far better trackers than those already tied up in his backyard.

Meanwhile, the talk about a lone killer – the "Midnight Assassin" – kept getting louder. Even if Jimmy Phillips and Moses Hancock had killed their wives – and most didn't believe they had – there was still a killer on the loose.

Many residents pushed Marshal Lucy to start stationing officers around the State Lunatic Asylum to ensure no one escaped at night. An editor for the *Waco Daily Express* was disturbed by the asylum's lack of security. He wrote, "It seems to us that the very first thing to be done would be to have the asylum closely watched day and night, without permitting either the officers or patients to know anything of it."

There were also calls for the police to investigate anyone in Austin of unsound mind who was *not* locked up in the asylum. That included an eccentric older man known as Dr. Damos. He walked up and down Congress Avenue daily, yelling about shipwrecks and the world's end. "It has often been the case that the harmlessly insane, who have been tolerated for years to walk freely about, have suddenly turned into bloodthirsty madmen," wrote the editor of Austin's *Texas Vorwaerts*, a German-language newspaper for German immigrants.

I'm assuming this editor wasn't a doctor or anyone who had ever treated the mentally ill.

Police officers did reevaluate and reinterview some of the more unusual suspects from the previous attacks on the servant girls, just to see what they were up to. One officer went looking for Maurice, the Malaysian cook, but when he went to the boardinghouse where he'd stayed, the landlady told him that Maurice had gotten a job on a ship bound for England and had gone to Galveston to meet the crew.

England? The officer asked if she was sure of his destination. The landlady shrugged and said that was what Maurice had told her.

He seemed to be one suspect they could check off the list.

THE NEWSPAPERS CONTINUED TO RUN WILD STORIES, speculating about the identity of the lone assassin.

A reporter for the *Dallas Mercury* wrote that the killer might be some supernatural figure from "the weird legends of the dark ages, where ghosts and vampires glutted their fiendish appetites with horrors indescribable."

A reporter for the *San Antonio Light* suggested that the attacks could literally be the work of the Devil. "Many hitherto have not believed in a personal Devil, but it looks like he has broken loose in the capital of Texas."

And then there was George Monroe, a successful publisher from New York, who was so fascinated with the murders that he convinced a former journalist turned novelist, Kenward Philp, to write a fictional short story about them. Philp was well-known in New York at the time. In 1870, he had written "The Bowery Detective," often called the first dime novel detective story.

George Monroe telegraphed newspapers all over the country, letting them know that after doing extensive research, Philp had come up with an "original theory" about a white man committing the Austin murders. Monroe offered the rights to print Philp's "shocking" story for only $6.

Many nationwide papers agreed to run the story, but the *Fort Worth Gazette* was the only one in Texas willing to pay for it. Other editors, including those at the *Daily Statesman*, refused to pay such an exorbitant fee without reading the story first, which Monroe would not allow.

In the story's opening paragraph, Philp described the murders as "a mess of horrors – more frightful than Edgar Allan Poe or Victor Hugo or Alexandre Dumas ever conjured up from their romantic brains." He then began a straightforward narrative about a New York reporter named Gerald Shanly, who came to Austin and eventually discovered that the murders were committed by "a gentleman farmer – a steely-gray-eyed man of powerful build, sallow complexion, six feet in height, slow-spoken, with bushy, standing-out black eyebrows."

The fictional newspaperman learned that, months before, the farmer's brother had been convicted of murder by a jury of both white and black men. Enraged by the verdict, he decided to exact revenge by murdering the wives, daughters, sisters, and nieces of the jurors. The farmer traveled to and from the home of each woman in a carriage driven by his servant, "a gigantic Negro," who took a circuitous route through town to confuse any bloodhounds that might be tracking them.

While Philp's story was arguably the first piece of American fiction about a serial killer, it wasn't exciting, frightening, or even good. In the end, the killer didn't even try and escape. He was quietly arrested at his farm and confessed to everything.

Poorly written or not, the biggest problem with the story was that it didn't come close to capturing the real mystery of the murders.

On January 31, that mystery only deepened when police in San Antonio were informed that the body of a black servant girl named Patti Scott had been found in her quarters.

When the police arrived, they found that Patti had been struck three times in the head with an ax.

But the fear that the Servant Girl Annihilator had packed up and moved to San Antonio was quickly dampened. This time, there was an obvious suspect – Patti's husband, William, whom she was divorcing. He was known to be a violent man and had "brutalized" his wife several times. He was once charged with trying to cut her throat with a razor.

But then fear returned when, after he was arrested, the police found no blood on him and were unable to break his alibi of being asleep at a local hotel when Patti was killed.

The police had to let him go, and the newspapers immediately began suggesting that the murder was connected to those in

Austin. A *New York Times* reporter even made a comparison between the wounds inflicted on Patti Scott and those on the Austin women. "There was the same deadly cut across the base of her skull that three of the Austin victims bore, and the blow on the crown of her head was identical with that in the Austin tragedies," he wrote and then concluded. "It is the general belief that the deed was done by the Austin murderer. This belief has created a perfect panic among the females of the city of San Antonio."

It wasn't a "general belief," not yet. But if the newspapers had anything to say about it, it soon would be.

The same kind of fear that spread through Austin now swept through San Antonio. Women hid behind locked doors while police officers and citizen's vigilance groups roamed the streets at night. Local editors blamed Marshal Lucy for pushing the killer out of Austin instead of catching him there. "Is it just for any city, when it fails to manage its own lawless elements, to shove them off to depredate on other cities?"

Mayor Robertson had no comments about this latest turn of events but couldn't have been too unhappy about it. Finally, the headlines about murder were no longer just about Austin. Sensing this was the perfect time to tout all the great things his city had to offer – and restore his reputation at the same time – he met with businessmen to devise new ways to promote Austin. Unfortunately, it was too late to do anything about the fiftieth celebration of Texas' independence, which was coming up in a few weeks. The committee the mayor had formed had disbanded after the Christmas Eve murders. Still, the mayor remained upbeat.

He and the businessmen decided to create an advertising pamphlet for the city titled "Austin – The Healthiest City on the Continent." The pamphlet claimed that only 331 people had died in Austin in 1885 – "a death rate of less than 12 per 1,000 inhabitants," which few other American cities could match. Only a dozen of those deaths "were from violence or unnatural causes." Of course, the pamphlet didn't offer any details about those deaths. Basically, it said that you needed to move to Austin if you wanted to live a long life. It read:

Austin, the admiration of strangers and the pride of all Texas, is the most beautifully situated and healthful city on the continent. Her elegant residences, broad drives, and clustering groves growing in tropical sunlight; and her modest but picturesque mountains, her changeful landscapes, her flowers and sunshine and balmy breezes, all tell of health and life and ripe old age.

Downtown merchants and shop owners – undoubtedly encouraged by the mayor – started offering early spring sales in hopes that people would come into the stores instead of standing on street corners talking about the murders. Charles Millett did his part, booking New York actress Blanche Curtis to play the lead role in a popular play called *The Farmer's Daughter*. The University of Texas invited all residents to attend a lecture by its physics professor, Dr. Alexander MacFarlane, titled "The Habitation of the Planets," which suggested that someday when it cools off, humans will be living on Mars.

Mayor Robertson was doing all he could to get things back to normal in Austin and leave the murders in the past. All he needed to make that happen, he believed, was for Moses Hancock and Jimmy Phillips to be convicted at their trials.

After that, this thing would finally be over, and the murders could become a part of a distant memory and be forgotten.

18. THE TRIAL OF JIMMY PHILLIPS

IN LATE FEBRUARY, A PRELIMINARY HEARING WAS held to decide if enough evidence existed to put Jimmy Phillips on trial for Eula's murder. He was led into the main courtroom of the grand two-story county courthouse, and he stumbled toward his chair. He didn't speak to anyone. His doctors said he was still "delirious" from his head wounds.

D.A. Robertson and the special prosecutor, T.E. Moore, laid out their case against him for the judge. They said his parents lied about Jimmy and Eula reconciling before Christmas and having a happy life. It was also significant, they stated, that no one in Austin had been able to come up with the name of any other man who would have wanted Eula dead.

It was a ridiculous case based on hearsay with no evidence. Just because no other suspect had been named in Eula's murder didn't mean that Jimmy did it. But Texas District Judge A.S. Wright, the elderly, stern man presiding over the case, nodded, tapped his gavel on his desk, and announced that Jimmy's trial would start in May.

But then, two days later, news spread across town that there was, in fact, a new suspect in Eula's murder. Believe it or not, the phony Pinkerton detectives, of all people, had found him. After six weeks of whatever they'd been doing, they'd finally had a break in the case. According to the newspapers, the Pinkertons had received a message from a "prominent citizen" alleging that one of the men Eula had been secretly meeting at Mae Tobin's house was a "distinguished politician." The message went on to say that the politician was a "prominent state officer and active candidate for the governorship of Texas" and that he knew "something about Eula's murder."

Only one man fit the description in the message – William J. Swain, the state comptroller planning to run against Governor Ireland in the next state election.

Naturally, reporters went straight to Swain for a comment – had he had sex with Eula? What did he know about her murder? For that matter, what did he know about all the other murders?

Swain insisted that he had never met Eula Phillips and hadn't even known who she was until her murder was printed in the newspapers. And he added that he intended to find the party who had gone to the Pinkerton detectives and spread "such underhanded slander" about him, vowing to hold them accountable in a court of law for such an "indignant and cruel outrage."

And it didn't take long for Swain and his staff to find the "prominent citizen" who'd sent the telegram. It had come from Waco and was traced to the home of Lawrence Sullivan "Sul" Ross, a slim, balding former war hero who had recently declared that he would be running against Swain for the Democratic Party's nomination for governor.

As you can see, politics was just as dirty back then as today.

Ross had made a name for himself in the past. During the Civil War, Ross fought in 135 battles for the Confederacy. Before that, in 1860, when he was a Texas Ranger, he'd led the rescue of Cynthia Ann Parker, a white woman who'd been taken by the Comanche when she was a child. The "rescue" made national news, but the real story was hidden for decades.

Lawrence "Sul" Ross

During the raid on the village where Cynthia – or "Narua," as she preferred to be called, which means "found one" in Comanche – the Rangers killed between six and twelve people, all women and children. Narua was forcibly taken from her husband and children and was returned to her biological relatives against her will. For the remaining ten years of her life, she mourned for her

Comanche family and refused to adjust to white society. She escaped at least once but was recaptured and brought back. The white settlers couldn't comprehend the idea that Narua considered herself Comanche. They believed her rescue had redeemed her from savages. Narua felt just the opposite. Heartbroken over her daughter's death from influenza and pneumonia, she lived only seven more years and died in 1871.

Not exactly the heroic "rescue" it was made out to be in the mid-nineteenth century.

Narua – the former Cynthia Ann Parker – who was "rescued" by Ross and the Texas Rangers.

But Ross was well-known and respected throughout the state, although he wasn't much of a politician. Reporters wrote about how terrible he was at giving speeches and pointed out that he had no real idea about how Texas should be promoted and improved. His campaign manager, Waco attorney, and long-time political operative George Clark admitted that Ross was "timid" about running for governor because he didn't believe he could win.

All this made it hard to imagine that Ross could beat Swain, who was already drawing large crowds at his campaign events. It was assumed that Swain was a sure bet for governor – unless some major scandal derailed his campaign, that is. And now, it seemed a scandal had arrived at just the right time. Across the state, people were reading new stories suggesting that William J. Swain, the man who wanted to lead Texas, could very well be one of the most bloodthirsty killers in the state's history.

Swain said he would be going to court to ask for a subpoena that required the telegraph operator in Waco to testify about which Ross "cohort" had sent the telegram to the Pinkertons. Ross' campaign manager, George Clark, hotly denied Swain's claim that anyone on his staff had sent the telegram. Ross' hometown newspaper, the *Waco Daily Examiner*, came to his defense, claiming Ross wanted to win the campaign "fair and square."

Using headlines like "A DASTARDLY OUTRAGE" and "THE INFAMOUS AND LYING DISPATCH," newspapers that backed Swain came to his defense, with some of them calling the sender of the telegram a "cowardly sneak" and a "cut-throat." The *Fort Worth Gazette* said that the whole affair was "one of the most damnable and infamous libels ever attempted in Texas."

Special prosecutor T.E. Moore issued a statement saying that during the investigation of Eula's murder, neither he nor D.A. Robertson had encountered any witness who mentioned Swain as the dead woman's lover.

As for the telegraph operator in Waco, he refused to reveal the source of the telegram, which to Swain's people was a clear sign that Ross – or someone on his staff – was behind this dirty trick.

When Ross began his gubernatorial campaign in Waco, just days after the rumor started circulating about Swain and Eula, he didn't mention Swain's name. His speech focused on the issues of the day – taxes, public schools, the fencing of cattle ranges – though he quickly mentioned that he would bring "dignity" back to the governor's office.

In contrast, Swain was barnstorming across the state, telling his supporters that he would not stand by while his detractors said "vile, low, and dirty" things about his character.

But the allegations about Swain and Eula refused to go away. Although Swain was supported by the *San Antonio Daily Express*, the newspaper acknowledged that the rumors about his relationship with Eula – even though they weren't true – may not make him governor."

Even Governor Ireland postponed endorsing him as his successor. He decided to wait until after Jimmy Phillips went on trial before saying anything. If Jimmy were acquitted, then Swain would still be a suspect, Governor Ireland knew, and he couldn't afford to endorse a man that people would suspect was a killer.

Mayor Robertson was distraught over the havoc created by the fake Pinkerton detectives. In early March, he paid them the balance they were owed for their work and sent them back to Chicago. He then met with the aldermen and told them they needed to pass more ordinances to defend the city from claims that Austin was an immoral place. One ordinance established "Sunday Laws," in which all businesses had to be closed every

Sunday from 9:00 A.M. to 4:00 P.M. saloons had to be closed all day so that residents would have more time to read the Bible and "improve their Christian attitudes."

Meanwhile, at the State Lunatic Asylum, Dr. Denton was also doing what he could to allay the fears that his hospital was a dangerous place filled with vicious madmen who were trying to escape. In fact, he told reporters that there had only been one escape in 12 years, and he added that plans were in the works for more gardens and winding paths on the grounds to ensure inmates felt an even deeper sense of calm.

Dr. Denton wasn't his usual self during these interviews, however. He could often speak for hours about the safety of the asylum and the good things his staff did for the well-being of the patients. But in early 1886, he seemed troubled for reasons that wouldn't become clear until later in the spring. Back in February, he'd quietly gone to a county judge and requested that an Austin resident – who was suffering from a "very distressing and deplorable" mental condition – be "involuntarily committed" to the asylum and "placed under restraints."

The Austin resident was none other than Dr. Denton's son-in-law and assistant superintendent, Dr. James P. Given.

Dr. Denton had said nothing to the judge about what had caused his son-in-law's insanity. He only said the young man was "bereft of his reason." Denton then made a strange request. He asked that James be removed from the Austin hospital and sent to the North Texas Lunatic Asylum, a hospital that had recently opened in the town of Terrell.

North Texas Lunatic Asylum in Terrell, where Dr. Given was sent after his father-in-law had involuntarily committed him.

The judge agreed, and James was transported to Terrell in a private railroad car. In his admissions report at the new asylum, James' cause of insanity was still not revealed. All that was entered in the books was that he suffered from "dissipation," which is a vague term used by asylum doctors of that era to describe a wide array of behaviors, from alcoholism to "hallucinatory activity."

After learning of James' fate, his friends were inconsolable. They described him as a "genial and accomplished gentleman" and "deservedly popular with all with whom he associated." He was a kind, honorable man, and diligent doctor who spent long hours meeting his patients' needs. There had been nothing in his behavior, friends said, that suggested he was unsound mind.

Was it possible that, within just a few weeks, James had become insane? Or had his insanity been hidden for a long time? And why, once his mental issues were discovered, was it so important to Dr. Denton that his son-in-law be sent to another asylum?

We can only speculate because records that detailed James' treatment at the new asylum were never added to the asylum's files – or they were later removed. It's been suggested that perhaps James contracted syphilis, which was untreatable in those days and was a major source of insanity. Maybe Dr. Denton wanted to hide this fact from the public to protect James' reputation and spare him from the ugly rumors that news of his condition would create.

Perhaps that's all it was. Or maybe Dr. Denton was trying to spare his family from rumors of another kind. Word could have easily spread that James' mental condition had transformed him into a murderous "maniac." We'll explore that possibility a little later in these pages.

Whatever the reason for Denton's secrecy, it worked. No scandalous rumors – of any kind – ever appeared in the newspapers about James Given.

He simply disappeared from Austin and was never heard from again.

JIMMY PHILLIPS' TRIAL BEGAN ON MAY 24. Hoping to get a seat in the courtroom, people began lining up outside the courthouse before the doors were opened. Once the hopeful spectators were

Jimmy's defense attorneys: William Walton (Left) and John Hancock.

Judge Alexander Walker

allowed inside, the room quickly filled. A reporter noted that the courtroom was "crowded to suffocation."

At the front of the room was a long oak table for the prosecution – D.A. Robertson and T.E. Moore.

Another table was reserved for Jimmy's defense team, William Walton and John Hancock, who were regarded as the best lawyers in Austin. Neither man liked the other – Walton had been a passionate secessionist during the Civil War, and Hancock was an outspoken abolitionist who lost his seat in the legislature because he wouldn't take the Confederate oath – but both were so outraged by Jimmy's arrest that they put aside their difference to defend him.

There were other tables in the courtroom for the press, including reporters from the state's large newspapers and those for the national wire services. The *New York World* and the *Chicago Tribune*, among others, promised their readers "full accounts" of what happened at the trial.

Jimmy was seated at the defense table. He was slumped over and staring at the wall, looking pale and haggard. He seemed to be still recovering from his wounds.

When Judge Alexander S. Walker entered the courtroom, the bailiff announced that the trial was now underway.

For weeks, the newspapers had been predicting how exciting the trial was going to be, like some melodrama filled with mystery, suspense, sex, and gruesome murder. In their opening arguments, Robertson and Moore did their best to make those predictions come true. They laid out a compelling narrative of a young, unfaithful wife and a jealous husband who drank too much. Jimmy's attorneys competed with a narrative of their own, telling the jurors that any number of men, from wealthy lovers to the notorious gang of black men, could have killed Eula.

Over the next three days, a steady stream of witnesses who knew Jimmy and Eula were brought to the stand, mostly to testify about Jimmy's abuse.

George McCutcheon, who owned the farm where Jimmy and Eula lived for a little while to keep Jimmy out of the saloons, testified that before the couple returned to Austin, he took Jimmy aside and told him to stop drinking.

"You are ruining yourself and making your wife miserable," he'd told him.

Jimmy replied that he worried his wife was seeing other men and asked McCutcheon, "Do you think Eula is too fast?"

McCutcheon said that he responded, "No, I think she is a good and virtuous woman, but she talks a little too much."

He then claimed that Jimmy told him, "If I thought she was not virtuous, I would kill her and then kill myself."

Jimmy's sister, Adelia, took the stand to say that Eula had been afraid of Jimmy – so fearful that she had once hidden for a few days in a home on the east side of town owned by a black woman named Fannie Whipple. She'd sought refuge there after Jimmy tried to attack her. The spectators in the courtroom gasped at this – Eula was so desperate to get away from her husband that she stayed in the home of a Negro?

More gasps from the audience occurred when Adelia testified that she knew Eula had met at least two different men at Mae Tobin's house. She insisted, though, that she didn't know their names. Nor, she added, did she know anything about what Eula might have been up to on Christmas Eve. But she said sadly, she could testify that Eula had been an "untrue wife."

When Mae Tobin, the prosecution's star witness, entered the courtroom, people reportedly rose from their seats and stood on tiptoe to get a look at her. She sat in the witness chair, and the room fell silent as she began to talk.

At first, she stuck to the same story she'd originally told Thomas Bailes, acknowledging that Eula had been to her home in the fall of 1885 to meet "young men and other men of uncertain age."

But now, she decided to name names.

Mae had recognized three of the men who had been with Eula. One was John T. Dickinson, the secretary of the state commission overseeing the construction of the new capitol building.

Another was Benjamin M. Baker, the state superintendent of Texas' public schools.

The third man was William D. Shelley, a clerk in the comptroller's office whose father just happened to be the law partner of John Hancock, one of Jimmy's defense attorneys.

A ripple of surprise went through the courtroom, and the spectators leaned forward in their seats, not wanting to miss anything, especially if Mae was going to confirm that William Swain, the comptroller himself, was one of Eula's lovers. But all the woman would say was that Eula had come to the house with two other men whose names she didn't know. She also reiterated that she hadn't been able to tell if there was a man in the carriage who was waiting for Eula on Christmas Eve when she'd come to the house only an hour or so before her death.

The newspapers ran huge front-page headlines the next day – "AUSTIN AGOG! A TEN-INCH BOMB EXPLODED IN AN AUSTIN COURT!" and "HIGH STATE OFFICIALS GIVEN AWAY – AND OTHERS SHAKING IN THEIR BOOTS." Mae Tobin herself was described as a "scarlet woman" and a "procuress" – a fancy name for a brothel madam – and one paper declared that her testimony had set off "one of the most extensive and profound scandals ever known in Austin."

For their part, the three men named by Mae Tobin expressed all the appropriate outrage, alleging their political enemies had paid Mae to testify they had been visitors to her house. Benjamin Baker even went so far as to pay for an ad in the *Daily Statesman* that insisted he "had no acquaintance with Mrs. Phillips, and never spoke to her in my life." The ad didn't help his situation at home – his wife soon left with the children to stay with her parents in East Texas.

Oddly, though, when the trial resumed, Jimmy's attorneys barely cross-examined Mae Tobin about Eula's visits. But they did tear into the prosecutors for presenting no evidence indicating Jimmy knew about his wife's secret life. Nor, they said, had they offered any evidence that linked their client to Eula's murder. When Roberston brought up the behavior of Bob the bloodhound when he got up on Jimmy's bed to sniff him, John Hancock got a big laugh from the spectators when he called out, "I wouldn't hang a dog upon the testimony of a dog!" More points were scored in Jimmy's favor when three doctors testified that he physically wouldn't have been able to wound himself so severely with an ax – especially on the back of his head.

The defense lawyers then introduced a new suspect. They suggested that George McCutcheon, the man Jimmy and Eula had stayed with on his farm, had come to Austin on Christmas Eve to commit the murder. They speculated that McCutcheon had been having an affair with Eula and that he once gave Eula money to go to a pharmacy and purchase chamomile flowers and extracts of cottonwood and ergot, which, when mixed, caused an abortion. Maybe, the lawyers shrugged, he'd decided to kill Eula before his wife found out about the affair.

On the stand, McCutcheon was asked by William Walton, "Is it true you were in the habit of having carnal intercourse with Eula Phillips while she lived at your house?"

McCutcheon's face became red with anger. "I decline to answer the question," he growled, adding that he had a solid alibi for Christmas Eve. He had been at a "stag party" that night near his farm and had been seen there by many other men. Still, McCutcheon was forced to admit that he did own a fast horse that could have carried him from his farm to the Phillips house and back before daybreak.

Jimmy didn't testify during the trial, but one of his attorneys did have him remove his shoes and socks, place his foot in a bucket of ink, and step on a pine board, leaving a footprint. It was displayed next to the bloody footprint that had been found outside the bedroom after the murder. Jimmy's foot was noticeably smaller.

T.E. Moore objected to this demonstration. He told the judge that it was flawed. He said that Jimmy was likely carrying his wife when he left that footprint, meaning his feet would have made flatter prints due to the extra weight. So, William Walton, who weighed 175 pounds, climbed onto Jimmy's back and asked him to step in the ink and make a second print with the extra weight. Once again, Jimmy's footprint was too small.

During closing arguments, Walton and Hancock told the jurors that since Jimmy's footprint didn't match the bloody footprint from the house, they had no choice but to acquit him. They painted a picture of Jimmy as a loving husband who had been working hard to stay sober and had tragically been attacked by the same man who'd murdered his wife.

After deliberating for a day and a half, the jury returned to the courtroom. Almost everyone in the room assumed the verdict would be "not guilty." The entire trial had been a farce. They were convinced that Jimmy would be leaving the courthouse a free man.

The jury foreman stood and announced that he and his fellow jurors had reached a unanimous verdict – "guilty of second-degree murder." Jimmy was sentenced to spend the next seven years in the state penitentiary.

The courtroom was stunned into silence as Jimmy was taken out and returned to the county jail, where he'd be waiting until the state prison wagon arrived to take him to the penitentiary.

Reporters filled out, mumbling to one another and scratching their heads, wondering how they would explain to their readers how such a verdict had been returned.

A reporter from the *Galveston Daily News* hinted that the jurors had been bribed or, at the least, had been given secret information about Jimmy and Eula that had influenced their decision. He wrote, "There is simply no way to account for the verdict unless there was some inside business that was made known to the jury privately."

A San Antonio reporter claimed that the deciding factor in the trial had been T.E. Moore's powerful courtroom performance. He noted, "His eloquence rather than the guilt of the prisoner caused a verdict of guilt."

The only thing the reporter for the *Daily Statesman* could say was that the "majority of Austin's citizens" believed the jury had "erred."

Hancock and Walton announced they'd be filing an immediate appeal. Walton was furious with D.A. Robertson, accusing him of turning himself from an upstanding young man into a "veritable thug" who had done anything possible "to win at all costs, leaving no human contrivance, no trick of the trade, no art untried to secure a conviction."

Robertson replied that he hadn't resorted to anything underhanded to persuade the jury of Jimmy's guilt. He said that no one – like his older brother – had asked him to do what he could to put Jimmy behind bars. He and Moore had simply done what the law required them to do – lay out the facts for the jury and allow the jury to decide on their own that no mysterious killer had come after Eula.

Robertson then said he would soon be convening a new jury, as the law required, to hear the case against Moses Hancock for the murder of his wife, Susan.

Many wanted to know why the prosecution hadn't presented any testimony about the identity of the man that Eula was with on Christmas Eve. Was it another prominent man? A rumor spread that a "rich cattleman" was with Eula that night, and he had paid Mae Tobin a lot of money to make sure she didn't mention his name in court. Who was this cattleman?

Robertson and Moore said they had uncovered no information about Eula's Christmas Eve lover. They said they had no proof of his identity and didn't want to speculate if it was some elusive cattleman or a state politician.

Which, of course, got the rumor mill started again that Eula's mysterious lover was none other than William Swain.

DURING JIMMY'S TRIAL, SWAIN HAD NOT commented on the proceedings, and he had nothing to say about the verdict. He didn't believe he needed to say anything. He still had the endorsements of most of the state's newspapers – a four-to-one advantage in newspaper endorsements over Ross, one reporter claimed. The Democratic Party nominating convention that would be held in Galveston was only two months away. Swain couldn't imagine that he could be ruined in that short amount of time by the ridiculous rumors involving him with murder.

To reassure voters they had nothing about him to fear, Swain went on another tour around Texas. In Rockdale, his staff arranged for the town's ladies to turn out "in full force" and cheer when he took the stage. He gave a speech that lasted for two hours and didn't take a single break. After hearing Swain speak, one reporter dubbed him a "full-fledged candidate" and said his opponent, Sul

Ross, was nothing more than a "kindergartener beating the brush." The reporter concluded, "Swain has served Texas and her interests too long and too faithfully to be defeated by an unwarranted effort to pull down and belittle the man."

But the rumors about Eula Phillips would not go away.

Newspapers supporting Ross pointed out that Swain had never followed through on his promise to hunt down whoever had sent the telegram that claimed he was with Eula on Christmas Eve. Meanwhile, Ross' campaign manager, George Clark and other operatives who worked with Ross had started spreading other damaging stories about Swain. They claimed he had violated state nepotism policies by hiring two of his sons to work in his office, that he had illegally used state stationary to write campaign letters, that a woman he knew was given a state "no-show" job, and that he was getting kickbacks from some of the construction suppliers who were used to build the new capitol.

Worse for Swain, though, was that Governor Ireland had never delivered his promised endorsement after Jimmy was found guilty of Eula's murder. He obviously believed his political future would fare much better if he kept his distance from Swain.

Thanks to this, when the Democratic convention was held in August at a roller rink in Galveston, it was obvious that Swain had lost a lot of support. Many of the 696 delegates openly told reporters they felt he had too much baggage to be the next governor. They'd decided that Texas needed a war hero to lead the state – not a murder suspect.

On the day of the nominating speeches, it was unbearably hot inside the roller rink. Sul Ross, suffering from a fever, only gave a disappointing 25-minute speech.

Swain followed him to the podium and gave a speech interrupted by applause from his remaining supporters many times. When he finished laying out his positions on the issues, he walked out to the edge of the stage and, in a voice "trembling with agitation," a reporter on the scene wrote, "and now and again swelling into a roar of rage," he lifted his arms and loudly declared:

This campaign has been the most disgusting in mudslinging and vituperative slander that has ever disgraced the footstool of the Deity. I have filled offices for fifteen years in this state. I have turned them over untarnished, and I defy any man to find a single blemish in the record that I have made for the state of Texas. But lying and contemptible scoundrels – men who would be thieves if they had the opportunity – have been slandering me from one end of the state to the other.

Swain then looked over at Ross' supporters and ended his speech by speaking directly to them. His voice was still shaking when he spoke: "Gentlemen, whatever you say about me, I can go home and make as good a soldier as ever fought in the Democratic ranks – and you can't touch me."

When he was finished, the newspapers reported that hats were tossed, his supporters waved handkerchiefs, and that "shouting and cheering lasted for fully two minutes."

But it was too late. Ross received 433 votes on the first ballot to only 99 for Swain, with two other candidates snagging the other 164 votes. Amidst shouting and cheers, Ross was carried onto the stage on the shoulders of his friends, where he gave a brief acceptance speech and then went straight to his hotel bed to rest.

Angered and bitter, Swain returned to Austin, where he announced that after completing his term as comptroller, he would be joining a local law firm that focused on real estate matters.

He would never, he said, run for public office again.

FOR THE REST OF THE SUMMER AND FALL OF 1886, Austin remained quiet – and then came November 10 and an announcement from the Court of Appeals of Texas, which was based in Galveston. The judges who made up the court announced that they had reviewed the appeal that Jimmy Phillips' lawyers had filed over his murder conviction. They agreed that the prosecution had not presented proof – as they promised they would at the start of the trial – that Jimmy knew anything about Eula's infidelity.

Nor, the judges ruled, had any evidence been presented by the prosecution that connected Jimmy to his wife's murder. The jury's verdict had been "reversed and remanded," and Jimmy's case was returned to Austin's district court for a new trial.

Jimmy was brought back to the county jail from the state penitentiary, and D.A. Robertson didn't object to him being released on bail so he could stay at his father's house with his young son, Tom, until trial. Roberston undoubtedly hoped that Jimmy would head to the nearest saloon, start drinking, and either tell someone he'd murdered Eula or, at the least, admit that he knew about her lovers and her trips to Mae Tobin's house. That would give Robertson the new evidence he needed to ensure Jimmy didn't get out of prison a second time.

Jimmy, though, said nothing and, by all accounts, didn't start drinking again. He seemed to be a sad and broken man, humiliated by his wife's affairs, and still suffering from the effects of his own attack. It wasn't long before the talk around town was overwhelmingly in his favor. It made no sense to anyone that he would have slaughtered his wife and left her the way she was found.

As the Christmas season approached, the one-year anniversary of the last two murders loomed for the residents of Austin. Some wondered anxiously if the Servant Girl Annihilator – or whoever had done the killings – would return for another Christmas Eve attack.

But he didn't. In fact, Austin was very quiet during Christmas Eve and Christmas Day, free even of "petty crime," a reporter for the *Daily Statesman* wrote.

On New Year's Eve, Sul Ross celebrated his inauguration as the new governor of Texas with a banquet and ball at the newly opened Driskill Hotel. From the platform, in his weak and reedy voice, he announced that he wanted his time to be known as the "era of good feeling in Texas."

Governor Ireland was at the ball, already talking about what he would be doing if he were chosen as a U.S. Senator later in the month. In those days, the members of the state legislature, not the voters, decided on who would be a senator.

He seemed very sure of himself, not knowing that many legislators had been receiving campaign contributions from railroad owners who weren't fond of Ireland. They hadn't liked him since he'd opposed a plan to subsidize railroads to build more tracks through rural parts of Texas. He was foolish enough to say he thought "the railroads were already making plenty of money."

When the vote for U.S. Senator took place at the end of January, the winner turned out to be a late entry in the race, John H. Reagan, a longtime politician and – surprise – a supporter of the railroads.

Ireland lapsed into a depression and returned to his home in Seguin, near San Antonio, to practice law. He never ran for office again and, like William Swain, became a minor footnote in the history of Texas.

19. HUNG JURY

IN LATE MARCH 1887, FOUR MONTHS AFTER Jimmy Phillips was released from the state penitentiary, D.A. Roberston filed a motion in state district court to have the case against him dismissed. Robertson never commented directly on Jimmy's innocence – he only said that he had no new evidence to support a conviction.

But Robertson, like his brother, was not a man who was willing to admit he'd done anything wrong. He was determined that someone would pay for the crimes that had haunted Austin for so long. Likely also pushed by the mayor and the vigilance committee to get at least one conviction, he announced he would be prosecuting Moses Hancock later in the year for the murder of his wife.

Moses' trial began in June. After Jimmy's trial, T.E. Moore was elected to the legislature. He no longer had time to act as a special prosecutor, so Robertson hired former U.S. assistant attorney Jack Evans to help him.

The first witnesses called by the prosecution were neighbors of the Hancocks, who testified that they heard no noise coming from the Hancock house on Christmas Eve. The implication was that if a man had entered their home, attacked Susan, and jumped over the back fence, they surely would have heard something. I'm not quite clear why they were so sure of this, but that's the testimony the prosecution presented.

Robertson and Evans also called a couple of neighbors who said they'd heard Moses – who had been out on bond since his arrest – tell a completely different story about what happened that night in his backyard than the one he originally told Marshal Lucy. They claimed Moses told them there had been two men standing over his wife and that one of them had pointed a pistol at Moses and advised him to stay back.

The key witness was Joseph Gassoway, who had known Moses for many years. I'm pretty sure they weren't friends, in any case. It turned out that Gassoway had been hired by Marshal Lucy – using money from the vigilance committee – to work as an undercover officer and keep tabs on Moses. Gassoway said that one night, while the two men were on a camping trip to West Texas, Moses had gotten drunk and started talking about how he wanted to hang private detective Thomas Bailes for having him arrested.

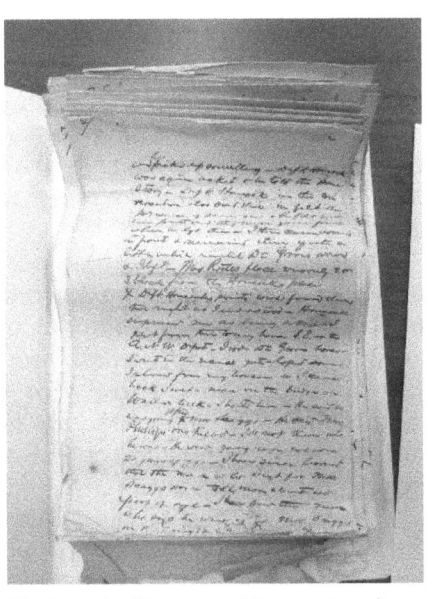

The handwritten court transcripts from the Moses Hancock trial at the Travis County archives.

According to Gassoway, Moses said, "Them damn sons of bitches down at Austin are trying to work up something on me, but they have not got anything, nor never will, out of me." He then allegedly asked Gassoway if he thought his daughters would "give him away." He then added that he would flee to Brazil if he had to so that the police and detectives wouldn't be able to find him.

Even if Moses really said this, I'm not clear how it makes him guilty. His statements could be interpreted in several ways. Sure, it *could* mean he killed his wife, but he never said so. He simply said he was tired of Bailes and others "trying to work something up on me," which, to me, translates to him not wanting to be railroaded by Bailes and the law. What he said about his daughters seems more like a concern that they'd turn against him, and what he said about Brazil sounds like something a drunk man would say if he felt that he was being framed and that was his only way to stay out of jail.

Moses' defense attorney was John Hancock – no relation – who had also defended Jimmy Phillips. He was so furious about Moses being prosecuted that he had taken the case for free. His co-counsel was an old friend, Bethel Copwood, an eccentric character who raised camels on his ranch outside town. Believe it or not, the U.S. Army had once toyed with the idea of using camels for their cavalry soldiers in the desert areas of the Southwest. Copwood, though, made more money selling his animals to the circus.

The two defense attorneys portrayed Moses as a man who had turned to alcohol after the murder of his wife to deal with his grief. He had only mixed up his stories about Christmas Eve because he'd had too much to drink when discussing what happened that night. They also accused Gassoway of inventing the camping trip story because he was interested in not only earning the money the marshal was giving him but also getting a piece of the reward money.

Moses didn't testify, but his oldest daughter, Lena, did. She said her parents had a good marriage and "lived happily together." She admitted that her mother had found fault with her father's alcohol consumption in the past, but He'd never once "laid on hand" on her mother and certainly had never struck Lena or her little sister. Her father sometimes had a bad temper but was still a good man.

Lena added that her mother had never found the courage to show her father the letter she had written, which said she would leave him and move to Waco. Instead, she had hidden the letter in a box of artificial flowers, where her aunt had found it. She and the authorities were wrong, Lena testified. Her father had no motive to murder her mother.

Just before they rested their defense, Hancock and Copwood offered a surprise witness – Travis County Sheriff Malcolm Hornsby. On the stand, the lawman testified about an event that took place on February 9, 1886, a little over a month after the Christmas Eve murders. One of his deputies, William Bracken, was called to a saloon in a black neighborhood east of downtown. Bracken had been called because a customer at the saloon named Nathan Elgin was "quite drunk" and "raising Hades in general." He had gotten into an argument with a woman, knocked her to the floor, and dragged her to a nearby house, where he started beating her. When Deputy Bracken arrived at the house, he tried to handcuff Elgin, but Elgin quickly turned and struck the deputy in the head.

Bracken went down but pulled his pistol and shot Elgin in the chest, killing him.

Sheriff Hornsby testified that when he arrived at the scene, he saw that Elgin was missing a little toe on his right foot. The sheriff said he recalled the bloody footprint outside Eula and Jimmy's room on Christmas Eve, and it looked as though a little toe was missing. He decided to have a plaster cast made of Elgin's foot and later compared it to the footprint from the Phillips house.

Hornsby said that, in his opinion, they matched.

And that wasn't all. He also said he believed that the footprints discovered in the alley behind the house where Mary Ramey was murdered also seemed to indicate that the little right toe was missing. Those footprints hadn't been preserved, but Hornsby speculated that they would match Elgin's foot, too.

This was explosive testimony – the Travis County sheriff was suggesting that Nathan Elgin was involved in at least two of the Austin murders and just might be the man some people were calling the "Midnight Assassin."

Who was Nathan Elgin, and why was he never mentioned before? Elgin grew up in Austin. When he was a teenager, he was known, according to the *Daily Statesman*, as "a kind of bad citizen." In July 1881, he and another African American man named Green Alexander were in a fight near the governor's mansion that almost turned deadly. After "cursing at each other for some time," Alexander drew a pistol and fired three shots at Elgin but missed. One year later, Elgin had been arrested and briefly jailed after he allegedly wrote a note threatening to kill a deputy sheriff.

That would have been quite the task since he could neither read nor write. Since then, no reports of Elgin having any trouble with the law have been reported. At the time of his death, he was married, had two children, and worked as a cook at one of the city's finest restaurants, Simon and Bellenson's on Congress Avenue. He was said to be a marvel in the kitchen, specializing in quail, venison, and "fine chops."

So, how did he end up accused of being a serial killer? No one knows, and there's no record of it anywhere. If I had to guess, though, I'd say that it was likely because he was conveniently dead and couldn't dispute any of the "facts" that were now being spoken about him.

Harry White, a deputy U.S. marshal who had studied and measured the footprints at the Phillips home, never mentioned a missing toe when he testified at Jimmy's trial. He only said that the "impressions of the hell and toes" were so light they were "indistinct." Thomas Wheeler, a notary public who took measurements of the same footprints, also testified at Jimmy's trial, and he never mentioned missing toes either.

No one did. And the toes in the alley behind the Weeds' home, where Mary Ramey was killed? Five toes were clearly seen, although one toe was "peculiarly shaped." Perhaps that's what Sheriff Hornsby remembered.

A reporter for the *Daily Statesman* who was at the trial wrote, "the rumors relative to Elgin and his crimes are false in every particular."

Defense attorney Hancock never mentioned Nathan Elgin's name at Jimmy's trial, so why do it now? Had he come to believe that Elgin was the "Annihilator" – or at least part of the gang of "bad blacks" murdering Austin women?

Probably not. Most likely, he was just doing his job. He was doing everything he could to get his client acquitted, using every means at his disposal, including flawed testimony from a confused county sheriff.

After the closing arguments and two days of jury deliberation, the jury was split right down the middle. A day later, the vote changed to eight for acquittal, three for conviction, and one who voted "doubtful." The foreman told the judge that no one was budging, and it was declared a hung jury and a mistrial.

It was now June 6, 1887, and after nearly two and a half years of police investigation, dozens of arrests, scores of lies, and mistaken testimony, no one had been convicted for any of the murders of Austin's women.

And then, one week later, on June 13, another attack occurred. Was it the same killer who had wreaked havoc in Austin for an entire year?

It certainly seemed like it.

20. "TWO YOUNG LADIES HORRIBLY MANGLED!"

THE TEXAS TOWN OF GAINESVILLE IS ABOUT 250 miles north of Austin, on the other side of Fort Worth, and not far from the Oklahoma state line. It was a cattle town, started in the 1850s, and because it was along the Chisholm and Shawnee Trails, cowboys took advantage of the saloons, gambling houses, and brothels in Gainesville. Local merchants profited even more in 1879 when the Missouri, Kansas, and Texas Railroad -- better known as the "Katy" -- arrived in town. By then, barbed wire had made Gainesville less of a Cowtown, and with a population of over 10,000, the town acquired most of the trappings of modernization.

By 1887, Gainesville had several railroads, the telegraph, the telephone, gas and electric lights, and heating. Cement sidewalks ran alongside the town's well-graded and graveled streets, illuminated by incandescent lamps.

A mule-drawn streetcar line ran along California, Dizon, and Harvey Streets, providing efficient transportation in the business and residential districts. There were also two sturdy iron bridges over Pecan and Elm creeks to improve travel in town further. Gainesville even boasted public water works. A dam had been built on Elm Creek to create a reservoir that provided the community with a clean water supply.

This was a wild western town no longer, but as the residents were just about to discover – a modern city had to deal with the modern problem of crimes that weren't committed by unruly cowboys and men who'd had too much to drink at the saloon.

In the early morning hours of June 13, Genie Watkins, the 18-year-old daughter of a wealthy Dallas cattleman, was in Gainesville visiting her friend Mamie Bostwick, whose father was also a cattle rancher and was also rich. The newspapers would describe both as "handsome girls" who "possessed very lovable dispositions" and were "quite popular in society." Genie attended high school in Dallas, where she "stood high in her classes," and Mamie attended a girls' boarding school in Tennessee.

In the middle of the night, Mamie's mother heard a "scuffling sound" coming from Mamie's bedroom. The three women were alone in the house because Mr. Bostwick was away on business in Chicago. She left her bedroom just in time to see "the form of a man jump through the east window." She rushed into her daughter's room and found Mamie and Genie on the bed, "weltering in blood." By the light of the full moon coming in through the window, she could see "gaping wounds upon the faces of both girls."

Genie had been struck with an ax over her right eye, and the force of the blow was so powerful that it "penetrated both frontal bones" of her forehead. Her right eye had been "driven from its socket" and was "lying upon her cheek, hanging only by a slight thread."

Mamie had also been struck but three times -- just under her right eye, in the right temple, and on the right side of her nose to the center of her mouth. Her upper lip was "almost entirely severed."

Mrs. Bostwick's bloodcurdling screams got the attention of the neighbors, and groups of people came running and alerted the police. Within minutes, the newspapers reported that the entire town "was in a state of confusion and excitement." Every police officer in the city was summoned to the home. Finding the two young women still alive, one officer removed his hat and fanned the girls, hoping to provide some comfort. The department's lone bloodhound was brought to the Bostwicks' backyard, where he sniffed around and then took off into a run. He led officers to a nearby creek bed, but it was here where he came to a puzzled stop.

Later that morning, all the town's stores and banks remained closed. A citizen's meeting was convened at city hall, where the first order of business was to start a reward fund that quickly added up to $200. All the men at the meeting were "deputized" by the Gainesville sheriff, some of whom were sent to the train depot to look for a man with bloody clothing who might be trying to leave town. Others were ordered to search the surrounding countryside, while others were tasked with house-to-house searches.

The search turned up nothing, but hope wasn't lost. That afternoon, the sheriff's son in Fort Worth arrived by train with his own bloodhounds. By then, officers had found "large footprints" in the Bostwicks' garden, and the dogs were taken straight to the scene. Unfortunately, since the ground around the house had already been trampled by so many people, the dogs found no trail worth following.

Although Genie Bostwick had never lost consciousness, she was so badly hurt by the attack that she couldn't remember anything that had occurred. Mamie lived for just over 24 hours before she died from her injuries.

After an inquest jury ruled that Mamie had been murdered by "a party or parties unknown," her body was released to her family and was taken by train back to Dallas. According to newspaper accounts, "at each town along the way, people turned out to show their sympathy for the fallen young lady." A procession several blocks long followed her casket from the railroad depot to the Floyd Street Methodist Church, where her funeral service was held. Those unable to get into the crowded church stood by open windows to hear a eulogy delivered by Reverend G.W. Briggs.

AWFUL.

A Foul and Most Devilish Crime --Two Young Ladies Fatally Wounded.

A Villain Enters their Sleeping Room and Uses a Hatchet --State Items.

Special Telegram to the Statesman.

GAINESVILLE, July 13.—About 12 o'clock last night, Miss Mamie Bostick, of this city, and her friend Miss Jennie Watkins, of Dallas, who was here on a visit to her aunt, Mrs. Willis, but who was spending the night with Miss Bostick, retired to slumber. Captain Bostick, the head of the family was absent in the Indian Territory, looking after his cattle interests there. About 2 o'clock this morning Mrs. Bostick was awakened by the noise of a struggle in the room, occupied by the young ladies. She went to the door of the young ladies' room just in time to see the form of a man jump through the window, and upon the bed lay her daughter and Miss Watkins weltering in their blood.

The bright moonlight which flooded the whole apartment revealed a gaping wound upon the faces of both girls. Mrs. Bostick began to scream immediately, and her cries soon brought

Back in Gainesville, the police were busy questioning suspects – "two Negroes and the rest Mexicans" – but the evidence against them was so slight, the *Dallas Morning News* reported, that all of them were released.

With the police investigation going nowhere, the same fear that had swept through Austin now seized North Texas. Residents in Gainesville and surrounding towns – even as far away as Fort Worth and Dallas – locked their doors and windows. Groups of armed men walked the streets from midnight to sunrise. A call was put out for the state legislature to pass a law that made it justifiable for every homeowner "to kill a man or any person upon his premises at night upon sight if he be attempting to hide his actions, no matter whether the object be theft or murder."

Naturally, the attack brought reporters to Gainesville. With articles under sensational headlines like "TWO YOUNG LADIES HORRIBLY MANGLED WHILE ASLEEP" and "A FIEND FROM THE DEPTHS OF HADES MURDERS GIRLS IN THEIR BED," they left no doubt that the Gainesville attack was connected to those in Austin.

In the same way that the *New York Times* had done with Patti Scott's murder in San Antonio, the *Daily Statesman* analyzed the similarities between the attacks in Austin and Gainesville, nothing that Mamie and Genie had been struck in "nearly the same anatomical region" – the right eye – as "women and girls assassinated in Austin."

The same correspondent from the *New York World* who had come to Austin after the Christmas Eve Murders also came to Gainesville and concluded that the killer from Austin had attacked the two young women. In his article, he wrote that "the time of night, the time of the moon, the fact that the victims in each case seemed without an enemy, the similarity of the wounds and the impenetrable mystery which overshadowed each of the crimes, all point to the same bloody hand in the awful work."

Sensing that Texas was just about to earn another black mark on its reputation – newspapers in the East were starting to call the killer the "Texas Jekyll" – Governor Sul Ross announced that he would add $1,000 to the reward fund raised by citizens in Gainesville. Soon, people started mailing letters to the governor naming men they believed had done the killings. A traveling salesman was named as the culprit, and one writer wanted the authorities to investigate the whereabouts of a stonecutter who was known to be violent with women. At least one writer brought back the old Comanche theory, claiming the crazed killer was hiding out in Indian Territory, which was just north of Gainesville and was not yet the state of Oklahoma.

But, of course, no arrests were made, which only made people more afraid, even hours to the south in Austin. Convinced that the killer was still among them, just waiting to strike again, the streets once again emptied at night, and people started staying home once more, huddled behind locked doors with loaded guns at hand.

One woman wrote to the *Daily Statesman* with an idea coming into fashion in the 1880s called "optography," or the imprinting of the last images seen before death on the eyes. In her letter to the paper, she stated that it was a scientific fact that the last image a murdered person saw remained permanently on the retina of their eyes.

It wasn't a "scientific fact," but it was certainly an exciting idea that was surprisingly accepted in the late nineteenth and early twentieth centuries. Most people knew little about photography at the time, as was anatomical knowledge of the eye. In 1876, a German physiologist, Franz Boll, identified purple rod cells on a frog's retina that turned yellow when exposed to light. It seemed possible that the eye could act like a camera and that the retina was like a photographic plate.

The retina had long been considered translucent – a window rather than a screen – and a German physicist, Willy Kühne, put the retina-as-camera theory to the test. His unfortunate subject was an albino rabbit, which he placed before a barred window for a three-minute exposure. He then decapitated the rabbit, removed its retina, and examined it. He claimed to perceive the bars on the window and created a sketch of this "optogram."

But Kühne didn't stop with rabbits. He obtained permission to study the retina of a man who was going to be executed by guillotine in November 1880. After his death, Kühne studied the man's retina and "had the satisfaction of seeing a sharply demarcated optogram print on its surface," wrote George Wald in *Scientific American*.

Kühne had trouble, though, identifying the supposed image. He said that it vaguely resembled the guillotine's blade – even though the executed man had been blindfolded just before his death.

Optography was eventually debunked as a forensic science, but it hung around much longer than it should have. However, when that Austin woman contacted the *Daily Statesman* and suggested that a photographer be hired to take a close-up photo of the eyes of the next person killed in Austin, she was actually on the cutting edge of criminal science. Many people believed that when the photo was developed, it would reveal the face of the killer, and the police could finally solve the murders. There is no record of this ever being seriously considered in Austin, though, especially at a time when Sergeant Chenneville's bloodhounds were the most advanced weapons in the police arsenal.

WHILE ALL OF AUSTIN SEEMED TO BE BUZZING with news about the Gainesville murders, there was one unusually quiet man – Mayor Robertson. Just as he did with the murder in San Antonio, he refused to say anything about the connection between the attacks in Gainesville and Austin.

Instead, he continued to promote Austin as "orderly and prosperous with a growing moral development and a future promising everything that is good and great." He announced that the city was growing more rapidly "in wealth and population" than

Atlanta, which was considered the greatest city in the South. When the Texas Medical Association members came to Austin for their annual convention, he gave a welcome speech in which he shamelessly bragged that Austin had become one of the safest cities in America.

But Robertson's days as a politician were almost over, and he knew it. The news had finally broken that he had not hired the famous Pinkerton Detective Agency of Chicago in 1886. William Pinkerton, the co-owner of the real agency, had received a letter from relatives of either Eula Phillips or Susan Hancock asking what his detectives believed had happened regarding their relative's death. Pinkerton replied with a letter of his own – which was eventually published in the newspaper – that said he hadn't sent anyone from his agency to Austin. Although an investigation by the city aldermen found that Roberston had acted "honestly and squarely" – and it was not his fault that the detectives he hired were "of little account" – many citizens were angry to learn that he had paid $3,328.27 with city funds to the fake Pinkertons to avoid embarrassment.

William Pinkerton, the head of the REAL Pinkerton Detective Agency wrote a letter announcing the people of Austin had been duped by an imitator.

In the fall of 1887, Robertson announced that he would not be running for reelection in December. He returned to his law practice with his dreams of being the man who led Austin into its golden age destroyed.

His longtime rival, Joseph Nalle, quickly declared his candidacy for mayor, describing his platform as one of "sound business and fiscal reform." He said he was the "people's candidate," and unlike the last administration, he would keep Austin "safe and secure." He won the election in a landslide vote.

One of his first acts to help Austin citizens feel safe and secure was to propose to the aldermen that the Austin Water, Light, and Power Company be authorized to set up 25 electric lamps on poles to better light up the downtown area. The aldermen agreed with the idea.

Meanwhile, Marshal Lucy asked Sergeant Chenneville to establish a mounted patrol division consisting of at least five officers who constantly rode through the city on horseback, always ready to race to the scene of a crime.

Austin would be ready if the Servant Girl Annihilator returned to his bloody work.

BUT HE DIDN'T.

In fact, by the spring of 1888, the murders in Gainesville had largely been forgotten in Austin, and life had returned to normal. The Driskill Hotel was consistently filled with travelers, businessmen, and politicians. Charles Millett had enlarged the stage at his opera house so he could bring in bigger companies to perform. Several new businesses had opened downtown, like a tobacco shop, another ice cream parlor, and a new hardware store that offered porcelain toilets for inside the house, replacing the outhouses that most families used.

On May 16, the new state capitol building – finally completed after six years of construction – was opened with a formal dedication ceremony. It was the largest statehouse in the entire country, a Romanesque-style monstrosity of polished red granite covering three acres of ground, with 392 rooms, 924 windows, 22-foot-high ceilings, and seven miles of wainscoting in a variety of woods. On the top of the capitol's dome, the Goddess of Liberty looked out over Austin, her head crowned in laurel and a sword in her hand. The stonecutters had exaggerated her facial features so they could be discernible from the ground, which was 311 feet away.

Trust me, you did not want to see that face up close.

One reporter described the ceremony to open the capitol as "one of the highlights of the century in Texas." Officials and dignitaries came from all over the state to be part of history. Six bands played at different times in the ceremony, and a chorus

In May 1888, the state capitol building was finally completed with parades and great fanfare.

treated the crowd to patriotic songs. Governor Ross offered a speech about Texas' "unbridled future."

The celebration lasted five days, each marked by parades, concerts, parties, and fireworks. Military drill teams came from surrounding states to perform. The famous Battle of Gettysburg Cyclorama – a giant, 360-degree panoramic painting inside a cylindrical platform depicting Pickett's Charge – was shipped to Austin from Pennsylvania and set up on the capitol grounds. On one afternoon, there was a lingering moment of silence for the fallen heroes of the Alamo.

At least 50,000 visitors from out of town arrived to witness the festivities, and many of them likely hired drivers to take them past the quarters where the murdered servant girls had been killed and past the Phillips and Hancock homes. They'd read the terrifying stories in the newspapers, and now they had seen where the women were axed and bludgeoned to death.

Many of them also likely whispered in fear about the possibility that the Servant Girl Annihilator was still somewhere in Austin, lurking in the shadows.

If he was, though, he never showed his face again. There were no more attacks on women – servant girls or otherwise – in Texas. The killer seemed to have moved on to satisfy his taste for blood somewhere else.

Many in Austin wondered where he might have gone, but content that at least he was no longer among them, terror faded, and the attacks became memories of a more fearsome time in the city.

And then, in the first week of September, a story came to Austin over the news wires. Far across the Atlantic, in the Whitechapel district of London, the body of a woman had been discovered, drenched in blood.

She had been cut up – just like the servant girls of Austin.

21. "JACK THE RIPPER"

THE DEAD WOMAN'S NAME WAS MARY ANN "Polly" Nichols, and she had been killed at 3:40 A.M. in Whitechapel, which was a district in London's East End.

At that time, Whitechapel was overflowing with immigrants and refugees from Ireland, Russia, and other areas of Eastern Europe. By 1888, more than 80,000 people were living in this small neighborhood, and with work and housing conditions worsening, most were plunged into poverty. More than half the children born in the East End died before they were five years old, and robbery, violence, and alcoholism were commonplace. These conditions drove many women to prostitution to survive.

It was estimated that there were at least 62 brothels and 1,200 women working as prostitutes in Whitechapel. There were also about 8,500 people sleeping in common lodging houses in Whitechapel each night – making them essentially homeless. The

The discovery of Polly Nichols' body

cost of a bed for one night was roughly four pence. Working as a prostitute was often the only way that a woman could come up with the coins to snag one of these "first come/ first served" beds for the night.

Polly Nichols was one of those women. She was a native of London who spent a good deal of the 1880s driftless and alone. Her marriage to a man named William Nichols had fallen apart after the birth of their sixth child when William began sleeping with a neighbor woman. Polly started drinking and was unable to stop. She left home and began a dismal journey through London's workhouses and hospitals, sleeping rough in Trafalgar Square with countless other homeless people, and ended up as a prostitute in the East End when she reached the end of the line.

On the early morning of August 31, she was stumbling toward a lodging house – having earned and then drunk away the four pence she needed several times that day – and ran into an acquaintance at 2:30 A.M. at the corner of Junction Street and Whitechapel Road. It was the last time she was seen by anyone but her killer.

Just over an hour later, two men walking west along Buck's Row saw what they thought might be an abandoned canvas cover lying on the street. Closer inspection, though, revealed it to be the body of a woman. Her throat was cut, and she was lying in a pool of blood.

But it was only when her clothing was removed at the local mortuary that the horrible incisions on Polly's body were revealed. Her abdomen had been sliced so deeply that her intestines threatened to burst out of her. The police were stunned by the unusual degree of brutality – it was unlike what they were used to seeing in this part of the city – but they had no idea then how common it would soon turn out to be.

WHEN THE REPORT OF THIS MURDER WENT out on the news wire, it was received in Austin by the *Daily Statesman*. In the story, it was noted that the police were already searching for a suspect – a Jewish immigrant named Pizer who was known to walk the Whitechapel Streets.

It seemed like nothing more than a one-off story, but the reporter couldn't help but notice the similarity between Polly Nichols' murder and the murders in Austin. He made note of that in the September 5 edition of the paper, pointing out how alike "the murders across the water and the servant girl murders in Austin" were to one another. The murders had been "perpetrated in the same mysterious and impenetrable silence," and the killer in London was described as a "short, heavyset personage," which was the same description given by Irene Cross' nephew when the man came into her quarters to murder her in August 1885.

But Texas was a long way from England. It seemed very unlikely that there could be any connection between the attacks.

Annie Chapman

THEN, A FEW DAYS AFTER THE STORY RAN IN THE Austin newspaper, the Whitechapel killer struck again.

One of the common misconceptions about "The Five" – as Jack the Ripper's historically accepted victims have been dubbed – is that they were all prostitutes. They weren't. The tragic homeless of Whitechapel far outnumbered the sex workers who lived out their terrible lives there.

The Ripper's second victim, Annie Chapman, once lived a better life. Far from the slums of Whitechapel, she had spent her youth – and later, part of her married life – in Windsor, not far from the royal castle. She had never been wealthy, but she'd had a decent life. But somewhere along the way, Annie's future veered off course, and she became estranged from her family and addicted to drink.

By 1888, she was isolated, starving, and suffering from chronic illnesses. On September 5, she got into a physical brawl with another woman, Eliza Cooper, over a disputed bit of soap. She was badly beaten, and her corpse would later show signs of it.

Her body was discovered on September 8, just after sunrise, in an unsecured yard behind 29 Hanbury Street. It is believed she went there looking for a place to sleep.

Like Polly Nichols, her throat had been cut. Annie's abdomen had been sliced open, and a section of the flesh from her stomach was pulled away from her body and placed over her left shoulder. Another section of skin and flesh had been placed over her right shoulder. An autopsy also revealed that her uterus and sections of her bladder and vagina had been removed.

Just like before, her killer left no clues behind.

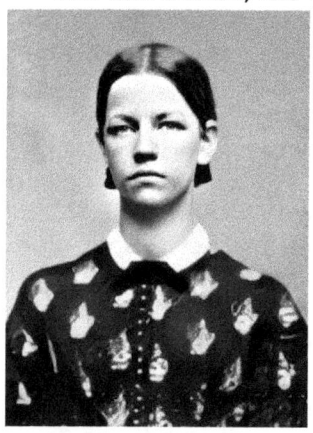

The Ripper's next two victims – Elizabeth Stride and Catherine Eddowes – were both killed on the same night or rather during the early morning hours of September 30, 1888.

Elizabeth had ended up on the uncertain streets of Whitechapel after an unfortunate early life and the death of her husband. The couple had attempted to prosper in the hostile environment of the East End with a coffee shop, but it closed after she became a widow, leaving her homeless.

She was last seen on Berner Street on the night before her murder, dodging an evening rain.

Elizabeth Stride

The next sighting of her was by a grocery man whose horse shied away from something in the street outside Dutfield's Yard. He got down from his wagon, lit a match, and peered closely, finding a woman with a sliced throat. No other damage had been done to her body, which led some police officers to surmise that she hadn't been a victim of the same killer – or that he'd been interrupted in his work.

It was the latter that was likely the case. The Ripper soon struck again; this time, he took his time.

ON SEPTEMBER 29, CATHERINE EDDOWES had been arrested for public drunkenness after a police officer found her passed out in the street. After a few hours at Bishopsgate police station, Catherine was slightly recovered from her binge and was ready to be released.

If only she had stayed behind bars, her life might have been saved.

Instead, though, she walked out of the station at just after 1:00 A.M. and started walking in the direction of Mitre Square, where her body would be discovered less than an hour later.

The state of her corpse was much worse than that of Elizabeth Stride. Her throat had been cut from ear to ear, and her abdomen sliced apart by one long incision. Her intestines had been pulled out and placed over her right shoulder. One section of her intestine had been completely detached and placed between her body and left arm.

Catherine Eddowes

Her left kidney and most of her uterus were also removed. Her face was disfigured with her nose cut off, her cheek slashed, and two cuts carefully removing her eyelids. Two triangular incisions—which pointed towards Catherine's eyes—had also been carved on each of her cheeks. A severed piece of one ear lobe was found inside of her clothing. The police surgeon who conducted the autopsy stated that, in his opinion, the mutilations would have taken at least five full minutes to complete by a man with surgical knowledge and medical skills.

BY THE NIGHT OF THE DOUBLE MURDER, nearly everyone in London knew the killer's name was "Jack the Ripper." That was a name that – not surprisingly-- came from newspaper reporters. The killings had quickly become the first major murder story in history that had international appeal, so journalists tried everything to keep the story on the front pages – including giving him a moniker that sounded shocking.

As the murders were being reported, the police, newspapers, and others received hundreds of letters about the case. Some letters were well-intentioned offers of advice as to how to catch the killer, but the vast majority were either hoaxes or generally useless.

Dozens of those letters claimed to have been written by the killer himself, but only three of them have been taken seriously – the "Dear Boss" letter, the "Saucy Jack" postcard, and the "From Hell" letter.

The "Dear Boss" letter was sent to the Central News Agency on September 25 and was forwarded to Scotland Yard. At first, the police assumed it was a hoax, but when Catherine Eddowes was found three days after the letter's postmark with a section of one ear cut from her body, the promise of the letter writer to "clip the lady's ears off" got their attention. But the letter writer – who signed his name as "Jack the Ripper" for the first time – promised to send some ears to the police, but he never did.

The infamous "From Hell" letter, alleged to be from the killer, Jack the Ripper.

The "Saucy Jack" card was postmarked on October 1 and sent to the Central News Agency. It arrived that same day and made mention of the "double event" – the murders of Elizabeth Stride and Catherine Eddowes – but no one knows for sure if this was written in advance of the murders or after, taking advantage of the publicity to claim "Saucy Jack" had killed the two women.

The "From Hell" letter was the most unsettling and disgusting of the three. It was sent to George Lusk, the leader of a Whitechapel Vigilance Committee that was also hunting the killer, on October 16. This letter's handwriting and style are unlike the other two, and it arrived with a small box, which George opened and discovered contained half of a human kidney. The writer claimed he'd "fried and ate" the other half.

Some say the kidney belonged to Catherine Eddowes, while others dismiss it as a practical joke. The kidney was examined by Dr. Thomas Openshaw of the London Hospital, who determined that it was human and from the left side of the body – but nothing else.

Years later, the police suspected that the first two letters were written by a journalist, coining the killer's name and keeping the story alive. However, no one could ever debunk the ominous "From Hell" letter, which remains a mystery to this day.

Just like the identity of the killer himself.

BUT JUST AS IT HAD BEEN IN AUSTIN, the London police had no shortage of theories about who the killer might be. Also, like in Austin, they had plenty of the "usual suspects" to round up when the search for the killer slowed down. It was just that the kind of suspects in London were a lot more "colorful" than the ones in Austin could ever be.

Tips poured into the Metropolitan Police Service about who Jack might be. Among the suspects were a crazed butcher; an insane Polish hairdresser; a lot of Jewish immigrants; a fanatical vivisectionist, which was a person who dissected animals for medical and scientific research; a Russian con man; an abortionist; and even an actor who was playing the dual role of Jekyll and Hyde in the stage version of Robert Louis Stevenson's book, which was being performed that fall at the Lyceum Theatre.

But there was a very different suspect many feared was Jack the Ripper thousands of miles away in Austin – the Servant Girl Annihilator. The *Daily Statesman* was busy printing stories suggesting that Scotland Yard was looking for the wrong man. The murders in Whitechapel were almost certainly the work of Austin's killer, who had also once committed two murders in the span of an hour.

"The peculiar mutilation of the bodies, the silence in which they are slain – no outcry – the impenetrable mystery that envelopes the assassin – all tend to make a case almost entirely similar to the series of Austin women murders," a reporter for the *Daily Statesman* wrote.

Using headlines like "IS THE LONDON MONSTER FROM TEXAS?" other American papers began speculating about the connection between London and Austin. The *New York World* – which had published dozens of stories about the murders in Austin –

concluded, "It is by no means impossible that the perpetrator of the Austin murders and the Whitechapel fiend are one and the same – a man gratified at the gush of blood, the warm quiver of flesh and the crunch of cold steel into the bones."

The *Atlanta Constitution*, the leading newspaper in the South, also argued that it was perfectly logical that the "Man from Texas" could have moved to London. An editor explained, "The fact that he is no longer at work in Texas argues his presence somewhere else. His peculiar line of work was executed precisely in the same manner as is now going on in London. Why should he not be there? In these days of steam and cheap travel, distance is nothing. The man who would kill a dozen women in Texas would not mind the inconvenience of a trip across the water, and once there he would not have any scruples about killing more women."

In the excitement, reporters and editors were skipping over the fact that there were considerable differences between the Austin and Whitechapel attacks. The victims in Texas had been attacked with knives, but the killer had also used bricks, iron rods, and, usually, an ax. Only a knife was used on the women in Whitechapel. Of course, this might be explained by axes being common tools in Austin – every home had at least one – but was not as common in London. In most cases, the Austin killer had used an ax that belonged to the owners of the property where he committed his assault. It was a weapon of convenience that didn't exist in the slums of London.

There was another similarity that writers didn't pick up on at the time, but it is more obvious today. The killer in Austin – except in two cases -- and the killer in London chose their victims from the lowest levels of society. In Austin, the killer chose African American servant girls, and in London, the killer's victims were prostitutes and homeless women.

But there were more differences between the killings than there were similarities. The Austin victims were bludgeoned to death with what seemed to be great anger. The London victims were literally sliced into pieces, and their organs were moved, strewn about, and even carried away.

And there were certainly no letters written by anyone in Austin taking credit for the murders or hinting that there would be more attacks to come.

But the timing of the attacks – coming so soon after the Texas attacks had ended – was too good for reporters to pass up. It was just too sensational, especially since the London police seemed to be bumbling around with no real idea about how to catch the killer. It wasn't long before newspapers in England joined in the frenzy. "A TEXAS PARALELL!" one headline read. The *London Daily News*, which was circulated all over the country, trumpeted, "THE MONSTER HAS QUITTED TEXAS AND COME TO LONDON!"

Likely because they didn't want to consider the idea that one of their own was dismembering women with such relish, many Englishmen eagerly embraced the idea that an uncivilized American was committing the Whitechapel murders – someone who had been raised surrounded by what one London writer described as "more pernicious cultural influences." As one letter writer to London's *Daily Telegraph* put it, it was easy to imagine that this American was "a Texas rough."

And surely, other letter writers declared, a proper Englishman would never have written the "Dear Boss" letter. The letter's crude grammar "most certainly suggested an American background."

Even Scotland Yard detectives were intrigued by the Texas theory – so much so that they decided to hunt down "three persons calling themselves cowboys" who had come to England the previous year as members of Buffalo Bill Cody's Wild West Show.

Cody had been asked to bring his show to England to perform at the American Exposition, a trade fair designed to promote the latest industrial, mechanical, and agricultural advancements from the United States. Cody and his entire cast – 209 people in all, including the famous female sharpshooter Annie Oakley and 90 "real Indians" – had sailed from New York on a steamship with 180 horses, 18 buffalo, ten elk, five Texas steers, four donkeys, and two deer.

In the 1880s, there were likely a half-dozen Wild West shows performing across America's eastern states and the Midwest, but no show was greater than that of Buffalo Bill Cody.

William F. Cody was born in Le Claire, Iowa Territory, in 1846. After a few years in Canada, his family returned to the Midwest and settled in the Kansas Territory. He started working at the age of 11 – after his father died – and became a rider for the Pony Express when he was 15. During the Civil War, he served in the

Union Army and then as a civilian scout for the U.S. Army during the Indiana Wars.

After leaving the army behind, he began appearing on the stage, and he founded his "Wild West" production in Omaha, Nebraska, in 1883. That show – in one form or another – ran for the next three decades, thrilling crowds across the United States and Europe. The show itself consisted of a series of historical reenactments mixed with feats of showmanship, sharpshooting, staged races, sideshows, and rodeo-style events.

William "Buffalo Bill" Cody

Essentially, it presented the "dime novel" version of the Wild West to crowds who'd never seen the real thing. They'd only read about cowboys, outlaws, wild Indians, buffalo stampedes, and shootouts in books and newspapers. Buffalo Bill brought all that to life for them.

Over the years, the troupe – which often included as many as 1,200 performers -- included many authentic personalities such as James Butler "Wild Bill" Hickok, Texas Jack Omohundro, Annie Oakley, prominent Native Americans, including Sitting Bull and Geronimo, as well as "real" cowboys recruited from the West.

Native Americans figured prominently in many of the reenactments and offered many of them a way to escape from the drudgery and starvation conditions of their reservations. In return, they played characters that attacked settlers and wagon trains as Buffalo Bill or one of the other actors rode in and saved the day.

The show also reenacted the riders of the Pony Express, stagecoach robberies, and buffalo hunting. Most productions ended with a melodramatic re-enactment of Custer's Last Stand, in which Cody himself portrayed the unlucky General Custer.

By the late nineteenth century, Cody was probably the most famous American in the world. No one symbolized the West for

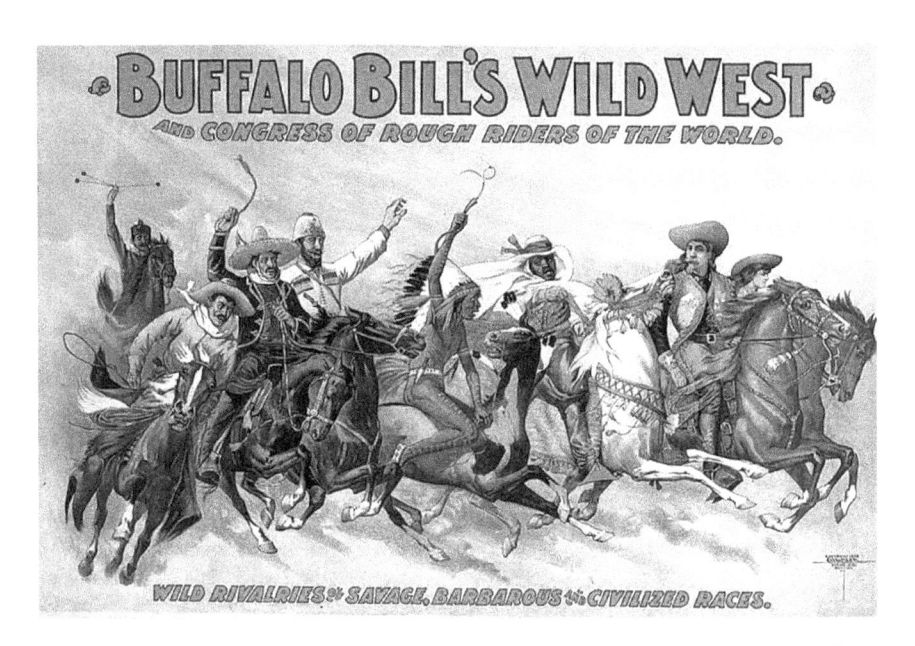

Americans and Europeans better than Buffalo Bill, and his shows were billed as entertainment triumphs for all ages.

On May 9, 1887, Buffalo Bill's Wild West show opened in London, giving international audiences their first glimpse of the American Wild West. At Earl's Court in the middle of London, the show played to standing-room-only crowds with as many as 30,000 people at every performance.

Buffalo Bill's Wild West Show performing in London, drawing as many as 30,000 people for each show, including Queen Victoria.

The show was so popular that even Queen Victoria attended. It was reportedly the first time since her husband's death a quarter century earlier that she had appeared in person at a public event.

All of Buffalo Bill's "performers" were real-life cowboys, known for their rough-and-tumble behavior and encounters with the London police.

The queen was so impressed that she returned to watch a second show on the eve of her Golden Jubilee festivities, this time with an assortment of Europe's kings, princes, and princesses, all in London for the celebration. At one point, the Prince of Wales and the kings of Denmark, Greece, Belgium, and Saxony were invited to climb aboard the "Deadwood Stagecoach" and ride around the arena with Buffalo Bill himself holding the reins.

However, during their time in London, many of Cody's men – who really were rough-and-tumble cowboys – developed reputations because of their rowdy behavior. One cowboy, Jack Ross, was charged with purposely breaking a window in a pub. Another, Richard Johnson, who was billed as the "Giant Cowboy" in the show, was charged with assault at another pub after he got into a fight with two constables, one of whom ended up in the hospital.

Buffalo Bill, at his most charming, managed to get both men out of trouble, and they were allowed to rejoin the show, which performed in other English cities before returning to the United States in May 1888.

But for unknown reasons, three other men who were or pretended to be cowboys stayed behind in England. Perhaps, police detectives surmised, one of them was not just rowdy but was an utterly deranged "Wild West killer."

And maybe he'd come from Austin, Texas.

The detectives found the three men, subjected them to lengthy interrogations, and eventually released them after they had established alibis for themselves.

But the detectives did learn something from the men that was interesting – apparently, four Lakota Indians from the show had been inadvertently left behind in London and were still loose on the streets.

One of them was Black Elk, who fought at Little Big Horn as a teenager and now performed as a chief in Buffalo Bill's show. The London police were curious to discover if Black Elk had grown so angry about being left behind in England that he'd allowed his "savage side" to take over and commit the gruesome murders.

Black Elk (Right) and another Lakota man in a photograph that was taken in a London studio.

When Black Elk and his fellow Lakota were tracked down, they were also about to account for their whereabouts on the dates of the Whitechapel murders. As an act of generosity, the British government made sure that the four Lakota were about to connect with another Western show traveling through Europe, this one run by a promoter named Mexican Joe. He was happy to hire the men until they earned enough money to pay their way back to America.

By then, I'm sure they were ready to be as far away from the "civilized" white world as they could get.

AFTER EXHAUSTING THE "TEXAS" LEADS OF rowdy cowboys and savage Indians, the London detectives assumed they'd hit a dead end – but they hadn't.

One afternoon, a detective spoke with an English sailor named Dodge, who said he'd been recently drinking in a pub called the

Queen's Music Hall. There, he'd met a man that he described as "about five feet, seven inches in height, 130 pounds in weight, and apparently 35 years of age." The man was a native of Malaysia.

According to Dodge, the man told him he'd been working as a cook on steamers that came in and out of English ports and that he recently "had been robbed by a woman of bad character in Whitechapel." The man then told him that "unless he found the woman and recovered his money, he would murder and mutilate every Whitechapel woman he met."

The story was reported in the London newspapers and went out to America on wire services. A reporter from the *Daily Statesman* – anxiously waiting for other news from England that could be tied to the Austin murders – ripped the story from the telegraph machine and started reading.

A Malaysian cook in London?

Hadn't there been a Malaysian cook in Austin during the murders?

He was quickly reminded of Maurice, who'd been employed at the Pearl House. After the Christmas Eve murders, he suddenly decided to leave town. The last thing anyone had heard, he was on his way to Galveston, hoping to get hired onto a steamer to take him to England.

In the next day's edition of the *Statesman*, there was a long article that appeared under the headline that read:

"A WONDERFUL COINCIDENT – BLOODY LINKS CONNECTING WHITECHAPEL WITH THE AUSTIN ASSASSINATIONS. A STRANGE STORY GRAPHICALLY TOLD OF CRIMES WITH A MALAY COOK AS THE CENTRAL FIGURE."

The article reminded readers that nothing was known about Maurice's past and that during his time in Austin, he "had rarely been seen about town." It mentioned that "three of the most bloody and cruel Austin murders" – those of Eliza Shelley, Mary Ramey, and Susan Hancock – had occurred "three or four blocks away" from the boardinghouse where "this Malay is said to have slept." For a few weeks, Maurice had been "kept under detective's eyes, hoping that something definite would be found to warrant his arrest." Yet, he had done nothing suspicious until he left Austin during an "unguarded moment."

An editorial accompanying the article stated that it wasn't just a coincidence. It was a "strong possibility" that the Malay cook from the Pearl House and the London Malay cook were "one and the same." The editor also speculated that this "inhuman wretch, wandering demon and bloody fiend" could very well be a member of "the secret order of thugs, in the East, who worshipped Bhavani, the goddess of crime, whose business and occupation is murder, with the cord and the silent knife."

Sound far-fetched? Definitely. There is no indication of where the editor came up with this idea or what evidence he could have possibly had to justify putting this speculation into print. It was completely fabricated and sensational, but sensationalism always sells newspapers.

Wildly racist newspaper stories claimed that Malaysian men like Maurice were savage killers, implying that he could have easily been the Whitechapel killer – and the Servant Girl Annihilator.

The insane articles from the *Daily Statesman* were quickly picked up by the wire services and cable across the Atlantic to London, where the newspapers there compounded the story with their own articles, as well as letters from readers who concluded it made perfect sense that a Malaysian was behind both the Austin and Whitechapel murders.

The racism was, of course, not confined just to the *Daily Statesman*. Articles written by London reporters stated that Malay men were bred to commit vicious killings, with one actually concluding that the mutilations of the women in Whitechapel were all done according to "peculiarly Eastern methods" designed "to express insult, hatred, and contempt."

Sir Charles Warren, chief of the Metropolitan Police, was swept up in the excitement of the story and ordered his men to "search everywhere" for the Malaysian cook, but he was nowhere to be found – if he was ever there at all. No one had been able to confirm Dodge's story, and no other witness ever came forward –

despite all the publicity – to say they'd ever met a Malay man who told a story about murdering prostitutes.

Eventually, police officials were forced to acknowledge that Dodge, the constable, or some enterprising reporter had likely invented the whole thing.

Whoever the Whitechapel killer was, his identity was just as great of a mystery as the man who'd murdered those women in Austin.

AND THEN, ON NOVEMBER 9, 1888, JACK THE RIPPER struck again.

Of all the Ripper's victims, his fifth and likely last, Mary Jane Kelly, remains the most mysterious. Her death made her famous, but her backstory is mostly unknown.

The photograph of Mary Jane's corpse on her bed, with almost everything about her that made her human entirely gone, is the last reminder of the Ripper's killings. In a break from his previous habits, the Ripper went inside to kill, and he apparently took the time to satisfy his murderous lusts because he knew he wouldn't be interrupted.

Mary had been living in a squalid room at 13 Millers Court with Joseph Barnett, a fishmonger with whom she had a relationship. But Joseph had moved out a few weeks earlier after learning that Mary had returned to prostitution to make money.

Living upstairs from Mary's flat, Elizabeth Prater heard a cry of murder at about 4:00 AM on November 9, but she did nothing about it. Mary's lifeless, mutilated body was discovered seven hours later.

Mary's face had been hacked beyond all recognition. Her throat had been severed down to the spine, and her abdomen was emptied of all its organs. Her uterus, kidneys, and one breast had

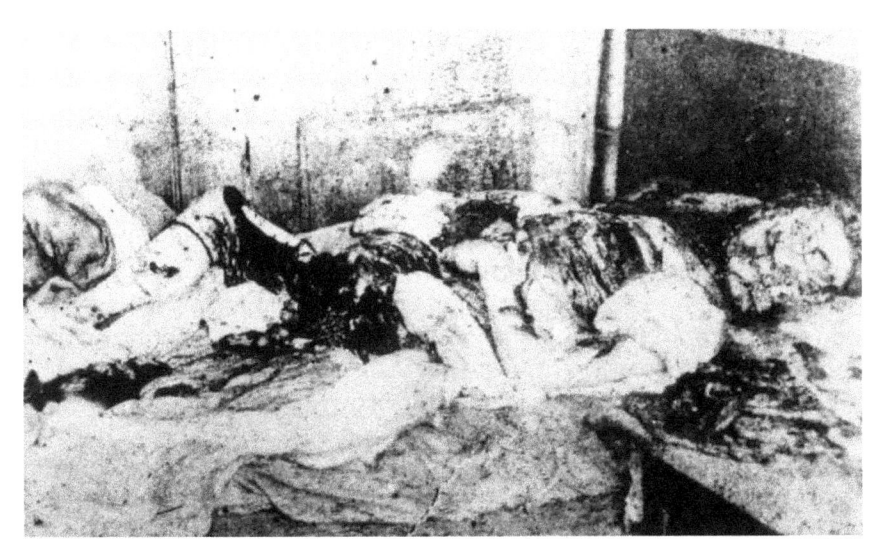

The gruesome crime scene photograph of Mary Jane Kelly.

been placed beneath her head, and the other viscera from her body had been placed at her feet. Sections of her abdomen and thighs were on a table next to the bed. The killer had removed her heart and had taken it with him when he left the scene.

One police inspector who later reviewed the case concluded that the gore-soaked scene at Miller Court had finally broken the mind of the killer. Perhaps it did. It is certainly true to say that nothing that remotely resembled this murder happened in the weeks, months, or even years that followed.

It seems to have been Jack the Ripper's last hurrah, which meant that any clue to his identity died with Mary Kelly -- but that hasn't stopped anyone from trying to figure out who he was.

MOST CRIME HISTORIANS BELIEVE THAT ALL FIVE murders described here were the work of a single killer. There were other murders – possibly as many as six more – that occurred in Whitechapel around this time, but most don't feel that can be strongly connected to "The Five."

Others argue that the idea of five victims is a myth and that only three of the murders – Nichols, Chapman, and Eddowes – were committed by the same man. And still others say there was no "Jack the Ripper" at all, but a group of unrelated murders that were all blamed on one man – a shadowy figure that was conveniently never caught.

Even so, the search for Jack the Ripper – the lone, crazed killer–has become a cottage industry in the century and a third since the murders occurred. There have been a lot of theories about his identity over the years.

Some claim he was a Whitechapel undertaker named Robert Mann, who examined the bodies after they had been found.

Sir Melville McNaughten, the Assistant Commissioner of the London Metropolitan Police, claimed to know the identity of the Ripper. He named Montague John Druitt, a country doctor's son and young barrister who inexplicably drowned himself in the River Thames in early December 1888, as the killer.

Another leading suspect was an artist named Walter Sickert. He took a keen interest in the crimes and told friends he believed he'd lodged in a room used by the killer because his landlady suspected a previous lodger of the killings. Even though his name has repeatedly come up, evidence shows that he spent most of the fall of 1888 outside England.

Some have also accused Prince Albert Victor, the Duke of Clarence and grandson of Queen Victoria, of being the Ripper. He allegedly had a child with a woman who lived in Whitechapel. The belief is that the Royal family and the government tried to remove any evidence of the child by killing it and anyone who knew about it.

Prince Albert Victor, the Duke of Clarence, is at the top of the Jack the Ripper suspect list for many researchers.

And there were butchers, doctors, and madmen also accused of the crimes. The theories just seem to have gotten wilder as the years have passed. There's even one outlandish claim that novelist Lewis Carroll – who wrote *Alice in Wonderland* -- was the killer because he made anagrams of Jack the Ripper in his books.

There have been American suspects, too, like H.H. Holmes, the famous American serial killer who would make a name for himself in the 1890s because of a so-called "Murder Castle" that he devised in Chicago around the time of the 1893 World's Columbian Exposition. Legend has it that he dispatched many of his victims at the "Castle" when the place was used as a hotel during the World's Fair. Holmes would eventually be arrested, tried, and executed for the murder of his criminal accomplice, Benjamin Pitezel. Before he was caught, he also killed three of Pitezel's children, as well as many of his lovers – possibly as many as 37 people in all.

The claims that Holmes might have been Jack the Ripper originated more recently, but documents exist that place Holmes in Chicago in the fall of 1888 – not in London.

Another American suspect was Dr. Francis J. Tumblety. Suspicion by police officials that he might have been Jack the Ripper emerged in 1913. Interest in the killings was still high, and cold case detectives were still looking for suspects.

Tumblety's name came up because he hated women, had medical skills, and was arrested around the time of the murders. He skipped bail and fled England -- and the murders came to an end.

But there are flaws with his theory, too – maybe. On November 7 – two days before Mary Ann Kelly's murder – Francis was arrested. We know he was released on bail, but we don't know when. Some say it was November 16, well after the murder, but others claim it was November 8. Thousands of police records were destroyed in the London Blitz during World War II, including these.

Dr. Francis J. Tumblety

Whatever the date, he skipped bail and returned to the United States. In the following years, Francis continued moving around the country, living in hotels, and leaving little record of himself behind. He finally landed in one place in St. Louis in April 1903, where he checked himself into St. John's Hospital and Dispensary, where he died on May 28, 1903.

EDWARD CHARLES SPITZKA, M.D.
PHYSICIAN AND BIOLOGIST
ALIENIST, WRITER ON MENTAL AND SPINAL DISEASES

Dr. Charles Edward Spitzka – America's most famous alienist.

And then, of course, is the theory that Jack the Ripper and the Servant Girl Annihilator were one and the same. Even after the London police dismissed the story of the Malaysian cook, the idea of the connection between the two cities continued to intrigue people, even those considered in the top tier of academia at the time.

In December 1888, about a month after Mary Jane Kelly was killed, Dr. Charles Edward Spitzka – America's most famous alienist – arrived at the Academy of Medicine on West 43rd Street in New York for the monthly meeting of the New York Society of Medical Jurisprudence, a society made up of the city's most esteemed doctors and lawyers. Although the group's meetings were usually about technical issues regarding medical testimony at criminal and civil trials, on that night, Dr. Spitzka was presenting a speech that laid out his theories about Jack the Ripper.

Spitzka, described by a colleague as a "brilliant doctor and a man of intellectual heft," had been raised in New York City. He had completed his schooling overseas at the medical schools at the University of Leipzig and the University of Vienna, specializing in the field of "alienism," as psychiatry was called at the time. The term came from the belief that some people's minds had become "alienated" from reality. When he returned to New York, he joined the city's Post-Graduate Medical School as a professor of nervous and mental diseases.

In 1881, he had been asked to conduct a lengthy examination of Charles Guiteau, the assassin who had shot President James Garfield. At trial, Dr. Spitzka made national headlines when he stated that Guiteau was a "moral monstrosity" who had been driven to kill for reasons beyond his mental control.

In 1883, Dr. Spitzka wrote a textbook called *Insanity: Its Classification, Diagnosis, and Treatment*, which became the standard for psychiatric writings in the era before Freud. In articles that he's written for medical journals like *Alienist and Neurologist* and the *American Journal of Insanity*, he had written that it was a mistake to believe that the criminally insane were "idiots" or "depraved half-human beasts." Even in their delusions, they possessed what Spitzka described as cunning and a "reasoning mania."

That evening at the Academy of Medicine, Dr. Spitzka started his lecture with some general comments about other mass murderers in history. He mentioned the Roman emperor Tiberius, who allegedly killed children and kept their heads for relics, and the story of "Bluebeard," who supposedly murdered his many wives/ He told the story of the Marquis de Sade, who tortured women in the 1700s, and summarized the cases of men who found a "voluptuous exaltation" when they committed murder – including a French man named Louis Menesclou who, in 1880, enticed a young girl with flowers before cutting her into pieces.

He then turned his presentation to Jack the Ripper, expounding on his behavior and describing how he would slaughter a woman without being seen, slip away, and then emerge a short time later to kill again. He told his audience that the Ripper's murders were so expertly committed that he had to have perfected his technique somewhere else before coming to Whitechapel.

And that very place, Dr. Spitzka said, had to be in Austin, Texas, which had experienced murders that were "terribly similar in every detail" to the Whitechapel murders, in which the victims were "so mutilated that they fell apart on being lifted up."

There was silence in the lecture hall as he continued, "I would suggest that the same hand that committed the Whitechapel murders committed the Texas murders." He went on to describe the killer as having "Herculean strength, great bodily agility, a brutal jaw, a strange, weird expression of the eye – a man who has contracted no healthy friendships, who is in his own heart isolated from the rest of the world as the rest of mankind is repelled by him."

Dr. Spitzka then gravely added that the most disturbing thing about the man was that there was no telling where this Texas killer was today. The alienist speculated that he may have already "discontinued his work" in London or moved on to another city to create his "bewildering horror."

"Perhaps," Dr. Spitzka said, "he has returned to the United States and is even right here in New York City. In fact, he could be sitting among us at this moment, just so he could hear the speech being made about him."

There was a lingering silence after Dr. Spitzka's final words and then the sound of shuffling as men stirred uncomfortably in their seats. A few of those in the hall broke out into quiet, nervous laughter, but Dr. Spitza wasn't laughing. He didn't even break a courteous smile.

Instead, he peered out into the audience, watching those who stared up at him, wondering if he might catch a glimpse of an unfamiliar face that might be that of a killer.

TWO MONTHS LATER, IN FEBRUARY 1889, the *New York Sun* printed a startling story from Managua, the capital city of Nicaragua. According to this story, the bodies of six women had been found in the city over a period of 10 days.

A reporter for the *Sun* wrote:

Like the women of Whitechapel, they were women who had sunk to the lowest degradations of their calling. They have been found murdered just as mysteriously, and the evidence points to almost identical methods. Two were found butchered out of all recognition. Even the faces were most horribly slashed, and in the cases of all the others, their persons were frightfully disfigured. There is no doubt that a sharp instrument, violently but dexterously used, was the weapon that sent the poor creatures out of the world.

The wire services picked up the story and reprinted it in newspapers everywhere. Reporters speculated that, as Dr. Spitzka had predicted, the killer was on the move.

In Austin, under the headline "IS IT THE FOUL FIEND HIMSELF?" a reporter for the Daily *Statesman* wrote, "From the surrounding circumstances, does it not seem possible that one and the same person – some wandering, bloody demon, who, after finishing his dreadful tasks, seems to vanish with supernatural skill – may be the author of the Austin homicides, the Whitechapel butcheries, and the Central American assassinations?"

It all seemed very exciting to crime buffs to think that the killer was wandering the globe, committing murders in various cities until the entire story was exposed as a hoax. The police in Nicaragua hadn't issued any report about prostitutes being killed in Managua. The editors at the *Sun* had made up the entire thing to try and sell more papers.

This was not the first time they'd done something like this either. They just knew that any scoop involving Jack the Ripper would give them huge newsstand sales – even if it were only for a day or two.

REGARDLESS OF THE HOAX, DR. SPITZKA didn't stop pushing his theory about the traveling killer. He published a paper for the Journal of Mental and Nervous Disease that reiterated the points he'd made during his speech in New York, claiming the killer had used Austin as his training ground, honing his skills until he was ready to travel to London, a much larger city, and become Jack the Ripper. He added more details in the article about the killer, describing him as a man driven by either "singular antipathies" or "romantic notions of revenge."

Other alienists, though, found Dr. Spitzka's theories difficult to believe. For one thing, the man's travel itinerary – Texas straight to England – didn't make sense. If he was obsessed with slaughtering women, wouldn't he have stopped somewhere in between Texas and England for some other murders? After committing seven murders in Austin in 1884 and 1885 – followed by the murder in San Antonio a month later and then the Gainesville attacks in July 1887 – would the killer have stayed hidden for a year before showing up again in Whitechapel in August 1888?

Would it make more sense, one of Dr. Spitzka's critics asked, if a disturbed man in London read about the Austin murders and then became inspired to carry out even more gruesome killings in Whitechapel? That seemed a more likely scenario than the same killer traveling a few thousand miles to kill women when he could have just killed more of them at home.

It was a question worth asking, but no one in Texas wanted to think about that. If this was true, then it seemed likely that the killer was still in Austin.

22. MIDNIGHT IN AUSTIN

IT WAS A QUESTION THAT HAUNTED THE RESIDENTS of Austin – what if the killer was still there? If he was, though, where was he, and what had happened to him?

More than three years had passed since an Austin woman had been attacked or murdered. Marshal Lucy was no longer conducting an official investigation into any of the murders because all the leads had dried up. There were no tips, telephone calls, or anonymous letters – there weren't even any rumors. There was nothing more the police could do.

District Attorney Robertson had given up trying to prosecute anyone for the murders. He didn't bother to re-try Moses Hancock or Jimmy Phillips and decided to stop pushing the grand jury for new indictments.

Many asked why Robertson backed off from taking anyone to trial. Had he known all along he didn't have the evidence needed to obtain a conviction? Roberton wouldn't say. It appeared that he'd decided to forget the murders had ever happened. And since they'd stopped, why stir things up again? Besides that, he was hoping to be appointed to the office of state district judge, and the last thing he needed was to have a rival remind people that he'd botched the prosecutions of the Austin murders.

There were a few people around town – mostly men in saloons, barber shops, and billiard halls – who continued to swap theories about the murders. Many still believed there had never been a "Servant Girl Annihilator." They were still convinced the murders had been committed by those uneducated "bad blacks" or that black men in town had been struck by a "killing mania" that made them act out.

The *Daily Statesman* – always happy to stoke the racist fires and print batshit crazy theories – ran a long interview with a detective from Memphis who visited Austin. He said that he'd been studying the murders and concluded that both lower-class black criminals and maybe a few well-regarded white men had been affected by some "mystical suggestion" that caused them to murder their wives and girlfriends.

AT LEAST SOME OF AUSTIN'S RESIDENTS HAD to have been relieved to know that only a few of the men who'd been suspects in the murders were still living in town by 1889.

Walter Spencer, Mollie Smith's boyfriend, was still living at his mother's home, working at the brickyard, and minding his business.

Anastazio Martinez, the mentally unbalanced Mexican dump picker, was still at the State Lunatic Asylum. According to reports, he spent his days quietly cultivating the flowers on the asylum's front lawn.

Oliver Townsend, the infamous but legendary chicken thief, had been sent away to the state prison to serve ten years for what appeared to be a trumped-up burglary charge. I guess they finally got him for something after all.

Not wanting to end up where Oliver and some of the other black suspects in the case did, Dock Woods packed up and left Austin for good.

THE WHITE SUSPECTS WERE GONE, TOO. Moses Hancock had closed his carpentry business, sold his home on Water Street, and moved to Waco. At least there, he didn't have to listen to whispers about how he'd gotten away with murder or have people stare at him on the street.

Jimmy Phillips and his son, Tom, moved to Georgetown, 40 miles north, where he'd gotten a job at a chair factory. He rarely talked about what happened on Christmas Eve 1885, except to sometimes complain about the recurring headaches from his head wound. He later married a young woman who lived across the street, raised four more children, taught them to play musical instruments, and started the Phillips Family Band, which performed at local events.

William Swain eventually moved to Houston. After his loss in the 1886 gubernatorial election, he had never been able to build a successful law practice in Austin. He'd also never been able to make people forget about the rumors that he had been Eula Phillips' lover – or that he might have been involved in her murder.

In 1888, a young woman named Maria Dowd rented a floor of a home owned by Swain's son, Walter. She got behind on her rent, became involved in a dispute over her lease with Walter, and was evicted. Before she left, she confronted Walter and snapped at him, "Your whole family is as low as can be. Your father was a midnight murderer, and you are no better!"

That was the last straw for William Swain, and once he left for Houston, he was rarely seen in Austin again.

MAE TOBIN HAD VANISHED. DESPITE THE DEAL she had made with Mayor Robertson allowing her to maintain her house off Congress Avenue in exchange for testifying at Jimmy Phillips' trial, new mayor Joseph Nalle ordered Marshal Lucy to escort the woman out of town.

Not long after, her house had mysteriously burned to the ground. A *Daily Statesman* reporter wrote:

When the last flames were extinguished and the smoking remains were examined, it was plain to be seem that no more scandals would be hatched within its walls; no more victims to murder would be selected from those who frequented its confines; and all that would be left of it was a charred and blackened mass of weatherboarding, odiferous carpets, and ruined second-hand furniture.

Mayor Nalle seemed determined to do everything he could to erase all memories of the murders. He proved himself to be a worthy successor to Mayor Robertson when it came to peddling nonsense to Austin residents. He declared in one speech, "Crimes of a serious nature are almost totally unknown in our midst. A sense of security dwells among the humblest as well as the highest, and a general observance of the law among all classes is a conspicuous virtue that is not passed unnoticed by those who come among us."

AND YET THE MEMORIES – AND THE FEARS THAT went along with them – never really went away. People were still buying electric burglar alarms, door locks, sleeping potions, and tonics for their nerves. At night, before they went to sleep, men placed rifles and pistols next to their beds.

One story was told about a widow, Mrs. Delores Johnson, who was described as one of the city's "kindest and most charitable ladies," always kept a pistol under her pillow. She and her late husband, Dr. Lucian Johnson, had been the employers of Eliza Shelley, who had been murdered in her quarters behind the Johnsons' home in May 1885. Mrs. Johnson had been horrified by that night and was determined that nothing like it would ever happen again. For that reason, she always kept that handgun close by.

But in July 1889, while Mrs. Johnson was changing the sheets on the bed, the pistol fell onto the floor, discharged, and sent a bullet into her abdomen, killing her on the spot.

The news devastated the people of Austin. By that one cruel twist of fate, Mrs. Delores Johnson had become the final victim of the Servant Girl Annihilator.

THE EFFORTS TO ERASE AUSTIN'S PAST CONTINUED as 1889 wore on. Throughout the year, Alexander P. Woolridge – City National Bank president and the man who'd led the vigilante committee that formed after the Christmas Eve murders – had been meeting with Austin's Board of Trade to discuss an idea that he believed could restore the city's reputation and be thought of once again as one of America's great cities. He encouraged the board – the precursor to the Chamber of Commerce – to invest in building a dam on the Colorado River, upstream from Austin, and send the runoff water through an adjoining power station to create low-cost electricity for the city.

Woolridge had devised the idea of the dam a year earlier, originally stating that farmers could use the runoff water to irrigate their land and grow more crops. But board members tabled the idea and instead wanted to promote Austin's temperate climate and its religious and social institutions. It was boring, but they wanted to erase the stain left by murders and scandals.

A year later, though, the banker had a much better idea with a power station that might encourage the owners of factories and manufacturing plants to move to Austin and take advantage of low-cost electricity. And there would be enough left to power homes and electric streetcars and allow the city to install as many streetlights as it wanted.

Mayor Nalle opposed the plan. He said that building a dam would cost at least $1.4 million, putting the city into a "ruinous" financial situation. Besides that, who knew how much the power station would cost?

But to the mayor's surprise, the Board of Trade was thrilled with Woolridge's idea – and so were Austin residents. During the December 1899 elections, they voted Nalle out of office and replaced him with John McDonald, a building contractor and supporter of the dam project. A new set of aldermen – also backers of the dam – won their elections, too. They quickly agreed to hold a bond vote to raise the money to build the dam and power station.

However, that vote wouldn't take place for another year, on May 6, 1890. Regardless, public support hadn't wavered. The bond package passed by an overwhelming margin, and hundreds of people turned out on Congress Avenue to celebrate. A reporter for the *Daily Statesman* described the scene: "A band played, and rockets were sent high up into the heavens. Great crackers fired and Roman candles and colored lights illuminated the whole city." The writer also noted that among those on the street that night were "scores of ladies, all in high feather and rejoicing with exceeding joy."

Were they there to celebrate the building of the dam?

Or were they celebrating the new electric streetlights that would finally be installed and allow them to finally walk the streets at night without fear for the first time in five years? Did they believe the Servant Girl Annihilator would no longer want to live in a city without dark streets?

The newspaper story didn't answer those questions. It didn't, of course, mention the murders at all. The story simply ended with the line, "Things are brighter and more hopeful for us than ever before in the history of Austin!"

WORK BEGAN ON THE DAM AND WENT ON FOR the next three years. Once it was finished, work began on the power station. Mayor McDonald and the aldermen met and decided to spend $153,000 on a "citywide lighting system." Instead of choosing a lower-cost plan that involved more electric streetlights on 20-foot poles -- like the ones that Mayor Nalle had installed when he first took office – McDonald and the aldermen decided to purchase arc lamps on very tall towers. With such tall towers looming over the city, there would be plenty of light, and drunks leaving the saloons on Saturday nights wouldn't be tempted to shoot out the lamps the way they had been shooting out the electric lights that lined the downtown streets.

In 1893, only one other American city – Detroit, Michigan – was still using the tall arc lamps, and officials there were getting ready to take them down and return to regular streetlights. Like other cities that had tried them, Detroit found the lights too costly to maintain. Arc lamps no longer captivated the country like they once had – except in Austin. The new lighting for the so-called "city of the future" would be behind the times as soon as it was installed.

The mayor and his staff cut a deal with Detroit to take 31 of the towers off their hands without questioning why they were getting rid of them. Made from wrought iron and cast iron, the towers resemble miniature Eiffel Towers. Each was 165 feet tall and

One of Austin's iconic "Moonlight Towers," which went up all over the city in the early 1890s.

weighed approximately 5,000 pounds. To keep them from blowing over in the wind, guy wires were connected from their triangular framework to the ground. On top of each tower was a ring of six high-powered carbon arc lamps.

Unlike other cities, which had installed the arc lamps only above their railroad depots and downtown shopping districts, officials in Austin decided they wanted them to illuminate as much of the city as possible.

On May 5, 1895, everything was finally ready. At 8:00 P.M., the switch was flipped at the power station, and the turbines started to turn, sending electricity toward Austin as engineers turned on the lights for a 90-minute test. A reporter for the *Daily Statesman* described the event: "There was a sudden blinding flash, and the town was in a blaze of white light that hid the rays of the moonlight with its brilliancy. In every nook and corner, the brilliant white lights sent their shooting rays and the whole face of creation was transcendent."

Startled, residents rushed out of their houses to stare at the white light filling the sky. It was so powerful – shooting out from each tower in every direction for more than 3,000 feet – that people could read the time on their watches and recognize the faces of neighbors three and four houses away.

The *Statesman* reporter went on to say, "From every section of the city, loud shouts of joy were heard. All up and down the

Avenue, gentlemen were sauntering along, meeting, shaking hands, and congratulating one another on the successful outcome of their long-cherished scheme."

The newspaper was quick to point out how excited everyone was to have the new lights but, once again, didn't connect the arc lamps to the murders. The only hint at the real reason for the lights was in a line that mentioned Austin's residents had spent years "groping around in that darkness that threatened the life and safety of all." They had walked streets "steeped in utter darkness," but now they had "every cause for rejoicing" because the fear of the night was gone forever.

Or at least everyone hoped that was the case.

THE PEOPLE OF AUSTIN HAD BEEN CHEERING when the lights were turned on for the test, but can you imagine living anywhere near one of the towers? With its lights blazing into your windows all night long?

In May 1895, that seemed a problem for another day, but people predictably began complaining about the lights in the following weeks. They couldn't sleep. They hated the buzzing sound that the lights made. They were bothered by the ash from the carbon that drifted down and gathered on things. Those with gardens worried the constant light would cause their corn and bean stalks to grow around the clock. The owners of chicken coops feared their hens would lay eggs around the clock until they dropped dead from exhaustion.

And the drunks that stumbled out of bars at night? The height of the towers didn't deter them. They continued to fire their pistols at the lights, whooping with delight.

But the complaints fell on deaf ears at the Board of Trade. They were so excited about the lights that they decided to change Austin's official nickname from "City of the Violet Crown" – in honor of its stunning sunsets – to "The City of Eternal Moonlight."

They published a pamphlet encouraging all Texans to move to Austin to enjoy the benefits of "the greatest illumination of electric light" ever seen in the state. Real estate developers got in on the act, building new homes under the "moonlight towers," telling potential buyers they'd never have to worry about crime.

Or getting a good night's sleep, I would have added.

One developer, Monroe Martin Snipes, told customers that the upper-class neighborhood he built in north Austin, dubbed Hyde Park, was the finest in the country. It not only had a moonlight tower, he said, but also "the coolest weather in Austin, the best streets, and absolutely no dust, mud, tenants, liquor, of Negroes."

IN 1898, THREE YEARS AFTER THE MOONLIGHT towers were installed, Marshal Lucy retired, saying his work was done. He took a job as a vice president of the American Surety Company. He passed away in 1927.

The new marshal, Robert Thorp, asked for Sergeant Chenneville's resignation, saying it was time for him to rest and relax. The old methods of police work were over, and fresh new ideas needed to take their place. But Chenneville wasn't completely giving up on law enforcement – it was all he knew. He went to work for a private detective agency in Austin called the Merchant Police and Southern Detective Agency and hung onto his bloodhounds in case they were ever needed again.

Chenneville died in 1904 after having served under five different police chiefs. When he passed away, his funeral was held at the Washington Fire Company No. 1 station.

Even after the two men left the police department, neither Lucy nor Chenneville spoke to the newspapers about the bloody events of 1884 and 1885. They never offered their opinions about the attacks and whether they believed they had been committed by one man or several. They never speculated – at least not publicly – about the existence of the Servant Girl Annihilator.

And they weren't the only ones who never talked. After he left office, Mayor Robertson never spoke about the attacks either. His brother, James, who did become a state circuit judge, also said nothing. Dr. Denton also never addressed the rumors that one of his patients had been leaving the State Lunatic Asylum at night to commit murder.

In addition, Denton never again spoke about this son-in-law, Dr. Given, the asylum's former assistant superintendent, who had been legally declared insane six weeks after the Christmas Eve murders. After being sent to the other asylum in the North Texas town of Terrell, he had died from what officials there described only as "paralysis." Had it been syphilis that had made its way to his brain? Dr. Denton never said, and by the time the moonlight towers were built, he had left the state asylum to open the Austin Sanitarium for Nervous and Mental Disease. This small private hospital catered mostly to wealthy women who suffered from things like headaches and hysteria.

They weren't the only ones who wanted to lock away the memories of the murders and never speak about them again. At least a half-dozen histories of Texas were written between 1885 and 1895, and not one of them referenced the murders that paralyzed the city for more than a year.

Historian Hubert Howe Bancroft – who'd sent his researcher J.W. Olds to Austin in August 1885 during the height of the murders – decided they weren't significant enough to fit into his 841-page book, *History of the Northern States and Texas: 1531-1889*.

Well-known Texas newspaperman John Henry Brown, who published the two-volume History of Texas from 1685 to 1892, also ignored the murders.

And I think we can safely understand why Mrs. Anna Pennybacker, a proper schoolteacher who wrote a textbook for the state's public schools in 1888 called *A New History of Texas*, didn't include the murders. I'm willing to bet that she didn't think it was proper for schoolchildren to read about women being slaughtered with axes, knives, bricks, and iron rods.

Even the young writer William Sydney Porter, who gave us the name "Servant Girl Annihilator," never returned to the subject. In 1894, when he started a humor magazine in Austin called *Rolling Stone*, he never mentioned the murders – probably because they weren't funny, so no surprise there. But even after he moved to New York City – after serving a three-year prison stint for embezzling money from an Austin bank where he worked briefly as a teller – he steered clear of the murders. In New York, he published nearly 500 short stories as O. Henry, and while many of his characters were based on people he met in Texas or prison, no serial killer was represented. He wrote about bums, swindlers, kidnappers, and safecrackers but never used the killings as inspiration for his writing.

Probably, the people who kept the story of the murders alive the longest were the country's alienists. When they met at New York's Academy of Medicine – the place where Dr. Spitzka first espoused his theory about the traveling serial killer – they periodically discussed the issue of "moral insanity," which at the time was considered a medical condition. This physical illness afflicted those who were in almost all ways normal, except they were unable to control certain emotions. At one meeting, several alienists declared that the servant girl murders were a prime example of the damage a morally insane made could cause with his "abnormal conduct." In this case, they believed, he was unable to control his deep hatred of women.

The alienists came up with a list of things that might make seemingly normal people with "unimpaired mental facilities" become morally insane and go on a murderous rampage. Some of the doctors believed that moral insanity might occur because someone was the offspring of "intermarriage among criminals and drunkards." Others said that it might be caused by some childhood injury, like a blow to the head or something similar, which destroyed part of their mental capabilities. Other alienists argued that some people were born with "impaired or defective nervous tissue" that led them to a life of crime. Dr. Graeme M. Hamfriend, a professor of nervous and mental diseases at the New York Post-Graduate Medical School and Hospital, stated in one speech: "As the artist and musician get their power of artistic creation from some brain conformation that was born in them, so this criminal gets his life tendency in the same way."

A few alienists advocated for a theory first formulated by the German alienist Richard von Krafft-Ebing. In 1886, he published a work called *Psychopathia Sexualis*, which was the first academic study of "sexual perversion" – page after page about rapists, sadomasochists, masturbators, homosexuals, pedophiles, and fetishists. After the Jack the Ripper murders, Krafft-Ebing updated his book to include a section about men who committed "lust murders." Krafft-Ebing was convinced these men found physical pleasure in the murder of women, followed by the mutilations of their bodies. For some alienists, the Servant Girl Annihilator was the perfect example of Krafft-Ebing's "lust murderer."

At their meetings, the alienists tried to come up with ways to identify and stop a morally insane monster like the Annihilator before he committed his murders. Dr. Allan McClaine Hamilton, the attending physician at the New York Hospital for Nervous Disease and often described in the press as a "famous insanity expert," advocated for a national sterilization program that he hoped would prevent such men from being born in the first place. He proposed that the state forbid marriages between habitual criminals, consumptives, and those with mental insanity in their family history. "The least that can be said," he told a reporter, "is that society has the right to protect itself from them just as it has the right to protect itself from mad dogs."

But Hamilton and his colleagues didn't have to be told that they had little chance of protecting innocent people from men who were able to conceal their depraved personalities behind a mask of normality – as mask like the one likely worn by the Servant Girl Annihilator.

AS THE CENTURY DAWNED, THE MURDERS continued to be ignored by Texas historians. But people in Austin hadn't forgotten him, at least not entirely. Children had devised their own name for the killer – Servant Girl Annihilator was a bit much for a kid to remember – and they just called him the "Axe Man." They dared each other to stay out after dark, warning that the Axe Man might be hiding in the shadows just out of reach of the arc lamps of the moonlight towers.

But that wasn't the only spooky story that people told. Many residents swore they had seen a ghostly woman in white walking the grounds of the state capitol at night. Others claimed to see the pale young woman near the end of Congress Avenue, where Mae Tobin's house of assignation used to be. They swore it was the ghost of Eula Phillips, warning other women not to take the same road to ruin that she had taken when she was alive.

Some saw an elderly black woman hobbling along the street – but she was no ghost. She was Rebecca Ramey, the mother of Mary Ramey, who had been killed in V.O. Wee's backyard shack. By the turn of the century, Rebecca was living with another daughter, Minnie, and she'd never really recovered from the attack. Her face was disfigured, and her brain was damaged. She was never the same again.

When Rebecca Ramey died in 1910, she was the last female survivor of the attacks who still lived in Austin. No one knows what happened to Lucinda Boddy and Patsy Gibson, the two servant girls who had suffered serious head injuries in Gracie Vance's servants' quarters. No one kept track of young black women in those days, but since the two were unable to work or care for themselves, they were likely sent to the county poor farm, where many destitute and damaged people lived out the rest of their lives. Without proper medical treatment, though, it seems unlikely they lived very long. If they died at the poor farm, they were buried in two unmarked graves near the back of the property and forgotten.

For years, the memory of the murders harmed the African American population of Austin. Jim Crow laws came sooner to the city than many other Texas towns because of white residents' fear and distrust of the "bad blacks." City aldermen passed an ordinance in the early 1900s that required the separation of whites and blacks on streetcars. There was also a proposal to move all black residents to the east side forcibly. If they were all in one place, many white citizens stated, the police would have less trouble keeping track of the city's worst criminals.

African Americans in Austin had no one to stand up for them. White officials routinely ignored the city's black leaders. In truth, for many years, there were no black leaders at all. After Albert Carrington had lost the aldermen's race to a white man in 1885, it would not be until 1971 that a black man was again elected to the city council.

And people wonder why the murders of black women were mostly ignored by the authorities in Austin until two white women were murdered.

TODAY, THERE IS NOTHING LEFT OF THE PLACES where the murders occurred. By the 1930s, the homes and servants' quarters were gone, destroyed in the name of progress. They were replaced by bigger homes, office buildings, banks, restaurants, and parking lots.

More people came to town, and the city grew beyond the illumination of the moonlight towers. A couple of them were dismantled because they'd become unstable, others were removed to make way for construction projects, and one was accidentally knocked down by a vehicle. During World War II, city officials ordered that a central switch be installed at the city's electrical department so the lamps could be immediately turned off in case of an air raid. But the switch was never used. The moonlight towers kept glowing, night after night, still protecting Austin citizens from what was out there in the dark.

And some of them are still there.

Austin has changed dramatically since the 1880s. There are more students enrolled at the University of Texas than there were residents of the city when the murders took place. Austin has become home to tech companies, ad agencies, and filmmakers. It's home to the annual SXSW Conference and Festival, to hundreds of bars and nightclubs, and to so many musicians, artists, and eccentrics that its motto has become "Keep Austin Weird."

A few landmarks from 1885 remain, too. There is the granite-pink state capitol, of course, as well as the governor's mansion; the Driskill Hotel; the columned administrative building of the State Lunatic Asylum, which is now the Austin State Hospital; Millett's Opera House, which doesn't show opera anymore; a few downtown buildings and a handful of homes that had been built for the city's wealthiest residents.

And a dozen or so moonlight towers. They are essentially useless now. The glow from their lamps is barely visible compared to the harsh glare from hundreds of lights much closer to the street. But still, they stand. In the 1970s, city officials got the towers designated state and national historical landmarks.

In the application to obtain the designations, though, the murders were never mentioned. They didn't explain that Austin residents of the late 1880s had wanted those towers built because they were still anxious about a madman who used the darkness to wreak havoc in their community. The applications described the towers as quaint, nostalgic relics of the past.

Were the killings purposely excluded from the applications, or had they been forgotten – the way that city officials hoped they would be? Many who grew up in Austin in the middle and second half of the twentieth century knew nothing about the Servant Girl Annihilator. There was nothing in the city's history about them, and newspaper files were much harder to access back then. If you had told the average person that Austin was home to America's first true serial killer in the 1880s, they wouldn't have believed you.

The information about the murders wasn't easy to find, but it was there. Mostly, though, no one knew to look for it. It wasn't until the late 1990s that researchers and historians began digging into the "other side" of Austin's history.

"Keep Austin Weird?" Yeah, I think the murders qualified as weird.

Honestly, though, it's not much of a mystery as to why Austin's city officials didn't want to talk about the murders and why they were happy to let everyone forget about them. The killings had been a stain on the reputation of the city for the police, for at least two mayors, and for all the upstanding people who lived in the community. It was not what anyone wanted Austin to be known for.

What is a greater mystery to me is why everyone just stopped looking for the killer. After arresting the same "usual suspects" over and over, scores of beatings and interrogations, and putting two obviously innocent men on trial, the authorities just shrugged their shoulders. They figured they'd done all they could.

The Servant Girl Annihilator - whoever he was - just walked away. Even taking into consideration the poor state of law enforcement in Austin at the time and the lack of forensic science, the killer had been living among them for an entire year, and yet, no one had a clue as to who he might be.

Or did they?

That's a question that deserves a closer look.

23. THE MAN FROM TEXAS

THE FIRST SERIAL KILLER IN AMERICAN HISTORY was not – as generally believed – H.H. Holmes, who we've mentioned within these pages already. The Servant Girl Annihilator pre-dated him by several years. In fact, it was nearly a decade after the murders in Austin came to an end that Holmes was arrested for insurance fraud, and his string of murders came to light.

The Servant Girl Annihilator was unlike any other killer in American history at that time. He was a depraved yet cunning monster who, on some nights, wanted only to scare women, who on other nights only wanted to attack them, and who, on seven nights between December 1884 and December 1885, decided to rip apart his victims with such speed and ferocity that they didn't even have time to scream.

This was no slobbering madman. He was utterly confident in his murderous skills and in the fact that he would not be seen – or at least identified. Of the eight people that he left alive at the various murder scenes, only two got a glimpse of him, and both were children. One thought the killer was black, and the other thought he was white.

But just because he was clever didn't mean he wasn't insane. On Christmas Eve of 1885, he attacked Susan Hancock just before midnight in the southern end of downtown, dragging her out into her backyard, only to be interrupted by her husband. Unable to satisfy his lust for blood, he immediately raced to the northern end of downtown – only blocks from the police department – and attacked Eula Phillips, dragged her into the backyard, and finished her off.

He committed two murders in less than an hour – but was only able to satisfy whatever drove him the second time.

It was exactly what Jack the Ripper had done on the night of that double murder in Whitechapel when he slaughtered Elizabeth Stride and Catherine Eddowes. Stopped from quenching his thirst for blood the first time, he quickly killed again.

But we'll come back to Jack the Ripper.

For now, let's explore some of the Servant Girl Annihilator suspects a little closer to home.

THE "BAD BLACKS"

BEFORE WE START DISCUSSING POSSIBLE SUSPECTS in the case, we must accept that we'll never really know who the killer was.

We can surmise, suggest, and imply all kinds of things, but we'll never know his identity, any more than we'll ever know what motivated him, why he chose his victims, how he decided which women he wanted to attack, and why, on Christmas Eve, he decided to kill two white women instead of the black servant girls that he'd killed so far.

It's all what Mayor Robertson called "the mystery of the murders," but that doesn't mean we can't dig into things a little bit deeper.

I'll start this section, though, by saying that I do not, in any way, believe there was a roving gang of "bad blacks" who were committing murders in Austin. That was a racist trope that was concocted to steer blame toward the African American community and to create an excuse for the police not to work as hard on the cases as they would have if the victims had been white. I'm not telling you anything you don't know – it was a racist time and place. By scaring the residents with the imaginary "bad blacks," the authorities were essentially saying what city officials in Chicago said during the Beer Wars of the 1920s, when bootleggers were being killed on an almost daily basis – "don't worry, you're safe, the gangsters only kill each other." In this case, though, it wasn't gangsters. It was the African American residents of the city.

I should probably also point out in this section that "the murders give Austin a bad reputation" wasn't the only reason why the Servant Girl Murders were forgotten over the years. The other reason is that all but two of the victims were black. Yes, the Annihilator did attack servant girls of different races – remember the Swedish ones that he harassed? – but he didn't kill them.

Before the white citizens of Austin paid much attention to the attacks, they had already caused a tremendous amount of panic within the African American community. It was a widespread fear that one's entire family might be wiped out while you were sleeping – anyone's family, not just those who were, or lived with, a servant girl. That terror, for some, turned out to be justified.

Would the police have worked harder to solve the murders if the victims had been white? Probably. And this is based on the sensation the murders became after Susan Hancock and Eula Phillips were killed. After that, it was obvious the investigation hadn't been taken as seriously as it should have been.

But even if the police had taken the murders seriously, could they have been solved? That's a nagging question to which we'll never have an answer. There aren't enough police records that detail the crimes in the way we'd need to analyze his methods. No one checked for fingerprints or did much to collect forensic evidence in 1885. We're only left with secondhand accounts and newspaper stories that can often be questioned for their accuracy, especially when it comes to white reporters writing about black victims at the time.

We can't know his motives. They were obviously driven by hate and madness. But hate for what? Women? The race of the victims? His own race?

Was the killer white? Was he black? We don't know.

In 1885, it was widely believed in Austin that the killer was black – at least among the white residents of the city. That way, they had something obvious to be afraid of, like the killer's skin color, for instance.

But did the black residents share this belief? There's no way for us to know. If you read the newspaper stories, the accounts from black witnesses made it sound like they believed that the killer was black, but was this the slanted view of the reporter or the witness telling a reporter – or a policeman – what they wanted to hear? Maybe.

Two children were spared during the attacks. One said the killer was black, and the other said he was white. As you'll see in the chapter ahead, a case could be made for either race.

For now, let's focus on black suspects. It's easy to do since the police only arrested black men in connection with the murders and attacks. That only changed after the Christmas Eve murders, when they accused Moses Hancock and Jimmy Phillips. The reasons for that were obvious – they were the husbands, who are always suspected first. If they'd had better alibis – and a less desperate mayor and prosecutor – I'm sure that black men would have been arrested instead.

After the first murder, that of Mollie Smith, the initial suspect had been her boyfriend, Walter Spencer. Normally, this would be standard procedure, but Walter had also been struck and injured by Mollie's killer in a way that, according to doctors, he couldn't have done himself. As we already know, Walter was eventually cleared as a suspect, along with a former boyfriend of Mollie's named Lem Brooks.

Those two arrests – along with all the arrests of random black men that followed – set the stage for the entire investigation. Every time there was an attack, the police would round up any African American man they could find who had a record, acted strange, or was just walking down the street after dark. The vigilance committee even recommended arresting black men for doing nothing – they just seemed suspicious.

Oliver Townsend was known for stealing chickens, not for assaulting women or committing assaults – and yet he became a prime suspect because he was "sneaky." And one last note on Oliver – after he was sent to prison on that bogus burglary charge, he escaped from a prison chain gang in 1895 and was never heard from again.

As for the rest of the men who were arrested as suspects after each of the murders, I couldn't find any information that suggested any of them ever went on to commit murder later in life.

There was no "gang of bad blacks" in Austin. Despite such a gang being the frequent topic of discussion and the object of fear on street corners, in newspapers, and at City Hall, it didn't exist. No evidence of it was ever uncovered by the police, detectives, or even the citizen's vigilance committee, which promoted it more than anyone else.

African American men, in general, were the "others" in Austin in the 1880s and, in this case, the "boogeymen" who were haunting the streets of the city with axes, knives, and iron rods in hand.

But what if the Servant Girl Annihilator was actually black?

Based on what we know – or don't know, in this case – the killer was just as likely to be black as he was to be white. I understand that a lot of the information out there about serial killers may dispute this. However, I think we must consider the possibility for several reasons, not the least of which is that African American serial killers do exist. They may not be as prevalent as their white counterparts, but they have committed their share of violence.

There are a few things about the murders that suggest the killer may have been black. The first thing is the race of the initial victims. In most serial murder sprees, the offender targets victims of the same race. This is not always the case, but it occurs most of the time.

Studies show that most serial killers choose victims from their same ethnicity group because this is mainly the race they interact with and are most comfortable with, allowing them to release their urges safely.

It could also be because the personal prejudices of the killer wouldn't allow him to interact with another race as an intended victim. He harassed the white Swedish servant girls but didn't kill them.

Suppose the killer felt safe or comfortable killing black women. In that case, he may have felt he was less likely to be caught -- or, in this case, because the police at the time didn't take the murders of black women and domestic servants as seriously as they would have taken the murders of white women. And what happened after Christmas Eve proves this to be true.

However, studies also show that when a serial killer does branch out beyond their comfort zone is when they are more likely to make mistakes, becoming more aggressive and more self-destructive. This again takes us back to the Christmas Eve murders when the killer decided to attack a white woman, Susan Hancock. This was his first time being interrupted during an attack, so he fled. Unsatisfied, he struck again a short time later and killed Eula Phillips.

And then, he left Austin. He may have killed in San Antonio and Gainesville, but the Austin murders came to an end. Did the killer self-destruct? Maybe. I don't believe that he was Jack the Ripper, but it is possible he killed again – but we'll come back to that.

The main reason we should consider the idea that the killer was black, however, is because of the way that he moved so freely through both the white and black neighborhoods of Austin. It was something that a white man – unless he was a police officer – couldn't have done. A police officer would draw attention in a black neighborhood in the 1880s because he was a cop. But a random white man would also draw an inordinate amount of attention. He couldn't walk freely through the east side – at least not without getting wary glances and, most importantly, being remembered by anyone who saw him.

In a white neighborhood, though, a black man in Austin could come and go as he pleased, at least most of the time. Almost every white home in Austin that was middle-class or higher depended on the servants- male and female- who worked for them. Black women cooked the food, cleaned the houses, and cared for the children. Black men worked on the lawn, tended to the animals, and chopped the wood. Regardless of how he dressed, a black man would not be out of place on the street, in the backyard, or around the servants' quarters. Not only would he naturally seem to belong there, but he would be largely "invisible" to the white homeowners and neighbors.

If the killer were black, it would make it simple for him to pick a home, study the occupants for a few days, return at night, commit murder, and vanish without ever being seen.

I hope you'll consider these things and keep them in mind because, at the end of this chapter, all the points I just made will seem very familiar when we talk about the possibility that the killer might have struck again long after the murders in Austin had been largely forgotten.

JACK THE RIPPER

ALTHOUGH I SERIOUSLY DOUBT THERE IS ANY connection between Jack the Ripper and the Servant Girl Annihilator, it's interesting to look at how it affected the public, press, and medical establishment on both sides of the Atlantic in 1888. Many people were convinced that it was the same killer. They were sure that after the murder in Gainesville – which we can't be certain was the Austin killer, but it's certainly possible – the killer traveled to London and kept killing there.

It's easy to understand how this happened. The world had never experienced a serial killer before. Even though the methods and motivations of Jack the Ripper differed from those of the Austin killer, there was enough that was similar in the two cases to cause concern. In addition, the Ripper murders were just as shocking as the Servant Girl Annihilator killings, and the press became just as important to how the public saw the murders. It just seemed too big of a coincidence to have two madmen killing women in such a small window of time – so they had to be connected.

There were only a few suspects named at the time who could be linked between England, Texas, and the murders. One was, of course, Maurice, the Malaysian cook. Frankly, I don't believe the sailor's story at all. I think the whole thing was cooked up by a newspaper reporter who knew that Maurice had briefly been a suspect in Austin, but let's go along with it for a moment.

Maurice was an enigma. There is little information about him in the newspapers of the day. There is no record of where he worked after leaving Austin, no record of boarding a ship in Galveston, bound for England, or anything else.

The "Maurice Theory" only came up because police in London sought leads. A cable from London to Austin was sent about "cattle boats" from Texas and docked along the Thames each week. Since there was some speculation during the Ripper murders that the killer might be a butcher – or connected in some way with cattle – he might be employed on one of these boats. That means, it was thought, the man could have come from America.

Naturally, reporters in Austin – hoping for a connection to the Ripper murders because that would sell a lot more papers – landed on the Malaysian cook who had once been followed and questioned by the police in Austin. His landlady said he'd gotten onto a boat bound for England or at least would look for one.

Editors at the *Daily Statesman* quickly seized on this and pointed out how Maurice, since he was Malaysian, was genetically predisposed to commit murder. They wrote that a Malaysian was:

...capable of the greatest excesses when his passions are aroused. Indeed, the blood record would make an Apache chief turn green with envy. Under the influence of religious excitement,

jealousy, losses at gambling or anything else the average Malay is suddenly seized with a mania to murder, and he starts out on what is known as "amok", and he slashes and cuts and eats and kills whomever he meets. This is when the "amok fever" is on him, but ofttimes when moved by jealousy alone he does his bloody work cunningly, deftly, and mysteriously.

This is from the article that the newspaper had headlined, A STRANGE COINCIDENT, which used the story of the Malaysian cook being sought in London as an excuse to resurrect the suspicions in Austin about Maurice. As the *Statesman* pointed out: "Three of the most bloody and cruel of the Austin murders occurred in the quarter of the city where this Malay was said to have slept."

But as we already know, the police put a tail on Maurice after the Mary Ramey murder and discovered that none of the rumors about him were true – he wasn't a drunk, he didn't roam the streets at night, and he wasn't a difficult man to get along with. His only crime was being different – he was "the other," which made him suspicious to the white residents of Austin.

"A Malay cook suspected in London. A Malay cook suspected in Austin. Strange indeed," the newspaper concluded its article.

But it turned out it wasn't strange at all.

THERE WERE OTHER AMERICANS SUSPECTED OF being Jack the Ripper. Earlier, I mentioned Francis J. Tumblety, so while I don't think this is a worthwhile lead as far as the Servant Girl Annihilator goes, we should take a closer look.

Tumblety wasn't a suspect until 1913, and his name only came up because he was known to hate women, had medical skills, and was arrested around the time of the murders for what were called "unnatural offenses." He skipped bail and fled England -- and the murders came to an end.

Francis was technically not an American. He was born in Canada in 1833 but moved with his family to Rochester, New York when he was very young. Although uneducated, he was clever and used skills he learned to make a living mixing patent medicines. It's unlikely any of his snake oil cures actually worked, but he did start calling himself a doctor and claimed to possess "Indian and Oriental secrets" of healing.

He was charming and handsome, and he used these attributes -- along with numerous lies and boasting -- to get into the finest hotels, wear the finest clothes, attend the best parties, and live well beyond his means. When bills came due, he merely skipped town without paying them.

In the late 1850s and early 1860s, Francis was living in Washington, DC, rubbing shoulders with the wealthy and well-connected in the capital city. It's said that it was during this time that his deep-seated hatred for women began to emerge.

During a dinner party that he hosted one night in 1861, Francis was asked casually by one of his guests why he hadn't invited any single women to the gathering. Tumblety replied that women were nothing more than "cattle" and that he would rather give a friend poison than see him with a woman. He then began to speak about the evils of women, especially prostitutes, which must have come as quite a shock to the upper society neighbors gathered in his home that evening.

An attorney, C.A. Dunham, who attended the party that night, later remarked that it was generally believed that Francis had been tricked into marriage by a woman who was later revealed to be a prostitute. This was thought to have sparked his hatred of all women, but none of the guests had any idea just how far his feelings of animosity went until Francis offered to show them his "collection." He led his guests into a back study of the house, where he kept his anatomical "museum." Here, they were shown row after row of jars containing women's uteruses.

In 1863, Francis visited St. Louis and was briefly arrested as a Confederate sympathizer. The Civil War was taking place at the time, and tensions were high in places like St. Louis, which straddled the line between Illinois, which was loyal to the Union, and Missouri, which was not.

After the war, Francis continued his swindles, making several trips to Europe during the 1870s and 1880s. He also traveled widely in the United States during this time. Did he go to Austin? I suppose he could have, but there's no record saying he did.

However, in the summer of 1888, we know he was in London and rented rooms on Batty Street, in the heart of Whitechapel. This was within easy walking distance of all the crime scenes.

He became a suspect to the police when they belatedly learned of a visit that he made to a pathological museum in

London, where he inquired about any uteruses that might be for sale. This put them on alert because some of the medical examiners in 1888 stated that they believed the killer had medical knowledge. They assumed Tumblety was an actual doctor, and they didn't know at the time that he had a collection of uteruses back home. He was apparently looking for more to add to his very weird collection.

On November 7 – two days before Mary Kelly's murder – Francis was arrested. It wasn't for murder but for "unnatural offenses," which was usually a reference to homosexuality. We know he was released on bail, but we don't know when. Some say it was November 16, well after the murder, but others claim it was November 8. Thousands of police records were destroyed in the London Blitz during World War II, including these. Whether Francis was Jack the Ripper or not depends on the date he got out of jail, but we don't know when that was.

Whatever the date, he skipped bail for his arrest and vanished, allegedly taking a steamer to France on November 24 and then returning to the United States.

But the story of Dr. Tumblety is not quite over.

For years after his return to America, Francis continued moving around the country, living in hotels, staying ahead of his creditors, and leaving little record of himself behind. He finally landed in one place in St. Louis in April 1903, where he checked himself into St. John's Hospital and Dispensary at 23rd and Locust Streets.

According to accounts, Francis was suffering from a long and painful illness, although it was never identified. Those who believe he was the Ripper say it might have been syphilis, which he contracted from a prostitute many years earlier, creating his hatred of women and sex workers. Whatever his illness, Francis remained at the hospital until his death on May 28, 1903.

Things get even stranger after that.

Court records show that Francis left an estate of more than $135,00 when he died. The hospital received $450 for room expenses, medical tests, and care, while the rest of his estate – aside from costs to a St. Louis undertaker – went to his niece, Mary Fitzsimmons of Rochester, New York.

There was only one challenge to the will – and it turned out to be rather strange, especially because of Tumblety's clear feelings on the subject. The challenge had come from an attorney in Baltimore named Joseph Kemp. He claimed that Francis had another will – written in 1901 – which left $1,000 from his estate to the Baltimore Home for Fallen Women. It was a charity that helped sex workers start a new life.

The claim was thrown out of court, but it is an interesting final note to the life of a man who some say was the most infamous killer of prostitutes in history.

But was he really? The jury is still out on that one. If Francis Tumblety was released from jail on November 8, the night before Mary Kelly was killed, then it's possible that he was the man the police were looking for. Is it likely? No, but it is possible.

THE OTHER AMERICAN SUSPECTS WERE, of course, the "three American cowboys" who were tracked down in London and cleared of the Ripper murders. We have no idea who they were – this information was never printed – or if any of them were from Texas or ever set foot in Austin.

There were also the "wild Indians" left behind by Buffalo Bill's Wild West Show in London, who the police believed would certainly be capable of such bloody acts as murdering prostitutes.

One of those men was Black Elk, the Lakota chieftain, who returned to the United States in 1889. When he did, he traveled to the Pine Ridge Indian Reservation in South Dakota, where he was named one of the nation's medicine men.

In 1890, the U.S. Calvary attacked the Lakota in what would become known as the Battle of Wounded Knee. Black Elk rode out onto the battlefield to care for the wounded and tried to stop the bloodshed. But he was injured by a stray bullet. He survived and lived to be 87, trying to the end of his life to promote peace between his people and the white men. He published an autobiography called *Black Elk Speaks*, now a classic of Native American literature. In his book, he said he joined the Wild West show and went to England because "I wanted to see the great water, the great world, and the ways of the white man."

However, he never wrote anything about the London slums, being taken to Scotland Yard, and being suspected of committing the Whitechapel murders.

He also, by the way, had no connection to Austin.

HOWEVER, THERE IS ONE JACK THE RIPPER SUSPECT who does have a connection to Austin – or at least to the region around it. But this is not an American suspect. It's a British one who may have been in New Orleans in late 1884 or early 1885 at the World's Industrial and Cotton Centennial Exposition – an event where the city of Austin had a chance to shine.

Please note that he *may* have been there. It's not certain, but true-crime historians have tried to make the case for it.

The suspect's name was James Maybrick, a wealthy and successful cotton merchant from Liverpool,

James Maybrick

England. This is the only link between Maybrick and the trade show, but it is important since the event brought in those in the field from all over the world.

So, it's not just possible that he was there. I might even admit that it's likely he was.

Maybrick was born in Liverpool in 1838. His father was an engraver, but James eventually succeeded in the cotton trading industry. His business required him to travel regularly to the United States, and in 1871, he settled in Norfolk, Virginia, to establish a branch office for his company.

He remained in America for the next six years and then, in 1880, returned to England. During the journey, he was introduced to Florence Elizabeth Chandler, the daughter of a banker from Mobile, Alabama, and their relationship quickly blossomed. Despite the difference in their ages – he was 42, and she was 18 – they began to plan their wedding, which eventually took place in July 1881. They had two children together -- a son, James Chandler, born in 1882, and a daughter, Gladys Evelyn, born in 1886.

James continued to divide his time between his company's American and British offices. However, these long absences caused difficulties within his marriage. It didn't help that he had mistresses in America or that Florence later learned of this and started having her own affairs.

In late 1884, the World's Industrial and Cotton Centennial Exposition – described earlier in the book – was held in New Orleans. "Texas Day" was held at the exposition in April 1885. The state had already been promoting itself as a major cotton exporter throughout the event. It's possible that James Maybrick could have traveled to Austin, arrived there by New Year's Eve, committed the first murder, and then stuck around through the end of the year on the pretext of establishing an office in the state capital. He also could easily have gone back and forth between Norfolk and England amid the murders.

If he was the Servant Girl Annihilator – soon to also be Jack the Ripper – that is.

In April 1889, James' health suddenly began to decline, and he died on May 11. The circumstances of his death were deemed suspicious by his brothers, and an inquest, held in a local hotel, came to the verdict that arsenic poisoning was the most likely cause, administered by persons unknown.

Suspicion immediately fell on his wife, Florence, and she was arrested a few days later. She went on trial at St George's Hall, Liverpool, and after lengthy proceedings, she was convicted of murder and sentenced to death. Later, questions were raised about the fairness of the trial, the use of arsenic in some medicines at the time, and the way the judge conducted the proceedings. This is likely why her sentence was commuted to life imprisonment. She received a new trial in 1904 and was released. She supported herself through various occupations until her death in October 1941.

Florence Maybrick

But how did James Maybrick become a suspect in the Servant Girl Annihilator and Jack the Ripper murders? For starters, he was in the right place at the right time – maybe – but really, it has everything to do with the "diary."

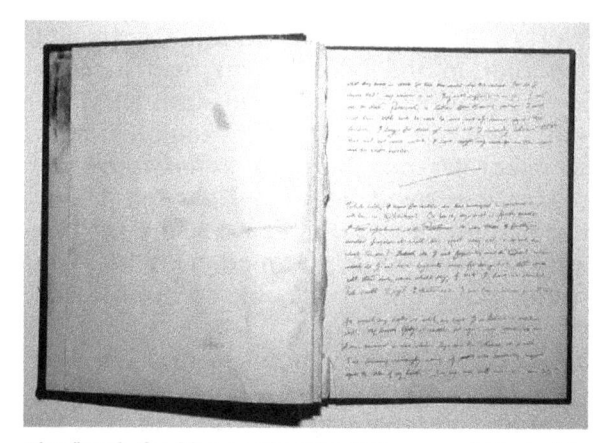

The alleged diary showed up in 1991. It had 63 handwritten pages and was signed by "Jack the Ripper." Handed down from friend to friend and said to have been discovered under the floorboards of a house, the diary was purported to belong to James Maybrick, but when studied, it was filled with errors and flaws. There were not only references to things that had been proven false, but the paper and ink were revealed to be no more than a decade old when it was found.

The "Jack the Ripper Diary," which named Maybrick as the killer, was revealed in 1991 – but turned out to be a hoax.

It's believed that whoever hoaxed the diary picked Maybrick as the killer because his death in 1889 fit neatly when it came to explaining the sudden end to the murders. Aside from that, the cotton broker was a strange choice. He had no medical knowledge, as experts believe the Ripper did. If he ever visited Whitechapel, there's no record of it -- just like there's no record of him ever visiting Austin.

It's an interesting theory, but nothing tangible suggests it can be true. As I mentioned, I really don't think there's a connection between the murders in Austin and London, but I can certainly understand how a possible link between them captured the imagination of the public in the 1880s.

THE ESCAPING MADMAN

ONE OF THE MOST POPULAR CONTEMPORARY theories about the murders in Austin is that one of the "lunatics" from the State Asylum was escaping at night, coming into the neighborhoods, and killing the servant girls.

It's no surprise that such stories were concocted. Mental illness was a complete mystery to most people in those days – including the doctors who were supposed to be treating those who suffered from it. Everything that was known about mental illness then was a theory. The ideas that Dr. Denton implemented at the state asylum were forward-thinking for the era – and they terrified the public.

Before the mid-nineteenth century, the mentally ill were hidden away from the rest of us, kept out of sight, and locked in cold basements and cages or chained to walls. Such places had been started with the best intentions but offered little chance of cure. Most were filthy, and inmates were placed in straitjackets, strapped into restraint chairs, or even locked in crates or cages if they were especially disturbed. Many of them spent every day in shackles and chains, and even the so-called "treatments" – which used ice, heat, water, and beatings -- were barbaric.

Not surprisingly, such techniques brought little success, and patients rarely improved. In those days, most mental patients spent their entire lives locked away. They lived in the state hospitals for decades, died in them, and were buried on the grounds.

By the 1840s, demands for change began to be heard, largely started by schoolteacher-turned-social-reformer Dorothea Dix, who began traveling across America around this time, lobbying states to build hospitals for the proper care of the "indigent insane." She knew just how bad things were. Her tours of America's asylums revealed that people with mental illness were often treated no better than criminals – and usually much worse.

Dix's humanitarian appeals were persuasive and well-timed: expansionist America was eager to create large civic institutions to serve as models for an enlightened society. Public schools, universities, prisons, and asylums were all part of this agenda, though the less-than-altruistic motives of politicians did not always match the high-minded rhetoric. Regardless, Dix bullied and cajoled one state legislature after another until they bent to her will.

In Texas, the legislature established the State Lunatic Asylum in 1856 with a board of trustees empowered to appoint a superintendent, purchase land, and construct facilities. Construction on the hospital soon began, but it wouldn't open until 1861.

State Asylum for Insane, Austin, Texas.

Once it did, the number of inmates quickly began to grow. The requirements that allowed people to be admitted to the asylum in those days would be unacceptable in the modern age. The "supposed exciting causes of insanity," as they were called at the time, ranged from "novel reading" to "abortion." According to one report, 623 patients were admitted between 1865 and 1868. The "exciting causes" of four of those were "extreme jealousy," seven were admitted for "overexertion," and 30 for "religious excitement." Early treatment emphasized fresh air, activities, and exercise. More sophisticated treatment methods, including medication, were extremely limited. Many of the residents remained at the hospital for decades, and new patients continued to be admitted on a regular basis.

Under such conditions, it was inevitable that the asylum would become overcrowded. It fell into a state of squalor and neglect and was run by inept, corrupt, and even sadistic bureaucrats.

Until Dr. Ashley Denton took over as superintendent in 1883, he was determined not only to update and renovate the hospital but also to take better advantage of what the building had already offered to make it a place of true "asylum" for the inmates.

The asylum was a palatial building with high ceilings, lofty windows, and spacious grounds, providing abundant light, fresh air, exercise, and a varied diet. Inmates would work in the fields and dairies, work being considered a form of therapy for them, as well as supporting the hospital. There were gigantic kitchens and laundries which, like the gardens and livestock, provided work and therapy for the patients and an opportunity to learn life skills. These were things that many, withdrawn into their illnesses, might never have experienced before. Community and companionship, too, were vital for patients who would be otherwise isolated in their own mental worlds, driven by their own obsessions or hallucinations.

The State Lunatic Asylum was no longer a place of isolation but rather a place of comfort and safety for the mentally ill.

It wouldn't be the only hospital like it in Texas. Before Dr. Denton arrived, overcrowding at the hospital in Austin had led to the call for another institution in North Texas. The state legislature passed a bill establishing an asylum in Terrell in 1883, specifying that it be located one-mile northeast of town.

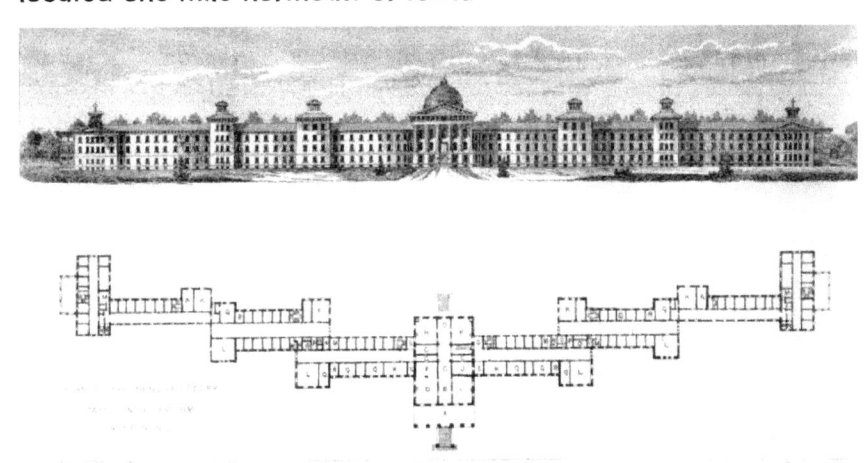

The basic design for "Kirkbride" asylums, like the institution in Austin.

The new hospital was built according to the "Kirkbride Plan." Dorothea Dix had been the catalyst for the first wave of asylum building, but Thomas Story Kirkbride provided the blueprint for their expansion. Kirkbride, who served as the superintendent of the Pennsylvania Hospital for the Insane in Philadelphia, drew on his own experience and travels in Europe to devise the model asylum.

As a skilled administrator, he was obsessed with asylum design and management. He believed that a well-designed and beautifully landscaped hospital could heal mental illness. If the insane were placed in a peaceful, structured environment, he believed, they had a much better chance of returning to the outside world as an improved individual. His belief – and his design–helped spread the idea that lunacy could be cured in a hospital, not at home.

The asylum building was the cornerstone of Kirkbride's idea. It consisted of a central administration building flanked symmetrically by linked pavilions, each stepping back to create a "V, like a formation of birds in flight, or as some have called it, a "bat-wing design." The layout was designed by sex, illness, and social class. The most disturbed patients were housed in the outermost wards, while those more socially adjusted lived closer to the center, where the staff lived. The stepped arrangement of the wards made the hospital easier to manage and provided abundant light with views of the outdoors. The location of the planned asylums – like the hospital in Terrell – was meant to be in the country, away from the city, offering privacy and land for farming and gardening. The land immediately around the asylum was used for pleasure, where the patients could take a relaxing stroll and admire picturesque views.

For many people, the Kirkbride building was the largest structure they'd ever seen. It was not even finished when the hospital opened in 1885.

It was a technological marvel of the time, offering modern amenities such as fireproof construction, central heating, plumbing, and gaslight. But it was not a hospital in the modern sense of the word. On the outside, it exuded grandeur, but inside, it resembled a dormitory. Each pavilion in the structure was three stories high, with one ward per floor. The ward had a long, wide hallway lined with small bedrooms. Each ward also contained a dining room, a parlor or sitting room, bathrooms, storage closets, and rooms for attendants. Patients spent most of their time in the hallways or common areas.

Dr. Denton used many ideas from the Kirkbride treatment plan when he took over the Austin hospital, although he didn't have the kind of building constructed in Terrell.

But, for the people of Austin in 1883, these ideas scared them the most – no walls, little security, garden paths were patients roamed about, and the chance the "lunatics" could escape at any time. Austin residents were familiar with how things ran at the hospital before Dr. Denton came -- when it was a dirty, overcrowded madhouse – and no matter how the place was praised in the newspapers, they could not stop being suspicious of it.

When women began to be murdered in brutal, bloody, seemingly insane ways, it was inevitable that they looked toward the State Lunatic Asylum as a place that might be hiding the killer.

Of course, Dr. Denton assured them this was not the case, but I imagine that his assurances fell on deaf ears. And, as it turned out, people were right to doubt him -- because Dr. Denton was keeping a very upsetting secret from everyone.

What happened to his son-in-law, James, remains a mystery. All that we can say for sure is that he was judged insane – presented as "bereft of reason" – in early 1886. He was removed from the Austin hospital and sent to the asylum in Terrell, likely to keep things quiet for the family.

Or was there something more to it than that?

How had James gone from being an upstanding doctor to a man with serious mental issues in just one year? Or had his insanity been hidden for a long time? And why, once his mental issues were discovered, was it so important to Dr. Denton that his son-in-law be sent to another asylum?

We can only speculate, of course. It's been suggested that James had syphilis, and his father-in-law wanted to spare everyone from the embarrassment his diagnosis would cause. Or maybe it was something worse.

James was born in Paducah, Kentucky, in 1852 but grew up in New Orleans. He attended medical school in Scotland at the University of Edinburgh. One of his classmates at the time was Robert Louis Stevenson, who later wrote *The Strange Case of Dr. Jekyll and Mrs. Hyde* – which might lead us to wonder how well the two men knew each other and whether James exhibited any behavior at the time that might have inspired the future work.

After becoming a doctor, James moved to Austin in 1876. He had an uncle, Dr. T.D. Wooten, who practiced in the city, helped his nephew obtain a job. James became the first-assistant physician at the asylum, initially working under a doctor named Wallace and then becoming the assistant superintendent when Dr. Denton took over a few years later.

In February 1885, he married Denton's daughter, Ella, and she gave birth to a son right around the time that Dr. Denton was forced to have James declared legally insane.

So, what happened? We don't know. Everything was kept secret, and when James died on August 25, 1886 – a few months after he was sent to Terrell – the newspaper listed only "paralysis" as the cause of death. His obituary went on to say, "he had been ill for several months, and seriously so for about two weeks." He was buried in the Denton family plot in San Marcos.

I confess that I couldn't help but wonder if the speed and secrecy with which Dr. Denton arranged for James to be locked up and sent out of town wasn't a way to hide the fact that James had been the Servant Girl Annihilator. I even surmised that he might have escaped from the Terrell institution to commit the murder in Gainesville, Texas, but then realized it had occurred ten months after he had died.

But what if the Gainesville murder – and the one in San Antonio before it -- wasn't committed by the same man that committed the killings in Austin? We don't know much about the other two murders. We only know that the situation was similar to Austin, but at that time, people were in a state of near hysteria, and the newspapers were more than happy to amp up the sensationalism and make it appear the killer was still at work. The same thing happened with the Ripper murders in 1888.

Is it possible that James Givens was the killer? Yes, it is. Nothing can contradict the idea that his sanity was already starting to slip in late 1884. He could easily have committed the murders throughout 1885 and then somehow revealed himself to his father-in-law in early 1886, which led to a speedy finding of legal insanity and James subsequently being locked up in an out-of-town asylum.

This could have been done not only to protect James but to protect the family name, too. Not long after, Dr. Denton left the state asylum and opened a sanitarium of his own. Notably, it didn't deal with serious cases. His clientele mostly consisted of wealthy society ladies who were treated for hysteria and the "vapors."

However, the problem with this theory is that there is no way to prove it. Records are scarce, and Dr. Denton did a very good job keeping things quiet. If James Given was the killer, there's no way that we'll ever know for sure.

But I'm definitely keeping him in the category labeled as "possible."

THE DOCTOR'S SON

AND JAMES GIVEN IS NOT THE ONLY suspect I'll put into that category. I have thought about this one a lot, and while some consider it far-fetched, I feel this is also someone worth considering as the possible killer – the son of the best-known doctor in town.

At the time of the murders, Dr. William Burt was the staff physician of the City-County Hospital in Austin. He was an esteemed physician and highly regarded in the city by officials and law enforcement. He not only conducted the autopsies on murder victims – including those of the Servant Girl Annihilator – but he also assisted the police by collecting evidence during postmortems. He was also on hand for the treatment of Susan Hancock after she was attacked, and his testimony at the inquest was important to the case.

During the year that the killer was active in the city, Dr. Burt was not only in charge of the hospital but also the county physician and the secretary of the Texas Medical Association. He was forced to deal with a case of smallpox in Austin, the possibility of a yellow fever outbreak, and a dengue fever epidemic. Mosquitoes spread the viral infection, and dozens of people, including Dr. Burt himself, became sick. He was well-regarded for his treatment of the poor and was beloved by the African Americans in Austin.

Unfortunately, he didn't live long enough to be able to look back on the Servant Girl Annihilator case and offer his opinions. Dr. Burt died on July 10, 1886, just a little over six months after the murders of Susan Hancock and Eula Phillips. I haven't found a cause of death – other than "illness" – but he was only sick for a week before he died.

But it's not Dr. Burt that I want to focus on here – it's one of his sons. Dr. Burt and his wife, Cynthia, had three sons, Silas, Horace, and William Eugene, who was born in September 1869.

This is not the first time that I've mentioned Eugene, as he was commonly known, in these pages. You might remember that he came along with his father to the Hancock house on Christmas Eve 1885, and he had been the one to find the ax in the backyard.

But did he know it was there all along because he had been the one that left it there?

If you've done the math, then you know that Eugene was only 16 when the Hancock murder occurred. This would have made him 15 the previous year on New Year's Eve when Mollie Smith was killed, and her boyfriend was attacked. It seems young to be a killer, but was it? Jesse Pomeroy was only 12 when he murdered two children in 1874, and he'd worked his way up to that by torturing and injuring others for a few years before graduating to murder.

William Eugene Burt, the son of Dr. William Burt, who was at the scene of at least one of the Servant Girl Annihilator murders.

But his discovery of an ax in the Hancock backyard was not why I added Eugene Burt to my suspect list – it was what he did in 1896.

According to relatives, Eugene had started acting strangely after the death of his father in 1886. At that point, they said, he'd begun to show signs of "marked depravity." But no one did anything about it, and they certainly didn't object when he married Anna Powers in 1891, and they had two children together, Elinor and Lucile.

So, if Eugene had started showing signs of "marked depravity" before his father died when he was only a teenager, would any of them have noticed?

Apparently, those signs of "marked depravity" continued to escalate over the next decade, and then, in July 1896, Eugene Burt exploded.

ANNA BURT KNEW THAT SOMETHING WAS WRONG with her husband. My guess is that she'd seen it coming for some time if the stories of his relatives were to be believed.

She had once awakened in the middle of the night to find Eugene standing beside the bed, staring down at her. She'd also been plagued with nightmares that warned her two little girls, Elinor and Lucile, ages two and four, weren't safe in the same house with their father.

But then, in June 1896, Anna was relieved by her husband's proposal that they move into a smaller house so that he could get back financially. She could see that he was making a concerted effort, and this put some of her fears to rest – even if the circumstances behind his money problems were worrisome.

Eugene had fallen into disrepute in Austin because he'd cheated his brothers, with whom he'd been a partner in a cigar store. When he was caught stealing and forging their names on bank drafts, Eugene abandoned his family and fled to New Orleans but was soon arrested. The *Daily Statesman* later editorialized that Eugene had exhibited "a total disregard to moral and legal obligations in his business relations." This had caused him to be regarded as "dull to a sense of business honor."

But no one outside the Burt family knew that this weak-willed, greedy, unsuccessful businessman hid a devil inside him. He was, even then, plotting a murder so terrible that it would again turn the attention of alienists across the country toward Austin as they tried to explain how such a thing could happen.

EVERYONE WHO SPOKE TO EUGENE ON SATURDAY, July 25, noticed nothing unusual about him. That morning, he finished packing his household goods, sold his carpets, and later informed his brothers that he was leaving on the midnight train for Dallas. He ate dinner at the Capitol Hotel – where he sought out the proprietor for a few games of checkers – which Eugene easily won. On the train, he ran into an old friend and schoolmate and seemed to be in good cheer. He told everyone that his wife and children had gone to San Antonio and that he would send for them soon from Dallas.

The only person who saw Eugene behave strangely that day was his cook, Minnie Simms, who later told reporters that he seemed very nervous, walked very fast, and frequently burst into tears. When she asked him what was wrong, Eugene explained that there had been trouble the night before, and Anna and the children had left suddenly for San Antonio. When Minnie started to make breakfast, he warned her not to use the water in the house's cistern because a cat had fallen in it the night before.

Later that evening, Eugene went to Dallas, and Minnie thought no more about her employer's behavior – or the cat in the cistern.

On Sunday, Anna's mother came to the house and was astonished when the cook informed her that her daughter and granddaughters had left town. She didn't believe Minnie and called the police, asking them to search the house. They did but found nothing.

On Monday, with still no word from her daughter, Anna's mother insisted the police return to the house. Some neighborhood boys had told *Statesman* reporters that a strange smell was coming from the basement, which had an outside entrance.

When Eugene's brother, Roscoe, finally entered the house on Wednesday morning, he was met with a terrible smell in the kitchen and the "ominous hum of myriads of flies" coming from underneath the floorboards.

Anna, Elinor, and Lucile were quickly found in the basement, floating in the water cistern. Their heads had been crushed by blows to the head. Handkerchiefs were tightly knotted around the necks of all three. The coroner initially assumed the victims had been strangled, though later it was determined Eugene had tied the cloths to reduce the flow of blood after he struck the fatal head wounds – with the blunt side of an ax. The handkerchiefs offered the first hint of how coldly and deliberately Eugene had planned the murders.

During another search of the house, blood was discovered that had seeped into the floorboards in the bedroom. Eugene had worked to make it appear clean to the naked eye but hadn't looked closely enough at the gaps between the wooden planks. Aside from that, though, there were no other signs that the murders had been committed there.

And that's when the police discovered that Eugene had mailed two large boxes to Houston. When police officers got there and opened the containers, they found the grisly remains of the crime. A bloody ax lay alongside blankets, sheets, and clothing that were soaked with gore. Eugene had carefully mopped up the bedroom and then had thrown the bloody towels into the shipping box that contained the rest of the evidence.

The cold premeditation of the murders had *Daily Statesman* editors working overtime to express their astonishment that such evil had returned to their town. "Murders that made Paris famous, when the Seine was wont to give up its dead each morning, were never more heartlessly cruel, and never in their perpetration was there more utter emancipation from every restraint of conscience," the paper stated on the day after the bodies were discovered.

Eugene was soon apprehended, returned to Austin, tried, convicted, and sentenced to die in October. But before he went to the gallows, the governor ordered that Eugene be given a new trial to determine if he was insane.

The trial took place in 1898, sharing national headlines with the rumblings of America's impending war with Spain. The *Daily Statesman* printed full court transcripts daily, with images, commentary, interviews, and once, even a drawing of Eugene's hand accompanied by commentary from a palm reader. His skull was measured and examined by phrenologists, but they could find nothing amiss. Jailers testified that they had spied on him but observed no unusual behavior. Physicians and alienists argued tediously for hours about the state of Eugene's mental health. On the witness stand, they fumbled around with the term "moral insanity," but they couldn't explain how a person could have all his faculties in order except the one that guarded against evil thoughts and deeds. One argued that there must be such a thing as temporary insanity, as everyone knew that a person might strike a dog or a horse when there was no rational reason for doing so.

Eugene's brothers testified that he'd suffered major trauma when their father died when he was a teenager. The boy who'd once had a bright disposition, they said, became withdrawn and ill-tempered. Clearly, Eugene had been emotionally cut off from his family and friends for many years, so no one knew just how damaged he actually was. A letter he wrote that was printed in the newspaper shortly before he was executed in 1898 illustrates the depth of his madness. "The outraged law is still outraged," Burt wrote because the real perpetrator of his wife's murder was "already punished by forces not of the law. He added:

Great God be thanked, the hellish brute that took from me the sweets of life, that snaped [sic] the human cords of my heart, that took from me and sent to heaven my loved ones, will never see the fulfillment of the ends of lawful justice. ... How happy to lay and dream ... to hear the howls and shrieks and screams of his tortured soul.

While the method of murder may differ, I don't think we can ignore the possibility that Eugene Burt's mental issues began before his father died. I wonder if it might have been easier for friends and family to point to a substantive event – such as Dr. Burt's death – to explain Eugene's behavior rather than try to understand mental science at a time when most doctors had no understanding of it.

Could Eugene Burt have been the Servant Girl Annihilator? Possibly. Was he? Probably not, but I don't think a person with a connection to the case who also murdered his wife and two daughters is someone we should ignore.

"HORRIBLY MUTILATED"

THOSE WHO DON'T BELIEVE THAT EUGENE BURT was the Servant Girl Annihilator will usually point to the fact that, if he was, he waited a decade before he committed another murder – three, actually, his wife and daughters. This seems unlikely to them, and usually, I'd agree.

Over the last 40 years or so, as law enforcement officials, clinicians, academicians, and researchers have worked to devise definitions of serial murder, they debated the requirements, like the number of murders required, types of motivation, and other aspects of the killers.

Typically, definitions of serial murder specify a certain number of murders, varying from 2 to 10 victims. This requirement distinguishes serial murders from other categories of murder, especially single homicide, which is by far the most common act of murder.

Most of the definitions also require a period of time between the murders. This pause or break between killings is necessary to distinguish between a mass murder, which is a one-time event, and a serial murder, which has multiple incidents. The separation between the murders is often described as a "cooling-off period."

This emotional cooling-off period between murders is a key behavioral characteristic that distinguishes serial killers from all other types of murderers. Psychologists see it as important because it serves as a time-out from murder when the serial killer disappears from the public eye and resumes his seemingly normal life and routine. In most cases, the life of a serial killer during a cooling-off period may appear to be completely normal to anyone who knows them.

Serial killers re-emerge from the cooling-off period to strike again when the urge to kill becomes overwhelming to them. A serial killer may not even understand his compulsion to kill but knows that it is both undeniable and uncontrollable when the urge arises. It's just like an alcoholic or drug addict who needs another drink or a fix – only giving into that need will calm their cravings.

The cooling-off period between murders is highly subjective and unpredictable. There is no set amount of time, and it can vary between killers. It might be days, weeks, months, and, yes, even years.

The murders of the Servant Girl Annihilator went on for an entire year. Many occurred on weekend nights and around the full moon, but not always. It wasn't the moon or the weather controlling the killer – it was something completely unpredictable.

And if the killer also committed the San Antonio and Gainesville murders – which I'm not convinced about – then the time between the murders was even greater.

But could the time between murders be long enough that Eugene Burt could be the killer?

Definitely.

After the serial killer Dennis Rader – who became known as "BTK," for "Bind, Torture, Kill" – was captured, he confessed to 10 murders that he committed over a span of almost 20 years, from 1974-1991. In between murders, he lived a remarkably normal-looking life with a wife and two children and was perceived as a pillar of his community in Wichita, Kansas.

Inwardly, though, Rader was secretly satisfying his sexual needs and delaying his compulsion to kill for months, even years, through fantasies in which he relived his murders with the aid of trophies taken from his victims, such as articles of clothing, identification cards, and jewelry.

As a result of this, the length of the cooling-off period between Rader's murders varied and often lasted much longer than other serial killers.

Could this have been what Eugene Burt did? If he was the Servant Girl Annihilator, perhaps the death of his father created a pause in the murders, and he found other ways to satisfy himself without killing until he one day concocted an elaborate plan to murder his family.

Or, have there been other murders we don't know about? The San Antonio and Gainesville murders came to the attention of the authorities because of their similarity to the murders in Austin, but also because they happened so soon after the Austin murders received national attention.

What if other murders in smaller towns happened later but didn't receive the same attention? Maybe we just haven't found them yet. Eugene may have committed even more murders than we have been able to link to his other crimes.

Eugene, even at his young age when he started, *could* have been the Servant Girl Annihilator and still killed his family ten years after the sensational murders stopped. His cooling-off period can't be an excuse as to why it *wasn't* the Annihilator.

So, with that said, Eugene Burt *could* have been the Servant Girl Annihilator, but he isn't the only one who might have might have been a killer with a long gap between murders.

Since I've offered the possibility that the Austin killer could have been in a cooling-off period after early 1886, it opens our pool of suspects much wider. Not only could there have been other murders that we don't know about, committed by the Annihilator, but we also have to consider the idea that he could have remained dormant until something set him off again.

If you think that I'm now leaning toward the idea that the Austin killer was Jack the Ripper, back in action after two years, I'm not. As I have already said, I don't think those crimes are connected.

But what if I can show you another series of murders that I do believe *may* be connected – murders that are much more like the Austin murders than they are to the Ripper killings? They were horrifying, brutal, and, in almost every case, claimed the lives of young African American servant girls.

To make the connection, though, we must be willing to say that the killer stayed out of the newspapers for 20 years. Is it possible? Yes, the killer could still be under 40 years old at the time of the second murder spree.

Is it likely? Maybe not, but as you'll soon see, the similarities in the murders are hard to ignore. I would say that even if the killer who stalked the black neighborhoods of Atlanta isn't the same one who wreaked havoc in Austin, he was almost certainly inspired by the events in Texas.

Downtown Atlanta, Georgia, in the early 1900s

WOMEN WERE DYING IN ATLANTA, GEORGIA, in the early twentieth century. In fact, more than 25 of them would die over the course of several years -- victims of one of the most prolific serial killers in American history.

It's one of the worst murder sprees in American history, and yet – like the Servant Girl Annihilator case – it's never achieved the infamy it deserves. The answer is simple, and it's the same reply you get about Austin – the victims were black.

By the early 1900s, Atlanta considered itself a shining example of the "New South." Less than four decades after Union General William Sherman had burned Atlanta to destroy the morale of

Southerners and impede the ability of the city to transport goods from place to place, nearly a dozen railroads were passing through Georgia's capital city. The city had risen from the ashes, rebuilt, and saw a boom in business that led to Inman Park and Peachtree Street being much sought-after neighborhoods for the wealthy.

Atlanta wanted to project itself as racially tolerant, touting Morris Brown, Atlanta University, and Atlanta Baptist as some of the best "black" schools in the country. Black-owned businesses were also cropping up, but for most of the city's non-white residents, life was far from idyllic. Most worked menial jobs like installing sewers, loading railroad cars, or cooking and cleaning in white households, then trudging home at night to dimly lit neighborhoods that looked nothing like the ones in which their employers lived.

Atlanta was, in truth, seriously divided by race. It even led to a riot in 1906 after newspapers reported that several white women had been harassed and attacked by black men. The stories weren't true but led to violence that ended with fires, looting, the destruction of black-owned businesses, black people attacked on the streets, and 40 deaths.

Between the riots and the Jim Crow laws that kept the city heavily segregated, Atlanta was not a great place to live for African Americans. So, not surprisingly, when young black and mixed-race women began showing up brutally slain, it wasn't cause for much concern in the local newspapers. Circulated largely among white readers and staffed exclusively by white reporters and editors, the three city newspapers were far more concerned about crimes among whites. So, it wasn't surprising that when the murder spree started, the press and the authorities didn't pay much attention to the victims.

At least, not at first.

And once they did, they started to refer to the murders as the work of a "Jack the Ripper-type," ignoring the fact that the body count was four times higher than the "Jack" who had wreaked havoc in the squalid alleys of Whitechapel in 1888.

The date when the Atlanta murders began remains unclear, but we do know the effect that the killing spree had on the black community in the city. For years, young women feared leaving their homes after dark; some feared even walking the streets during the daytime. Black community leaders began to unite in their insistence that the Atlanta Police Department commit as many resources as possible to track down the killer – or killers – and bring an end to the murders.

Atlanta became the scene of murder after murder. The Ripper's victims were all young black or mixed-race women in their twenties. While there were no fewer than six men arrested for the crimes, no one was ever sure if the killings were the work of one man or multiple men. At least one man was convicted of one of the murders, although it's never been clear from the newspaper stories which murder he was alleged to have been involved in.

By the time it was over, two dozen women were dead, and their killer had vanished into history.

Sound familiar?

THE "ATLANTA RIPPER'S" FIRST VICTIM IS believed to have been Delia Reid on April 5, 1909. She was found in a trash pile on Rankin Street.

Months later, on September 7, the mutilated body of an unidentified black woman was found in Peachtree Creek. Was it linked to the other crime and the murders that followed? It's impossible to say because the newspapers barely covered her death, and the police conducted nothing that could be mistaken for an actual investigation.

There were more African American women killed in 1910. On March 5, Estella Baldwin was found dead. She had died from a "concussion of the brain" – struck by the blunt side of an ax. On Monday, October 3, Maggie Brooks' body was found at the intersection of the Atlanta and West Point Railroad track and Hill Street. She had been beaten to death, and her skull fractured.

It isn't certain from the newspaper stories if any of these murders were later linked to the "Ripper" or even to a single unknown assailant. Like the murder of Delia Reid, they received little press coverage and only a passing interest from the police.

But it's evident that they alarmed the black community in Atlanta and made many of them, especially the women, afraid to walk the streets after dark.

The incidents also alarmed black city leaders. In July 1911, a group of black pastors included their names on a list of women killed in Atlanta that was part of a petition to the governor and the mayor to stop the violence and apprehend the killer.

The next murder occurred just as 1911 was beginning. On Saturday, January 22, the body of Rosa Trice was found in the Pittsburg neighborhood. The left side of her skull had been nearly crushed. She had been stabbed in the jaw, and her throat was cut so deeply that her head was almost severed. After slaughtering Rosa, the killer dragged her body to within 75 yards of her home on Gardner Street. Two hours after her body was found, her husband, John, was arrested for the murder but was released the following night. He had a solid alibi, and there was no evidence against him.

On Sunday, February 19, 1911, the killer struck again. The body of a black woman, who was never identified, was discovered in some woods in Grant Park. She was believed to be about 25 years old; her throat had been slashed, and her skull was bashed in with the blunt side of an ax, just as Rosa Trice's had been.

Atlanta was quiet for the next two months, but the killer struck again on May 28. The body of Mary "Belle" Walker was found just steps away from her home on Garibaldi Street. Her sister found her mutilated corpse after Belle failed to return home the night before from her job as a cook at a home on Cooper Street. There was only a brief mention of the murder in the *Atlanta Constitution*. The two paragraphs were buried on page seven under a note that read, "Negro Woman Killed; No Clew to Slayer -- Was Found With Her Throat Cut Near Her Home."

In the early morning hours of Thursday, June 15, the body of Addie Watts was found in some bushes at Krogg and Dekalb

It wasn't until the death of Mary "Belle" Walker, a cook who enjoyed minor fame as a local beauty, was killed that the Atlanta newspapers started to take notice of the crimes.

Streets, near the tracks for the Southern Railway. The police believed that she had been struck in the head by a brick or a coupling pin from a railroad car before the killer slashed her throat. After the slaying, he pulled her into the bushes near the tracks and abandoned her body there.

It was only after Addie Watts had been killed that the city's newspapers began to speculate that the murders of the "negresses" were the work of a single killer. On June 16, the *Atlanta Journal* ran a headline that questioned if a "Black Butcher" was at work in the city. Even though the article was only four paragraphs long, it compared the Atlanta murders to the London murders of 1888. The last line read:

> *On account of the number of recent murders of Negro women, policemen advance the theory that Atlanta has an insane criminal, something on the order of the famed "Jack the Ripper."*

Just ten days later, the "Ripper" was moved to the front page. But it took another murder to make that happen. On Saturday, June 24, Lizzie Watkins became his next victim. Her body was found around 11.00 A.M. the next morning in a clump of bushes. Also, like Addie Watts, her throat had been cut, and her body was dragged to the spot after she was killed.

The Atlanta newspapers were finally willing to admit that the murders were the work of a monster.

AS THE NEWSPAPERS FINALLY STARTED TO PAY attention to the murders, they examined the similarities in the crimes that had occurred, noting that five Saturdays in a row had seen the murder of a young black or mixed-race woman.

Through these articles, the public was told for the first time that during each assault, it appeared each of the women had been choked unconscious, after which her throat was slit from ear to ear, and "the carving of the victim -- always in the same area of the body -- begins."

None of the women were apparently raped, but from the nature of the mutilations – which were not specified at the time due to the "delicate" nature of the reader -- it was suggested that the crimes were sexual in nature.

The first possible break in the case came on Saturday, July 1. Emma Lou Sharpe, 20, was at her home on Hanover Street, waiting for her mother, Lena, to return. It was a Saturday evening, and Emma Lou was worried. Her mother had left an hour before to fetch some groceries and still had not returned. This was a cause for concern after the recent murders. Frantic with worry, Emma Lou set out toward the market to search for her mother. When she arrived there, though, she was told that Lena had never come in. Emma Lou was walking toward home along the dark street when a stranger approached her. She later described him as "tall, black, broad-shouldered, and wearing a broad-brimmed black hat."

Feeling apprehensive as he approached her, Emma Lou was startled when he asked her how she was feeling that evening. She replied that she was well and tried to move past him, but the man blocked her path.

"Don't worry," he said to her. "I never hurt girls like you."

And then he stabbed her in the back, and the man ran off, laughing. Bleeding, Emma Lou ran, screaming for help, alerting some neighbors who came to her aid.

Emma Lou survived the night, but her mother did not. Lena's body was found shortly after her daughter's attack. The corpse was in a pool of blood, with her head nearly severed from her body.

The killer had struck again, but he had been seen this time.

Detectives working the case almost immediately deduced that the same man who had stabbed Emma Lou had also killed her mother and just might be connected to the other victims.

The newspapers had no choice but to pay attention to the Sharpe murder and assault. This prompted the *Atlanta Constitution* to declare on July 4, "Theory of Jack-The-Ripper Is Given Further Substance." The story beneath the headline recounted, in detail, how Emma Lou came face-to-face with the man police believed was the "Ripper." The story noted, "While the ordinary Negro murder attracts little attention, the police department was upon the alert last night, doubtless expecting a repetition of the long series of crimes which have baffled every effort of the detectives."

Undertaker L.L. Lee offered a $25 reward for the capture of the man who killed Lena Sharpe. He also asked other black business owners to increase the reward fund, making it more enticing and hopefully getting people to talk and assist the police in capturing the killer.

The authorities now seemed certain that the murders were the work of a single killer. "It's the work of the same man," said Coroner Paul Donehoo.

As another Saturday approached, the *Journal* asked the question on everyone's minds: "Will 'Jack the Ripper' Claim Eighth Victim This Saturday?" The story quoted an unnamed veteran policeman. He told the reporter, "It's coming. The Negro will kill a woman before midnight Saturday."

Drawings of the suspected "Ripper," taken from descriptions by the few witnesses who managed to get a look at him. Like everything else in the investigation, the portrait led nowhere.

And he was right – almost.

On Saturday night, July 8, 22-year-old Mary Yeldell left the home of W.M. Selcer on Fourth Street, where she worked as a cook. As she was walking past an alley, she heard a whistle. She stopped, looked toward the dimly lit passage, and saw a man approaching her that she described as "tall, black, and well-built, moving with a cat-like tread." Mary ran back to the Selcer house, screaming. Mr. Selcer met her at the door and then grabbed his revolver. He ran to the alley and, surprisingly, found the man still there. Selcer ordered him to raise his hands or be shot, but the man turned and darted back down the alley. The police were called, but their search turned up nothing.

If, like Emma Lou Sharpe, Mary had encountered the "Ripper," she had been fortunate to survive without injuries. The Yeldell incident appeared to have broken the killer's Saturday night string of murders, but the "Ripper" was far from finished.

On Tuesday morning, July 11, a workman named Will Broglin noticed some loose dirt on his normal route to work. The disturbance led him to a pool of blood in the road at the corner of Atlanta Avenue and Martin Street, near the new Orme Street sewer. The blood spatter trail led to a small gully about 30 feet away, and there he found the lifeless body of Sadie Holley, who worked at a local laundry. Sadie's skull had been smashed by a rock, and then she had been dragged to the ditch, where her throat was cut so savagely that she was nearly decapitated. Her shoes had been cut from her feet, and one of her hair combs was found near the bloody rock that she'd been beaten with.

The police were summoned, but there were few clues to assist the investigation. The disturbed dirt first noticed by Will Broglin pointed out the direction in which the killer fled, but that was all.

Dozens of the morbidly curious flocked to the crime scene within 20 minutes of the discovery of the corpse. By the time Coroner Donehoo arrived at the scene, the crowd had swelled to more than 500.

Sadie Holley had the dubious honor of being the first "Ripper" victim to appear on the front page of the *Atlanta Constitution*, which had maintained for weeks that the murders weren't connected. But now, they had changed their tune. "CRIME GRIPS ATLANTA" they printed, along with "Negro Woman Slain, and No Arrests are Made." The paper now made up for lost time by recounting all the killings from the previous year and insinuating they were all committed by the same man.

No matter what the newspapers printed, the effect was the same -- hysteria. Since so much of the confusion in the case had been directly caused by an official lack of interest in the murders of black women, police patrols were beefed up. However, the increased patrols were mostly for show since there was no real pattern for when and where the killer would strike. The newspapers were suddenly interested in the case, and their accounts mourned the victims, noting that all of them, "with one exception," were "hard workers and generally respected by both races alike. The character of the victims is largely responsible for the indignation at the murders, which has been so evident among the better class of Negroes."

Atlanta residents and newspaper editors alike were chastising the police for not finding the killer. By mid-July, Mayor Courtland Winn began publicly leaning on the police chief and chairman of the police commission. "Why the police are unable to cope with the situation is more than I can understand," the mayor said.

The police were determined to carry on with the idea that they were doing something, and within 24 hours after the discovery of Sadie Holley's body, they arrested Henry Huff, a 27-year-old laborer. Huff had been seen with Holley the night she was killed, police said. A cabman named Will Williams claimed that he'd had Huff and Holley in his cab that night, and they were quarreling. He let them off, he said, near where the murder took place. Not only was he spotted at the scene of the crime with the victim, police said, but he had scratches on his arms and was wearing trousers with dirt and blood on them when he was arrested.

Not long after Huff was arrested, the police also picked up Todd Henderson, 35, at a saloon on Decatur Street. An informant had told police that Henderson had been seen with Sadie in a drug store on the night she was killed. Emma Lou Sharpe was brought into the station to listen to Henderson's voice and try to tell if he was the man that she'd met on the street who'd subsequently stabbed her. When Henderson spoke, a reporter for the *Atlanta Constitution* wrote that she "shrank back." Even though a reporter from another newspaper said that her identification wasn't solid, Emma Lou noted otherwise. She told reporters, "That's the man... If that's not the right man, I'm badly mistaken."

On the other hand, Henderson was quoted as saying that if he were the "Ripper," he would have started on his wife because she gave him lots of trouble. *The Georgian*, as other papers did when quoting African Americans, took great pains in spelling out their speech phonetically in ways that reinforced blatant racist stereotypes. For instance, Henderson's simple statement was "translated" by the paper to read, "Gee, if I wuz 'Jack the Ripper,' I sho wud hev begun on my wife. Fur she's gibe me lots ob trubble."

The police found his "joke" about as funny as I find newspaper racism from the early 1900s. However, they did find it suspicious that he told them he hadn't owned a straight razor or a penknife in over a year, but they discovered that on the morning after Sadie's murder, he had dropped off a razor to a barber to have it sharpened.

The cases against Henderson and Huff were circumstantial, but the police turned them over to the prosecutor anyway. They believed perhaps a grand jury could figure out which man to indict.

But were either of them the right man?

> **NEGRO "JACK THE RIPPER."**
>
> **SERIES OF MURDERS OF HALF-CASTE WOMEN.**
>
> **From Our Own Correspondent.**
> NEW YORK, Monday.
>
> Terror reigns among the negro population of Atlanta, Georgia, where on Saturday night an unknown "Jack the Ripper" for the eighth week in succession murdered and mutilated a half-caste woman.
>
> The victim, like her seven predecessors, was discovered on the Sunday morning with the head nearly severed from her body in a dark alley. Her daughter states that on Saturday evening she also was pursued by a tall, powerfully built, well-dressed negro who, as she ran, stabbed her in the back. This is the only clue the police have obtained of the appearance of the author of this singular series of crimes.
>
> In each instance the murderer, after dusk on Saturday evening, seems to have approached behind his victims, who are all good-looking half-castes, and, having seized them by the head, severed the jugular vein with a razor before mutilating the body. It is evident that the man has a knowledge of anatomy.
>
> The outrages have caused intense excitement among the negro population, whose preachers have succeeded in working them into a state of frenzy by exploiting the murders in their exhortations from the pulpit.

Even the police didn't think so.

ON THURSDAY, THREE DAYS AFTER THE HOLLEY murder, eight plainclothes patrolmen were assigned to night duty. Police chief Henry Jennings explained his department's challenges in tracking down the killer. "The police department is handicapped, seriously so, by its small size, but even if we had more men, we could not stop crime," Jennings said.

A reporter from the *Constitution* seemed exasperated by the situation. "The police department has nothing to say in explanation of its inability thus far to cope with the situation, further than the simple declaration that it is doing its best." The story went on to say that the white community was "aroused" over the killings as well -- killings that "have served to intensify the servant problem."

Atlanta's black community was more than simply "aroused" over the murders. Faced with the lack of results from the police, they urged the city council and the governor to add to the reward they had already established for the capture of the killer. Their petition was endorsed by many prominent white residents of the city, including Asa Candler, founder of Coca-Cola and a future mayor of Atlanta, and the week ended with Governor Hoke Smith offering a $250 reward for the Ripper's capture.

However, the chances of an additional reward accomplishing anything were slim, largely due to the kind of racism on display among Atlanta city officials.

Nash Broyles, the city recorder, also served as a local magistrate. At the trial of Jim Murphy, a black man charged with threatening to cut his wife's throat, Broyles said, "There is no such thing in Atlanta as a negro 'Jack the Ripper.' It is just such cases as these that result in these murders of Negro women. I am satisfied that every one of the several Negro women slain recently in Atlanta were murdered by a different man. There are least 1,000 Negro men in Atlanta today who stand ready to cut the throats of their wives at the slightest provocation."

When asked to explain why so many murders took place on Saturday nights, Broyles had a clever answer. Saturday night, he said, is the black man's "big night" -- the time when he "tanks up."

City officials at the time were a disgrace.

THE POLICE NOW HAD TWO SUSPECTS IN custody. However, the hysteria created by the murders took a toll on the city's black community, especially on the young women who worked as servants for other families in the area.

On the outskirts of Atlanta, six women were frightened by a man they thought might be the "Ripper." The man, they said, appeared out of nowhere as they were passing a field on their way home. All the young women were black, and all were domestic servants – a demographic the "Ripper" often targeted for his victims. When they saw the man, they screamed and ran away, shrieking so loudly they could be heard blocks away.

Mrs. McAdams on DeKalb Avenue heard the screams and called the police. Officers soon arrived by motorcycle and interviewed the shaken young women. They described the man they saw as tall and black, wearing a black hat and a white, long-sleeved shirt. They were convinced – after all the murders in the city – they had been stalked by the "Ripper" himself.

The police searched the area but found nothing. The press suggested that the whole incident had been a practical joke, but it didn't matter – the fear caused by the prankster was proof that young black women were unnerved by what was happening in the city. If the murders were not solved and the crime spree ended, no one would feel safe about leaving the house after dark or even in broad daylight.

For politicians, business leaders, and socialites of Atlanta, the fear being generated in the black community was of great concern. It was not because they were worried about the safety of African American citizens – their fears were much greater. If young black domestics were afraid to walk the streets, who would cook for them, care for their children, and clean their homes? The murders were now threatening to wreak havoc on the homes of white residents of Atlanta.

Something had to be done, and the arrests of Henderson and Huff seemed to be a step in the right direction. Although there was almost no real evidence against either man, the arrests managed to temper some of the criticism being directed at police and government officials.

But even with two men in custody, "Ripper" mania continued throughout July 1911. More meetings were held in black churches, and gatherings had now started to occur that were attended by white community members, too.

The moniker of the "Ripper" had been coined by journalists but now was being used by almost everyone. Each time a murder or attempted murder occurred that summer, the police and the press questioned whether it might be the work of the "Ripper."

It usually wasn't, but people were afraid.

AS THE CITY BAKED UNDER THE SCORCHING summer sun, Fulton County prosecutors moved forward in their cases against Henry Huff and Todd Henderson – the two black men who were both being blamed for the same murders.

On August 9, Huff was indicted by the grand jury, who also indicted a third man named John Daniel. Huff would stand trial for the murder of Sadie Holley, but there is almost no information that can be found about the arrest, investigation, and arraignment of John Daniel. All that we know if that he was held and indicted for a murder that was attributed to the "Ripper."

It was obvious to most people that the arrests were made under intense political pressure. The authorities had to do something. All three men had been arrested based on the accounts of witnesses – of various levels of believability – who put them at or near the crime scene. It was circumstantial evidence, at best, but the police and the city government were desperate.

As the grand jury handed down the indictments – and small moments of relief were felt at having three possible "Ripper" suspects off the street – things became eerily quiet in the city.

The "Ripper" murders had ceased. Could one of the men behind bars actually be the "Ripper"?

Before anyone could celebrate, it became clear that the last weeks of August were nothing more than the calm before the storm. Before the month ended, another young woman was found lying dead on the streets of Atlanta.

> **ANOTHER VICTIM OF RIPPER.**
>
> Thirteenth Negro Girl, Mutilated by Mysterious Murderer, Found in Street at Atlanta, Ga.
>
> Atlanta, Ga., Nov. 21.—[Special.]—The thirteenth negro girl fell a victim to Atlanta's "Jack the Ripper" last night. The body was found in an alley leading off a principal street. It was mutilated in the same manner as all the others have been. The police believe that the ripper is a maniac.

On the morning of August 31, Atlanta residents woke to the news that Mary Ann Duncan, 20, was found dead in an area west of Atlanta called Blantown. The killing had all the signs of another "Ripper" murder. Like Sadie Holley, her shoes had been removed and were missing. Mary Ann's throat had been cut from ear-to-ear. She had no family to identify her, only a few friends.

This latest slaying appeared in newspapers two days later. The *Constitution* reported, "After a lull of six weeks, the crime wave in the city rose again Thursday night and another negro woman, the ninth in less than as many months, was murdered by some 'Jack the Ripper,' who cut her throat from ear to ear." The article added, "two negroes were arrested by detectives yesterday, but there is no direct evidence to hold either, and one of them is held for the investigation of certain alleged statements concerning his knowledge of the crime."

Police officials told reporters they had evidence against the suspect that looked "promising." It wasn't. The two men were soon released, and this crime also went unsolved.

When this murder made the newspapers, it became clear to the public that the "Ripper" – despite official claims – was not behind bars. There was no denying its similarities to the other murders. It had also been carried out in a lonely, remote spot. Blantown was an isolated area between the Southern and Atlanta, Birmingham, and Atlantic Railroad tracks. The missing shoes were also an eerie connection to an earlier crime.

Again, this begged the question: if the killer had struck again, were Huff, Henderson, and Daniel innocent? Or was it possible they were guilty of the murders for which they were accused, and a new killer had picked up where they left off?

Could the "Ripper" be more than one man? It wasn't impossible – but it was unlikely. The Atlanta "Ripper" was almost undoubtedly just one man.

THE COOLER AUTUMN WEATHER BROUGHT crisper air to Atlanta, but it also brought more murders.

On October 17, another attack occurred, and, in this case, the victim was beaten to death with a blunt object.

Ellen Maddox, a cook for a family in Inman Park, was walking home from work and was near the Atlanta Stove Works on Irwin Street when she was attacked from behind. She was hit in the back of the head so brutally that the newspapers reported, "Her head was almost crushed, and her face beat out of all resemblance to a human being. Not once did she catch a glimpse of her assailant."

Officers Brannen and West arrived on the scene around 7.00 P.M. and visited Ellen at Grady Hospital soon after. Although she was badly beaten and near death, she told the officers, "He ran up behind me and hit me and then..." but she died before she ever finished her sentence.

On Sunday, October 22, the body of Eva Florence was found in a field at Rockwell and Elizabeth Streets. She had last been seen by friends the night before as she was leaving the streetcar they'd all been riding in. She was likely killed while walking home. Her head had been beaten, and she had been stabbed in the neck. Her brother, a waiter named John Clowers, posted a $100 reward with the police for the apprehension of the killer.

According to the newspapers, the police weren't convinced that Eva was a victim of the "Ripper." Although she was a young black woman, killed in an isolated spot, they said that the wound on her neck was a stab, not a slash, so they claimed this ruled out the "Ripper's" involvement.

I'm not sure that I agree with that, considering the murder matches all the other signatures of a "Ripper" murder, but perhaps the police knew more than what was being released in the papers at the time.

Regardless, the murder of Eva Florence was also never solved.

On Friday, November 10, Minnie Wise, who was described in the newspaper as a "comely mulatto girl," was found dead in an alleyway. She had been bludgeoned with a rock and dragged into a field on Connelly Street, where her throat was cut. She was then dragged about 20 feet to where she was discovered, near the corner of Georgia Avenue. The index finger on her right hand had been severed at the middle joint, and her shoes were missing.

The reports of these new murders caused fear and panic to grip the city once again. As pressure mounted on the police chief, mayor, and city council, newspapers nationwide began running stories about the "Atlanta Ripper." Letters began pouring in from professional and amateur detectives, offering their assistance in catching the killer of Atlanta's young black women. Mayor Winn was doing what he could to avoid embarrassment.

In a letter in reply to one of those outside detective agencies, he struck a defensive tone: "Atlanta is known throughout the country as one of the most law-abiding cities of its size in the United States, and its police and detective departments are second to none. It is true that in some instances criminals escape arrest for a time, but even escapes of this kind occur in all cities."

While the mayor was taking an increasingly sharp tone in his response to critics and those offering help, leaders in the black community used their time to renew their calls for help from state government and for the hiring of black detectives to assist in capturing the "Ripper."

Things were looking bad for Atlanta and were about to get worse.

JUST ONE WEEK AFTER MAYOR WINN'S SHARP reply to the detective agency, the killer struck again. It was almost as if he was responding to the confusion and chaos in the city.

It turned out to be Atlanta's grisliest murder so far.

On Tuesday, November 21, the body of Mary Putnam was found in a deplorable state in a ditch at Stewart Street and University Avenue. She had been buried under some loose dirt but could be easily seen from the street.

Her throat had been cut so deeply that her head had nearly been severed from her body. Her heart had been cut out of her chest and was lying next to her on the ground. She had been disemboweled, and an autopsy would later reveal that she had also suffered a crushed skull. Like other victims, she had likely been bludgeoned, dragged to another spot, and then murdered.

Prints were discovered on the ground around the corpse, so the police brought in a bloodhound to try and track the killer. The dog followed the trail for nearly 200 yards, but then it disappeared.

Mary had recently arrived in Atlanta. She had moved to the area to keep house for an elderly black man, whom the police did not consider a suspect. Even though she hadn't had much time to make friends, more than 1,000 people came to see Mary's body at the undertaker parlor.

One of the mourners was Mary's stepson, Walter, who did not identify himself or his stepmother at the time. It was not until after he returned to his job as an elevator operator that he informed a passenger. Walter said he feared he would be arrested if he spoke up earlier.

Sadly, he was probably right.

This most recent slaying caused more frustration for police and city officials. Meanwhile, black clergy, black civic leaders, and members of the black business community continued to be dismayed by the inability of the police to find the killer.

Pastors warned their female congregants about going out at night. Reverend C.M. Tanner stated, "As long as 'Jack the Ripper' stays at large, his misdeeds will be carried on. As his mania for killing seems to be directed at women alone, his murders can be checked through them. Stay indoors, and your lives will be saved, for venturing out at night moans only to invite the monster's ravages."

As difficult as this advice was to follow, given that many of the young black women of Atlanta had domestic jobs that required them to travel during the nighttime and early morning hours, it was a logical conclusion to reach.

It also further illustrated the lack of faith that the black community had in the city police.

The churches raised another $1,200 to add to the reward for the "Ripper's" capture. The pastors continued to clamor for black detectives to be retained to help track down the murderer, but their pleas were brushed aside.

THE END OF NOVEMBER BROUGHT AN END to the trial of Henry Huff, who had been indicted for one of the "Ripper" murders. The state had moved forward with the case despite the evidence being flimsy. They were able to prove that Huff was intimate with Sadie

Holley, the woman he'd been charged with killing, and had produced witnesses to say that he had been with her on the day she died.

Aside from that, they had nothing – and the jury knew it. They returned with a "not guilty" verdict, and Henry Huff was a free man.

Then, in the early morning hours of December 8, a young black woman named Zella Favors was found on the front porch of her home on Taylor Street. Although still barely alive when she was discovered, she died soon after at Grady Hospital. Zella's head had been bashed in by some blunt object, and then her throat had been cut.

Two detectives were assigned to the case, and when they arrived on the scene, they found a trail of blood that led from the porch to Pratt Street, where Zella had been seen talking to a man earlier in the night. Witnesses were unable to describe him, but the police believed that Zella was another victim of the "Ripper" and that he might have been one of her acquaintances. There is nothing that reveals how they came to this realization – aside from her witnessed conversation with the stranger – but detectives were becoming desperate to find any clue that might lead them to the killer.

A few days after this latest murder, Reverend Henry Hugh Proctor of the Atlanta Congregational Church -- the most outspoken black critic of the investigation -- took to his pulpit to denounce the crimes – and the police, who had still not arrested a definite suspect. He used his sermon to try to stir people to action and to raise more money to pay for a special detective force to aid in the hunt for the murderer. Once again, he begged the city to hire black detectives to assist the regular police force.

But, once again, no one listened.

The bloody year of 1911 ended, but the one that followed would not be much better.

BY THE START OF 1912, THE KILLER HAD CLAIMED at least 15 victims, and although the police department had done its best to find him, its efforts had failed. Leaders in the black community had tried to help in the effort, but they remained ignored and unanswered. Reward money had been raised but was never claimed. No solid suspects had been found. Henry Huff and Todd Henderson had both been tried for two of the "Ripper's murders, but Fulton County juries had found them innocent and let them go.

As 1912 began, there was hope that things would change – but they wouldn't.

On Friday, January 12, the body of Pearl Williams was found in a vacant lot at Chestnut and West Fair Streets, only a block from her home. Pearl's throat had been cut from ear to ear. The newspaper simply reported that the murderer was "uncaught."

It was the first "Ripper" murder of the new year.

On February 17, a second young black woman was killed. Alice Owens, who lived on Piedmont Avenue, was also found with her throat cut. She had been killed near Jonesboro Road, on Bowen Avenue, and then her body was dragged into a nearby gulley, where her assailant had gruesomely mutilated her remains.

The police investigated and soon arrested Alice's husband, Charlie, for the murder. In addition, two more black men were also arrested on suspicion of being involved in the killing. They were quickly released. Charlie Owens remained in jail for the next week but was also released. There was no evidence against him. He was simply arrested because he was the husband and, of course, because he was black.

That spring, a Fulton County grand jury reached a peculiar conclusion. On March 3, 1912, the *Constitution* reported that a grand jury had concluded that the "Ripper" was a myth. They had examined all the cases attributed to the "Ripper," they said and concluded that the killer did not exist.

> **RIPPER JACK IS DECLARED A MYTH**
>
> Grand Jury Finds That Each Slaying Was Result of Jealousy.
>
> Jack the Ripper is a myth! Such is the decision of the Fulton county grand jury after a two months' investigation of the murders of sixteen negro women who were killed during the past year.
>
> The jury declares that after a close study of the cases it has arrived at the conclusion that each murder was committed by a different man, and that in...

In a statement, the grand jury announced:

The jury declares that after a close study of the cases, it has arrived at the conclusion that each murder was committed by a different man, and that in each case it was the result of jealousy following immoral conduct. In almost every instance, the presentments declare, the woman killed was wither separated from her husband or was single, at the same time being guilty of immoral conduct, and that it was almost every case the result of revenge following jealousy.

The story – which was only four paragraphs – didn't explain how the jury had reached this conclusion. However, it's not hard to understand, and I don't believe the reader needs me to pick apart its ridiculous and inaccurate details. I think we can all see it for what it was – blaming the victims in the case because the authorities couldn't find the person who was responsible.

If anyone thought that declaring the "Ripper" was a "myth" was going to stop him from killing anyone else, they quickly found out they were wrong.

On Easter Sunday, April 6, the body of Mary Kate Sledge was discovered by two young men who were walking through a field near Pryor Street on the way to church. Mary Kate – described by the newspapers as a "pretty, 19-year-old octoroon" – was found face up in a cluster of bushes near the road. Her skull had been bashed in, and her throat had been cut. After the police searched the area, they found a spot where they believed she had been attacked. Her body was then dragged into the bushes and mutilated. Her clothing was found neatly folded next to her body.

According to the coroner, it had all the earmarks of another "Ripper" murder – whether the grand jury believed he existed or not.

On Monday, April 15, it was discovered that the "myth" had struck again. The body of an unidentified black woman was discovered in the Chattahoochee River under the Southern Railway bridge. She was found by the chief engineer of the nearby Chattahoochee Brick Company, and he and two of his men pulled the body from the river. Her throat had been slashed, and around it was a string with a key tied to it.

Her identity was never discovered, but the coroner estimated her to be about 15 years old. She had only been in the water a short time, so he was able to surmise from her wounds that she was likely another victim of the "Ripper."

Another murder followed. On May 11, the body of Marietta Logan was found hidden behind some bushes at the corner of

Atlanta Avenue and Fraser Street. She had been stabbed twice in the throat, severing her jugular vein. Her body had also been dragged a short distance after her death.

The "Ripper" murders were far from over.

AS THE POLICE HAD DONE IN AUSTIN, THE ATLANTA department continued arresting black men for the various murders but then had to let them go due to a lack of any solid evidence. Finally, though, the press announced on August 11 that the killer had been found with a headline that read, "JACK THE RIPPER BELIEVED TO BE A MODERN BLUEBEARD WITH 12 WIVES AS VICTIMS."

The article started with a question: "Is Lawton Brown, a lanky, well-dressed negro with small, sharp eyes that dart about nervously as though he were in perpetual fear, a modern Bluebeard who has murdered a dozen wives within the past year?"

Lawton Brown – whose real name was Henry Brown – had been arrested and, while in police custody, had confessed to the murder of Eva Florence, who had been killed in November 1911. Detectives Coker and Hambly had been assigned to the case, and soon after arresting Brown, they began putting together a larger and more complicated case against him – one that went far beyond just the murder of Eva Florence.

They announced to the press that Brown was being held on suspicion of committing 12 of the "Ripper" murders. Not only had Brown killed these 12 women, but he had also been married to all of them and had lived with each of them individually for a short time.

As the detectives pressed Brown for more information, he proved to be very familiar with the locations of all the murders in the Atlanta area. He could name all the victims and even how they had been killed. He even went on to say that he had witnessed two of the murders and proceeded to describe them in graphic detail. He stopped short of admitting to any of the murders – except for Eva Florence – and when asked why he didn't go to the aid of the victims of the murders he'd witnessed, he simply said that he'd been too afraid to get involved.

But where did the police get the idea that Brown was the "Ripper" and had at least 12 wives? The idea was given to the detectives by two women who came into the police station claiming to be his wives. One of the women said that during the time she had lived with him, she believed he was the murderer that was described by the newspapers. She said that Brown had come home on successive Saturdays – the same Saturdays when murders took place – wearing bloody clothing. She said it was a great relief that he had been caught and was now behind bars. The other woman – a cook, the same occupation as several of the "Ripper's" victims – said very little but "did show concern about the situation," a reporter noted. When detectives asked Brown about these women, he had nothing to say.

The more that police spoke to Brown, the more convinced they were that they had the right man. Dr. M.C. Martin was called to evaluate the prisoner, and he assessed that Brown suffered from an "unexplained mania."

To the police, this just meant that he fit the bill of a deranged killer, but to alienists, it told a different story. They believed that Brown had a mental illness and would agree to anything the police suggested to him, including that he had murdered 12 women.

In October, Brown went on trial for the murder of Eva Florence, but as had happened with the Henderson and Huff trials, the jury refused to convict him.

During the trial, doubt was cast on Brown being the murderer because of his mental condition. Doctors believed that Brown confessed to the murders for notoriety, an assertion backed up by witnesses who testified that Brown was a conceited braggart and "crazy." The defense also produced a witness named John Rutherford, who testified that detectives had put Brown through the "third degree" during questioning. Rutherford said that detectives had chained Brown's arms to a chair and then struck him in the head until he confessed.

For his part, Brown said he often suffered "hallucinations," and it was clear to the jury that he would admit to just about anything if he were pressured.

The jury believed the defense and returned a verdict of "not guilty." The Atlanta authorities had failed again – the "Modern Bluebeard" Lawton Brown was not the killer they'd been looking for.

The "Ripper" was still on the loose.

ATLANTA ENDED ANOTHER YEAR ON EDGE, and while the winter passed quietly, spring brought more carnage to the city.

On Tuesday, February 11, 1913, the body of a young black woman, estimated to be around 20 years old, was found at Fair and Christian Streets. The victim had suffered a cut to the face as well as a terrible slashing of the throat and bruises on the head and chest. An inquest determined that her killer had stabbed her in the head repeatedly until his knife had broken. He had pinned her down in a "vise-like grip" while the assault was carried out.

Based on the footprints found near the body, as well as the marks of a small rubber-tired buggy, police believed that the killer had returned to her body and turned it over, possibly to make sure that she was dead.

Even though the young woman had been nicely dressed in a blue corded suit, brown stockings, and high-top patent leather boots, her identity was never discovered.

> **ANOTHER VICTIM OF RIPPER.**
>
> Thirteenth Negro Girl, Mutilated by Mysterious Murderer, Found in Street at Atlanta, Ga.
>
> Atlanta, Ga., Nov. 21.—[Special.]—The thirteenth negro girl fell a victim to Atlanta's "Jack the Ripper" last night. The body was found in an alley leading off a principal street. It was mutilated in the same manner as all the others have been. The police believe that the ripper is a maniac.

In March, the Atlanta newspapers reported the death of Laura Smith, who was a servant for a family who lived on Ponce de Leon Avenue. The mixed-race young woman had been murdered on her way to work. She was found in an alley near Pine Street and Merritt Avenue.

Like all the others, her throat had been cut, and her body had been badly mutilated.

In August 1913, the "Ripper" struck again. His victim was Martha Ruffian, who had once been a maid for Mrs. Daisy Ople Grace. Interestingly, Martha had been a witness against her former employer when Mrs. Grace was accused of killing her husband.

Martha lived in a house in an alley off Ponce de Leon Avenue with her husband, J.C. The two of them had been separated for over a month. Martha was killed inside the house and dragged about 50 feet through a pea patch to where her body was discovered. A trail of blood was left behind. The body was found in a clump of bushes with a single knife wound to the throat.

The police briefly suspected a man named Alex Smith for the murder. He had been staying with Martha in the days before the murder, and, conveniently, he was black. But they couldn't turn up any evidence against him and were forced to let him go.

Martha Ruffian's murder would also never be solved.

The rest of the year was quiet, but the murders weren't over. The "Ripper" was still out there, and he still had a taste for blood.

IN THE SPRING OF 1914, THE "RIPPER" – or at least someone pretending to be the killer – emerged from hiding. He began attracting the attention of the police using the city's firefighters.

On the night of March 7, firefighters at Fire Station House 2 received at least three false alarms. All three alarms came between midnight and 1.00 A.M., and all came from fireboxes on the south side of Atlanta.

After the third alarm, Chief Courtney went out to investigate and found the alarm had come from a box at Whitehall and Richardson Streets. Stuck to the box was a note signed by "Jack the Ripper." In the letter, he threatened to "cut the throats of all Negro women" who were on the streets after a certain hour of the night. He also issued a warning to all the pawnbrokers in the city and even went so far as to threaten the life of every woman in Atlanta. He further said that all idlers – the homeless and drunkards – on the streets should beware of his wrath.

Police investigators believed the letter had also been posted at the two earlier boxes. It was a windy night, and it had likely blown off those boxes. It was only at the third false alarm that the note had stayed in place to be found.

The newspapers believed the letter was genuine and had been left by the "Ripper."

Was it? No one knows, but it did keep the "Ripper" in the nightmares of Atlanta residents for a little while longer.

THE SUMMER OF 1914 BEGAN QUIETLY IN Atlanta, but it didn't stay quiet for long. Soon after Independence Day, the murders started again. Two more women were killed that month, and both had all the signs of being victims of the "Ripper."

On Sunday, July 19, the body of a woman was found in Murphey Woods. An officer named Haslett reported that her throat had been cut, and she had been mutilated with one of her breasts found slashed off by a knife or razor.

On Sunday, July 27, another black woman's body was found in the woods north of the intersection of Greensferry and Lawton Streets. Her throat had been cut, and her body had been slashed repeatedly by a sharp blade. Two days later, the police identified her as Mary Roland, and although a man named Henry Harper was arrested and held for a time, her murder was never solved.

The murders were a minor sensation in the newspapers, and they proved that the public had not forgotten about the killer, even if he had been much quieter in recent years.

But they wouldn't remember for much longer. The newspapers fell silent about the "Ripper" for the rest of the year, and most believe the Roland murder was the last one committed by the killer.

Was it? Or was the "Ripper's" story not over yet?

As easy as it would be to end the "Ripper's" story with Mary Roland's murder and claim that his killing spree came to an end in the summer of 1914, it's impossible not to see the similarities in other murders that occurred over the next several years.

Even the newspapers liked to invoke his name occasionally. A year after Mary Roland was killed, the Atlanta newspapers reported another attack on a young black woman. They used "Another Victim Taken By 'Jack the Ripper'" when they printed the story. The woman had been found in a ditch alongside the road at Sixteenth and Cherry Streets and had been slashed in several places by a straight razor. She was never identified, and the crime was never solved – other than to say that "the murder had every aspect of the old 'Jack the Ripper' murders of several years ago.

The next month, the press attributed another murder to the "Ripper." Under a heading that read, "Ripper Busy Again; Another Negro Woman Victim of the Slasher," it was reported that a maid named Lucy Farr had been found dead near the corner of Ponce de Leon and Penn Avenues and that she had been stabbed in the head numerous times. This led "police to believe that another 'Jack the Ripper' crime has been committed in Atlanta.

More times passed, and on the morning of Sunday, June 24, 1917, two boys picking blackberries discovered the partially hidden body of an unknown black woman just beyond the Atlanta and West Point Belt Line railroad tracks, just 300 yards from Stewart Avenue. Her skull had been crushed and battered by a heavy, sharp object, probably an ax.

The newspaper added, "The details of the murder bring to mind the string of terrible "Jack the Ripper" murders which occurred two years ago, in which a number of Atlanta negro women lost their lives."

Next, a group of schoolchildren discovered the body of an unidentified black woman near the Clark University campus on Monday, October 1, 1917. She was lying in a mud puddle, her head had been crushed, and there were "numerous other marks of violence about her person."

In November 1917, a scrubwoman named Laura Blackwell was murdered with an ax. Found in her home on East Fair Street, Laura's head had been crushed, her throat cut, and her clothing set on fire. A suspect named John Brown was soon arrested, and newspapers noted, "Brown is accused of one of the 'Jack the Ripper' murders which puzzled the police about two years ago. The woman was found in the rear of East Fair Street with her throat cut and head crushed, wounds similar to those inflicted on several other negro women, victims of 'Jack the Ripper.'"

In March 1918, Brown went to trial and was sentenced to life in prison for the murder. He was later granted a new trial and convicted again in 1920. The police mentioned that they thought he might be guilty of other murders linked to the "Ripper," but there was, of course, no evidence to link him to any other crimes.

But while Brown was on his way to the penitentiary, the body of an "unidentified dark mulatto" was found at the top of a densely wooded hill above the West Point Belt Line Railroad tracks near Grant Street on March 17, 1918. She had been stabbed in the neck by a sharp object, and the ground beneath the body was saturated with blood. Nearby was a small, half-open pen knife, but the police ruled it out as the murder weapon.

The last paragraph of the newspaper report about the crime made it clear that the police feared she had been another "Ripper" victim. It read, "Detectives state that about five years ago during the 'Jack the Ripper' excitement when so many negro women were found murdered, that a body was found almost exactly at the same spot and no clue was ever found to the crime."

On April 30, 1918, the body of a 35-year-old black woman was found in a ditch near the Southern Railway tracks by a farmer named R.P. Wood from nearby Hapeville. Her skull had been fractured, and her throat was cut.

And the list of possible murders continued.

On Sunday, March 16, 1919, Queen Esther Jackson was attacked and stabbed several times by a mysterious assailant. She told police that she had stepped out into her yard on East Harris Street for a drink of water from the hydrant when an unknown black man had come out of the darkness and stabbed her. She died from her wounds on March 19 at Grady Hospital.

After that, the murders seemed to stop for the next five years, only starting up again in 1924.

On Sunday, May 4, the body of an unidentified 25-year-old woman was found along the Southern Railroad tracks between Peyton and Chattahoochee Stations. She had a knife wound to her temple, and there was evidence that a struggle had taken place before she was killed.

The newspapers mentioned that the crime was similar to the "operations in and around Atlanta a number of years ago by the mysterious 'Jack the Ripper' who was credited with more than a dozen murders."

On Friday night, September 5, 1924, the badly decomposed body of a young black girl was found lying face down in a vacant lot on Pryor Street, steps away from the Southern Railroad tracks. Her throat had been slashed from "ear to ear." The *Atlanta Constitution* reported that three black women had been found with their throats slashed in the previous two weeks, and, in each instance, the shoes and stockings of the victims had been removed.

Three days later, on September 8, the newspapers printed "Another Ripper Victim Reported." An unidentified woman had been found on Stewart Avenue the previous night with a bullet wound to her head, her throat cut, and "terrible slashes" to her wrists and back.

If she truly was another "Ripper Victim," then the length of time between the killer's first victim and his last was a span of more than 14 years. This might make it one of the longest-running murder sprees in the criminal history of the United States.

And even longer than that, if we believe the man might also have committed murders in Austin in 1885.

But this murder really does seem to be the killer's last. The murders ceased after 1924, and memories of the murders began to fade. Atlanta and the rest of the country soon had other things to worry about, including the Great Depression. The "Ripper" became a mostly forgotten figure in Atlanta's distant past.

No reward was ever collected for his capture.

No real suspect was ever tried and convicted.

To this day, the murders remain unsolved.

BUT WERE THE MURDERS COMMITTED AFTER THE summer of 1914, the work of the man who started in 1909? I'm not convinced that those later killings – perhaps even some of the ones publicized during the spree – were committed by the "Ripper." We'll likely never know just how many victims he claimed in Atlanta. The murder rate in that much larger city was very different than that of Austin, which was a smaller town.

Since there were many more murders reported in Atlanta at the time, things are messy when it comes to pinning down the "Ripper's" body count. The newspapers of the era – once they finally admitted that someone was preying on young black women in the city – were quick to sensationalize nearly every violent crime as the work of Atlanta's elusive "repeat murderer."

For instance, the murder of Lucinda McNeal was credited to the "Ripper." She was killed on February 3, 1911, by her husband, Charles, who sliced her up with a straight razor, one of the "Ripper's" weapons of choice. After a long night of drinking, Charles had cut his wife so badly that he nearly decapitated her. Lucinda had the misfortune to die at the height of "Ripper mania," and this has caused her to be listed as one of his victims erroneously.

In the case of Minnie Wise, who was murdered in November 1911, she was married to a jealous man who often threatened to kill her for flirting with other men. When she turned up dead, the police suspected that her husband had used the unsolved "Ripper" murders as a cover for his wife's murder.

Pearl Williams died after her throat was slashed on January 19, 1912. Her body was found the following day in a vacant lot at the corner of Chestnut and West Fair. She had only been a block away from home when she was murdered. The police arrested Frank Harvey on the day after Pearl's murder. He had been heard arguing with her a short time before. He was overheard saying that she had promised to marry him and that she wouldn't marry anyone if she didn't. He later confessed to the murder.

Alacy Owens was murdered on February 15, 1912, but her husband, Charley, was arrested soon after, even though the evidence against him was circumstantial. His first trial ended in a hung jury. He was convicted in a second trial, though, and given a life sentence. Interestingly, most newspaper accounts of the time reported that he had been sentenced for one of the "so-called Ripper murders committed in Atlanta during the last 18 months." The papers never mentioned that the victim had been his wife – or that he had nothing to do with the other murders.

Another small problem that exists when trying to come up with an exact count of the "Ripper's" victims is that the police depended entirely on the findings of the Fulton County Coroner Paul Donehoo during the height of the murders.

Paul Donehoo was legally blind.

While he had attended Atlanta Law School and graduated in 1911, he never obtained a formal medical degree. Most coroners complete their reports and findings by visual inspection. In Donehoo's case, he had to depend on the verbal and written descriptions of others, who may or may not have a slanted viewpoint, who may have missed evidence, or not understood what they were seeing.

To further complicate things, Donehoo stated unequivocally several times that the murders were the work of a single killer, which could have led police officers and detectives to try and connect cases that weren't actually connected.

While I do believe that most of the murders were the work of a single killer, I have been looking back at them for more than a century in the future, using written accounts, reports, and newspaper articles, all of which have their own issues. I could easily be just as mistaken as Paul Donehoo, using the accounts of others who may have been biased in their writings about the case.

But even so, I think something evil was going on in Atlanta in the early 1900s. I do believe there was a serial killer there claiming the lives of young black women.

And I also think it's possible that the killer could have been the same man who claimed the lives of young black women in Austin years before.

I did not go back and forth during the recounting of the Atlanta murders, pointing out the similarities between the crimes because I knew they would be obvious to anyone reading about them.

But I know that "obvious" doesn't always mean "probable," so before I mention the flaws in the theory, let's look at some important things.

I believe that, when looking at the facts and considering the era when the murders took place, the Atlanta killer was almost certainly a black man. Even if we ignore Emma Lou Sharpe's description of the man who stabbed her and killed her mother, it would have been difficult for a white man to move so freely and relatively unnoticed through Atlanta's black neighborhoods. Once the killings started, any unknown person – especially a white man – would have attracted attention, wary glances, and even outright violence. Since the "Ripper" was able to kill undetected, even after the city was fully on alert, he was almost definitely a black man.

This is the same belief that I have about the Austin murders.

The location of the bodies, almost always found in the vicinity of railroad tracks or someplace connected to the railroad, suggests that the killer either worked for the railroad, traveled about the area on freight trains, or at least didn't stray far from the area he was familiar with. As the trains would run in and out of Atlanta, usually on the weekends, it's possible that the "Ripper" was not an Atlanta resident but simply came into the city via the train. His schedule may have changed, too, which is why the murders started on Saturday nights and then switched to the early days of the week.

Austin was also a railroad town, as discussed earlier, so it's possible that – if he were the same man – he'd had a railroad job for years.

What drove the killer when he picked his victims? As in Austin, we don't know, but it was likely a deep, abiding hatred and possible fear of women. Both killers chose women to whom they had easy access and were vulnerable members of society. Black women, most of whom were servant girls in both cities, were easy targets. They had no choice but to be out on the street in the early morning or late-night hours because of their jobs.

The police departments in both cities were in impossible situations with the murders. They usually arrived at a crime scene or site where the body was dumped after dozens of people had already traipsed through it, looking at the body, potentially moving or destroying evidence, or carrying away objects for souvenirs. There was no forensic science at the time – even the common use of fingerprinting was still a few years away – but even so, any usable evidence was wiped away before they could usually take control of the scene.

After each subsequent murder, patrols were strengthened, but since the killer seemingly had no particular pattern for how he chose his victims and then struck, the police were at a serious disadvantage. When they did make an arrest, they were criticized and accused of making those arrests out of desperation. The newspapers and the public criticized the police, the mayor, and the city's aldermen for failing to solve the crimes.

Several things were similar between the two murder sprees, but we're always going to come back to the question: would the killer have waited 20 years to become active again in another city?

As much as I defended this possibility, deep down, it seems unlikely. We don't know who the Atlanta "Ripper" was any more than we know who the Austin "Servant Girl Annihilator" was. I'll never stop believing that the possibility exists that it could have been the same man, even though logic suggests that it was probably two black killers who preyed on their victims in much the same way.

Or maybe not, right?

Regardless of whether the murders were committed by one killer or two, they remain unsolved today.

THE END OF THE LINE

I'VE OFTEN WONDERED WHAT WOULD HAVE happened if the Austin KILLER had started murdering women today instead of in 1885. Would he have been caught after the first murder, that of Mollie Smith? The same murder today would mean that the police would have an array of forensic tools at their disposal – DNA tests, blood typing, fingerprinting – and they'd be able to study the security footage from street cameras and people's high-tech doorbells. Dozens of officers would follow up on the tips, and databases and experts would offer information and profiles about the killer.

But what if the murders committed today were the work of the first documented serial killer in American history? As the *New York World* reported in 1886, the Annihilator did "give a new story to the history of crime." There had never been a criminal like him before. He operated with no apparent motive, slaying his victims for no other reason than for the pleasure he received from it. He created chaos in the city and then disappeared, faceless and elusive, leaving a mystery in his wake.

Would a modern police force approach a brand-new type of killer in the same way the Austin police did in 1885 – clueless, overwhelmed, and mystified?

Who knows? They just might. The Servant Girl Annihilator might be as mysterious now as he was back then.

Obviously, I don't know who the killer was. Was he a black man from the city's impoverished east side? Was he a lunatic from the asylum – or Dr. Given himself? Was he some itinerant madman who spent a year in Austin and moved on? Was he the depraved son of one of the city's most prominent physicians? Or was a person we'd never suspect, whose daily life gave no indication that he was a serial killer?

I don't think we'll ever know. I don't believe the answer is filed away in the old records of the Austin police department or lost in the forgotten letters, archives, or diaries of someone who lived in the city in the 1880s.

Some mysteries will just never be solved – I think the mystery of the Servant Girl Annihilator is one that we're just going to have to live with.

BIBLIOGRAPHY

Abrahamsen, David – *Murder and Madness: The Secret Life of Jack the Ripper*, New York, NY, Donald I. Fine, Inc., 1992

Askins, Col. Charles – *Texas, Guns and History*, New York, NY, Winchester Press, 1970

Barkley, Mary Starr – *History of Travis County and Austin, 1839-1899*, Waco, TX, Texian Press, 1963

Barr, Alwyn – *Black Texans*, Norman, OK, University of Oklahoma Press, 1996

Beavan, Colin – *Fingerprints: The Origins of Crime Detection and the Murder Case That Launched Forensic Science*, New York, NY, Hyperion, 2001

Begg, Paul, Martin Fido and Keith Skinner – *The Jack the Ripper A-Z*, London, UK, Headline Book Publishing, 1991

Begg, Paul – *Jack the Ripper: The Facts*, New York, NY, Barnes and Noble, 2004

Bell, Neil R.A. – *Capturing Jack the Ripper*, Gloucestershire, UK, Amberley Publishing, 1014

Bondeson, Jan – *Rivals of the Ripper*, Gloucestershire, UK, The History Press, 2016

Bonn, Scott A., PhD – "How Serial Killers Cool Off Between Murders," *Psychology Today*, August 2019

Brown, Dee – *The American West*, New York, NY, Simon & Schuster, 1994

Campbell, Randolph B. – *Gone to Texas*, London, UK, Oxford University Press, 2012

Clavin, Tom – *Follow Me To Hell*, New York, NY, St. Martin's Press, 2023

Cole, Simon A. – *Suspect Identities: A History of Fingerprinting and Criminal Investigation*, Boston, MA, Harvard University Press, 2002

Cotner, Robert C. – *The Texas State Capitol*, Austin, TX, Pemberton Press, 1968

Cullen, Tom – *When London Walked in Terror*, New York, NY, Avon Books, 1965

Custer, Elizabeth B. – *Tenting on the Plains, or, General Custer in Kansas and Texas*, New York, Harper Brothers, 1895

Dary, David – *Red Blood and Black Ink: Journalism in the Old West*, New York, NY, Alfred A. Knopf, 1998
--------------- – *Seeking Pleasure in the Old West*, New York, NY, Alfred A. Knopf, 1995

Drago, Henry Sinclair – *The Legend Makers: Tales of the Old-Time Peace Officers and Desperadoes of the Frontier*, New York, NY, Dodd, Mead, 1975

Enss, Chris – *Entertaining Women: Actresses, Dancers, and Singers in the Old West*, Guilford, CT, Rowan & Littlefield, 2016

Erdoes, Richard – *Saloons of the Old West*, New York, Alfred A. Knopf, 1979

Evans, Stewart and Paul Gainey – *Jack the Ripper: First American Serial Killer*, New York, NY, Kodansha International, 1995

Fehrenbach, T.R. – *Lone Star: A History of Texas and Texans*, New York, NY, MacMillan, 1968

Fennessy, Steve - "Atlanta's Jack the Ripper," *CL Atlanta: Creative Loafing*, October 2005

Flanders, Judith – *The Invention of Murder*, New York, NY, St, Martin's Press, 2011

Frankel, Glenn – *The Searchers: The Making of An American Legend*, New York, NY, Bloomsbury, 2013

Franz, Joe B. -- *The Driskill Hotel*, Austin, TX, Encino Press, 1973

Freeberg, Ernest – *The Age of Edison: Electric Light and the Invention of Modern America*, New York, NY, Penguin Press, 2014

Friedman, Lawrence M. – *Crime and Punishment in American History*, New York, NY, Basic Books, 1993

Galloway, Anne – "Moonlight Memories," *Texas Highways*, May 1995

Galloway, J.R. – *The Servant Girl Murders*, Austin, TX, Booklocker, 2010

Gard, Wayne – *Rawhide Texas*, Norman, OK, University of Oklahoma Press, 1965

Guidebook Through the World's Cotton and Industrial Centennial Exposition at New Orleans, Harrisburg, PA, Lane S. Hart Printer, 1885

Gwynne, S.C. – *Empire of the Summer Moon*, New York, NY, Scribner, 2010

Haley, James L. – Passionate Nation: The Epic History of Texas, New York, NY, Simon & Schuster, 2006

Halttunen, Karen – *Murder Most Foul: The Killer and the American Gothic Imagination*, Cambridge, MA, Harvard University Press, 1998

Harrison, Shirley – *Jack the Ripper: The American Connection*, London, UK, John Blake Publishing, 2003

Hendricks, George D. – *Badmen of the West*, San Antonio, TX, Naylor, 1970

Hollandsworth, Skip – *The Midnight Assassin*, New York, NY, Henry Holt and Company, 2015

Horan, James – *The Pinkertons: The Detective Dynasty that Made History*, New York, NY, Crown, 1967

Hume, Robert – *The Hidden Lives of Jack the Ripper's Victims*, South Yorkshire, UK, Pen and Sword History, 2019

Humphrey, David C. – *Austin: History of the Capital City*, Austin, TX, Texas State Historical Association, 1997

Jenkins, James – *Murder in Atlanta: Sensational Crimes that Rocked the Nation*, Atlanta, GA, Cherokee Publishing Company, 1981

Johnson, Forrest Bryant – *The Last Camel Charge*, New York, NY, Berkeley, 2012

Karolevitz, Robert F. – Doctors of the Old West, Seattle, WA, Superior Publishing, 1967
--------------------------- – *Newspapering in the Old West*, Seattle, WA, Superior Publishing, 1965

Kasson, Joy S. – *Buffalo Bill's Wild West*, New York, NY, Hill and Wang, 2001

Kerr, Jeffrey – *Austin, Texas: Then and Now*, San Antonio, TX, Promised Land Books, 2005

Krafft-Ebing, Richard von – *Psychopathia Sexualis*, New York, NY, Arcade Publishing, 1965

Lane, Roger – *Murder in America: A History*, Columbus, OH, Ohio State University Press, 1997

Langford, Gerald – *Alias O. Henry: A Biography of William Sydney Porter*, New York, NY, MacMillan, 1957

Lavender, David – *The Great West*, New York, NY, Houghton Mifflin, 1965

McDade, Thomas M. – *The Annals of Murder*, Norman, OK, University of Oklahoma Press, 1961

Neihardt, John – *Black Elk Speaks*, Albany, NY, University of New York Pr4ess, 1932

Newton, Michael – *The Encyclopedia of Unsolved Crimes*, New York, NY, Checkmark Books, 2009

Pinkerton, Matthew – Murder in All Ages, etc. Chicago, IL, A.E. Pinkerton & Co., 1898

Prassel, Frank Richard – The Western Peace Officer, Norman, OK, University of Oklahoma Press, 1972

Quarles, Benjamin – *The Negro in the Making of America*, New York, NY, Simon & Schuster, 1987

Rickards, Colin – *Bowler Hats and Stetsons*, New York, Bonanza Books, 1966

Robinson, Charles M. III – *The Men Who Wear the Star: The Story of the Texas Rangers*, New York, NY, Random House, 2000

Rubenhold, Hallie – *The Five: The Untold Lives of the Women Killed by Jack the Ripper*, New York, NY, Houghton Mifflin Harcourt, 2029

Sanborn Fire Insurance Maps – *Austin, Texas*, 1885

Sitton, Sarah C. – *Life at the Texas State Lunatic Asylum*, 1857-1997, College Station, TX, A&M Press, 1999

Skrabanek, D. – *The Servant Girl Annihilators*, Wimberly, TX, S&S Press, 2014

Smyth, Frank and Myles Ludwig – *The Detectives*, Philadelphia, PA, J.B. Lippincott Company, 1978

Streeter, Floyd B. – *Ben Thompson: Man with a Gun*, New York, NY, Frederick Fell, 1957

Sugden, Philip – *The Complete History of Jack the Ripper*, New York, NY, Carrol & Graf, 1994

Swanson, Doug J. – *Cult of Glory: The Bold and Brutal History of the Texas Rangers*, New York, NY, Viking, 2020

Thorwald, Jurgan – *The Century of the Detective*, New York, NY, Harcourt & Brace, 1964

Tolbert, Frank X. – *An Informal History of Texas*, New York, NY, Harper Brothers, 1951

Taylor, Troy – *Horribly Mutilated*, Jacksonville, IL, American Hauntings Ink, 2021

--------------- – *Murdered in Their Beds*, Jacksonville, IL, American Hauntings Ink, 2013

--------------- - *Victims of the Ax Fiend*, Jacksonville, IL, American Hauntings Ink, 2020

Underwood, Corinna – *Murder and Mystery in Atlanta*, Charleston, SC, The History Press, 2009

Ward, Geoffrey C. – *The West*, New York, NY, Little, Brown, 1999

Wells, Jeffrey -- *The Atlanta Ripper: The Unsolved Story of the Gate City's Most Infamous Murders*, Charleston, SC, The History Press, 2011

West, Paul – *The Women of Whitechapel and Jack the Ripper*, Woodstock, NY, Overlook Press, 1992

Whittington-Egan, Richard - *Jack the Ripper: The Definitive Casebook*, Gloucestershire, UK, Amberley Publishing, 2013

Wilson, Colin – *The Mammoth Book of the History of Murder*, New York, NY, Carroll & Graf, 2000

Wilson, Colin and Damon Wilson – *The Mammoth Encyclopedia of the Unsolved*, Carroll & Graf, New York, NY, 2000

Worsmer, Richard – The Rise and Fall of Jim Crow, New York, NY, St. Martin's Press, 2003

Yadon, Laurence J. and Dan Anderson – *Ten Deadly Texans*, Gretna, LA, Pelican Publishing, 2009

Zelade, Richard – *Austin Murder and Mayhem*, Charleston, SC, The History Press, 2015

-------------------- - *Guytown by Gaslight*, Charleston, SC, The History Press, 2014

Newspapers

Atlanta Constitution (GA)
Atlanta Georgian (GA)
Austin Daily Capitol (TX)
Austin Daily Statesman (TX)
Austin Daily Sun (TX)
Dallas Daily Herald (TX)
Dallas Morning News (TX)
Fort Worth Gazette (TX)
Galveston Daily News (TX)
Houston Daily Post (TX)
National Police Gazette (NY)
New York World (NY)
San Antonio Daily Express (TX)
San Antonio Light (TX)
Waco Day (TX)
Waco Daily Express (TX)

SPECIAL THANKS TO

April Slaughter: Cover Design
Becky Ray: Editing
Samantha Smith
Athena & the "Aunts" - Sue, Carmen & Rocky
Orrin and Rachel Taylor
Rene Kruse
Rachael Horath
Bethany Horath
Elyse and Thomas Reihner
John Winterbauer
Cody Beck
Tom and Michelle Bonadurer
Lydia Rhoades
Cheryl Stamp and Sheryel Williams-Staab
Joelle Leitschuh and Tonya Leitschuh
Scott and Hannah Robl
Jake and Emily Fink
Dave and Donna Nunnally
And the entire crew of American Hauntings

ABOUT THE AUTHOR

Troy Taylor is the author of books on ghosts, hauntings, true crime, the unexplained, and the supernatural in America. He is the founder of American Hauntings Ink, which offers books, ghost tours, events, and the Haunted America Conference, as well as the creator of the American Oddities Museum in Alton, Illinois.

He was born and raised in the Midwest and divides his time between Illinois and wherever the wind decides to take him. See Troy's other titles at: www.americanhauntingsink.com

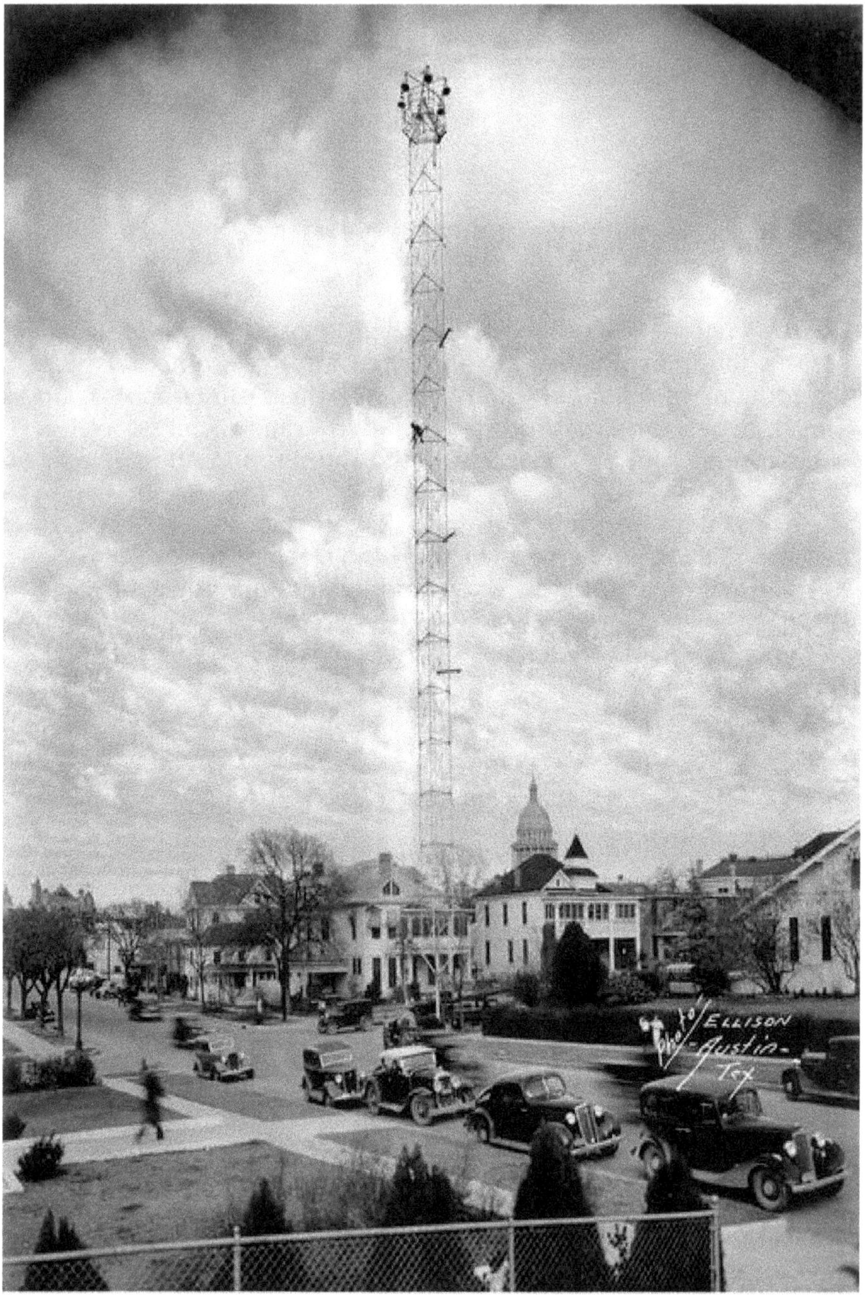
Photo/ELLISON
-Austin-
Tex

Milton Keynes UK
Ingram Content Group UK Ltd.
UKHW050630150424
441175UK00006B/314